F C

PAPERBACK

MULTIETHNIC
BOOKS

for the

MIDDLE-SCHOOL CURRICULUM

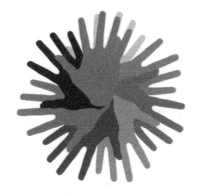

CHERRI JONES
and **J. B. PETTY**

An imprint of the American Library Association · Chicago · 2013

CHERRI JONES is head of the Curriculum Resource Center at Meyer Library and a professor of library science at Missouri State University. Her research, publications, and presentations focus on multiethnic children's and young adult literature, early childhood literacy and storytelling. Jones founded and directs the Children's and Young Adult Book Review Board of Missouri. She served as president of the board of trustees of the Springfield–Greene County Public Library District and cofounded the Club de Cuentos Early Literacy program in Springfield, Missouri. Jones earned her MLS from the University of Chicago. **J. B. PETTY** is professor emeritus of Missouri State University. Her career in librarianship spanned thirty-five years. She worked in school and academic libraries, serving children in a variety of grades, and coordinated a library science program, teaching library science courses on the graduate level. Her research has focused on multicultural literature for elementary and middle-school students. She is the author of numerous journal articles and reviews, as well as a chapter in Venture into Cultures, 2nd ed. (EMIERT/ALA Editions). Since 2000 Petty has made annual presentations on multicultural literature for middle-schoolers and for public and school librarians. She served as president of the Arkansas Library Association (1997) and received their Special Service Award the following year. In 2010 she received the Special Service Award from the Missouri Association of School Librarians. She earned her MLS from the University of Missouri–Columbia and her doctorate in library science from Texas Woman's University.

Printed in the United States of America

17 16 15 14 13   5 4 3 2 1

Extensive effort has gone into ensuring the reliability of the information in this book; however, the publisher makes no warranty, express or implied, with respect to the material contained herein.

ISBNs: 978-0-8389-1163-1 (paper); 978-0-8389-9476-4 (PDF); 978-0-8389-9477-1 (ePub); 978-0-8389-9478-8 (Kindle). For more information on digital formats, visit the ALA Store at alastore.ala.org and select eEditions.

Library of Congress Cataloging-in-Publication Data

Jones, Cherri, compiler.
  Multiethnic Books for the Middle-School Curriculum / Cherri Jones and J. B. Petty.
    pages   cm
  Includes bibliographical references and index.
  ISBN 978-0-8389-1163-1 (alk. paper)
  1. Middle school students—Books and reading—United States. 2. Junior high school students—Books and reading—United States. 3. Multiculturalism in literature—Bibliography. 4. Reading (Middle school)—United States. 5. Young adult literature—Bibliography. 6. Cultural pluralism in literature—Bibliography. 7. Ethnic groups in literature—Bibliography. 8. Minorities in literature—Bibliography. 9. Teenagers—Books and reading—United States. 10. Middle school libraries—United States—Book lists. I. Petty, J. B., compiler. II. Title.
Z1037.A1J69 2013
028.5′5—dc23

                    2012040938

Cover design by Kimberly Thornton. Images © Shutterstock, Inc.
Text design by Adrianna Sutton in Adobe Garamond Pro and Eames Century Modern.
♾ This paper meets the requirements of ANSI/NISO Z39.48-1992 (Permanence of Paper).

We dedicate this book to the countless librarians and teachers

who are strongly committed to introducing children and young adults to

"the right book at the right time."

CONTENTS

ACKNOWLEDGMENTS

We have so many librarians and teachers to thank, but first and foremost we'd like to thank Dea Borneman, head of the Haseltine Library at Greenwood Laboratory School, Missouri State University (MSU) and an associate professor of library science, for her unflagging support and the many booktalk sessions she presented with us. Emily Furtak, supervisor of the Curriculum Resource Center, Meyer Library, MSU, and our student assistants helped track down many titles and, along with numerous other colleagues, held down the fort during Cherri's sabbatical. All were immensely patient as we met, discussed, and wrote reviews for titles we were reading. Ellie Mason painstakingly created a helpful and comprehensive list of series book titles. Teachers, librarians, and administrators in the Springfield (Missouri) Public Schools provided advice and gave us direction. Although they are more numerous than we can count, we especially thank Catia Gilpin, teacher at Phelps Center for Gifted Education for her encouragement and her close reading of the "Social Studies" chapter; Ann Wollenmeyer, district science facilitator; Margaret Butler, middle school librarian, Cherokee Middle School; Denise Kelly, district English–language arts facilitator; and Jennifer Renegar, district mathematics facilitator. Members of the Missouri Association of School Librarians and the Southwest Region Association of School Librarians in Missouri have listened to, discussed, and critiqued our reviews for over a decade, and we thank them for their thoughtful input. Steve Hinch, MSU associate professor in Reading, Foundations, and Technology; Judy Gregg, MSU adjunct professor in Reading, Foundations and Technology; Mara Cohen-Ioannides, MSU senior instructor in English; Suzanne Walker-Pacheco, MSU professor of Sociology and Anthropology; and Lilias Jones Jarding, professor of Environmental Studies and Political Science, Oglala Lakota College, all offered suggestions and answered questions along the way. Jim Coombs, associate professor and Meyer Library Maps librarian, offered solid geography advice for the social studies chapter. Professor Linda Esser of the School of Information Science and Learning Technologies, University of Missouri–Columbia, has provided ongoing support and encouragement when we couldn't see the end of the project. Our thanks go to Meyer Library's Circulation and Interlibrary

Loan staff, the staff of the Library Center, Brentwood, and Midtown Branches of the Springfield–Greene County Library District, and the staff of the Oak Bend Branch of St. Louis County Public Library for their cheerful assistance as we requested and picked up literally hundreds of books in the past few years! Our deep gratitude goes to our editor, Stephanie Zvirin. Without her support, vision, and suggestions the book probably would not have come to fruition. Finally, we'd like to thank our families for supporting this project, giving us time to work, providing suggestions, and maneuvering around the stacks of books that often took over our households!

INTRODUCTION

The purpose of this book is to make it easier for teachers and librarians to infuse curricula with multiethnic literature. We provide a vetted list of recommended multiethnic titles for grades 5–8, organized by curricular area. Why multiethnic literature? Aside from the positive benefits attributed to multicultural and multiethnic literature by scores of researchers (see appendix C), promoting understanding and empowerment through books is a long-standing passion for both of us. We've talked with countless educators during the preparation for this book and have consistently heard the comment, "We need a sourcebook like this."

Issues in defining multicultural/multiethnic literature are many and complex. As have others (see appendix C) through the years, we struggle with our own definition. However, when we examined national curricular standards, we found ethnic diversity most nearly fit the meanings behind the standards. Thus, for the purposes of this book we decided to focus only on diverse ethnic groups in the United States and various places around the world.

Junko Yokota's yardsticks for authenticity have guided our selections. These include "richness of cultural details, authentic dialogue and relationships, in-depth treatment of cultural issues, and the inclusion of members of 'minority groups for a purpose.'"[1]

We are aware of the controversy concerning authors who write outside their own culture. We believe that personal experience, immersion, or extensive research can allow authors to do so. Therefore, we have included such titles. We looked for source notes and/or qualified advisors for both fiction and informational books to ensure accuracy and authenticity. At times, we contacted authors to request background information.

We have read a large percentage of the multicultural children's and young adult books published since 2000, preparing countless booktalks for teachers and librarians. Because of our combined experience in research and in reading multicultural books for children and young adults, we trust (mostly) our choices. Even as we realize some of our selections (and omissions!) will be criticized, we believe they represent an array of books with broad appeal to tweens and younger teens.

WHO WE ARE

Cherri, of Finnish and Icelandic descent, remembers the first year of busing for school integration in Denver, Colorado, where she grew up in the 1960s. She couldn't understand the fuss; she rode a bus to school, what did it matter that African American kids rode a bus to her school, too? Then in high school she tried to convince an African American friend that, of course, he'd be welcome in her home. "Maybe," he said, "but would I be welcome if I were to come to pick you up for a date?" That one simple question brought home the subtleties of racism.

J. B. grew up in the segregated South in the 1940s and 1950s. When she was 4, her father bought a small neighborhood grocery in Camden, Arkansas. The family lived in quarters at the back of the store. The African American family that lived behind them had a daughter her age. Not allowed to go into one another's yard to play, the girls played with their dolls through the fence. J. B.'s question was, "Why?"

Each of us grew up in white middle-class families. We were avid readers and read widely. The adults around us viewed the world one way; the characters in our books often gave us another perspective. We found our way into librarianship, where we saw the power of even one story to change a life. We each kept up with new research on the positive effects of a well-developed program of multicultural education. J. B. even focused her doctoral dissertation on how school librarians in Arkansas promoted multicultural understanding in their schools. When we met in 1998, we were new to the library science department faculty at what is now Missouri State University. It took us about five minutes to realize we were destined for a long friendship! We soon found ourselves regularly presenting booktalks on multicultural children's and young adult books. In 2001, we decided to narrow our focus on that difficult, transitional period in a child's life: preadolescence. This book, then, stems from our years of research and reading for ages 11 through 14.

Between us, we have read over two thousand books from the years 2005–2011 to find the titles we recommend here. We have read every book for which we have a review.

WHAT WE INCLUDED

Organization

We organized this book with teachers and school librarians firmly in mind; this arrangement can also benefit public librarians. Titles are placed in chapters where we, our advisors, and our editor felt they most readily fit with the curriculum; a quick look at the table of contents will give readers a place to start. For example, titles with themes such as bullying, sexual orientation, and sex roles are in chapter 1, "Health"; titles in which a particular sport plays a key role are in chapter 4, "Physical Education." Readers are encouraged not only to look for subjects in their specific curricular areas, but to utilize the index to find additional titles on a subject that might be listed under another curricular area.

Bibliographic Information

For most books, we include the title, author, copyright date, number of pages, publisher, designation as fiction (F) or nonfiction (NF), and grade levels. Although in the bibliographic statement we use (NF) Grades or (F) Grades to indicate the category of the book, in the body of a review we chose to use the term *informational books* rather than *nonfiction* because this is the term used by teachers and national content area associations. We do not include the ISBN because we know online sources readily provide all available book versions, from paperback to trade to library binding.

Series Books and Informational Titles

As we began exploring series books, we realized not every book in a series fit our chosen parameters. For example, from the current list of 107 titles in one series, only twenty-nine could be termed multiethnic; and of these twenty-nine, only some are appropriate for the middle school curriculum. We found that not all books in a series are created equal. Quality varies by author. Sometimes we were not able to find or read all in a series. If we read all the titles in a series that fit one curricular area, and could recommend all, we wrote a review for that series to conserve space. We encourage teachers and librarians to explore individual titles of series before making blanket purchases of an entire set.

We deemed some series titles to be *report books*, but if their content was valuable and appealing enough for classroom use we included them. We are heartened by some publishers' recent new standards requiring source notes, photograph and illustration credits, and author information. We've noted these areas (or the lack thereof) in our reviews. A complete lack of documentation led us to eliminate titles that otherwise were appealing.

Grade Levels

As most of us know, assigning grade levels to books can be tricky. We decided to err in the direction of breadth. We debated, but opted to include the best of the picture books we read for this age group. We know many middle school social studies teachers use picture books in their classes to introduce specific topics; other teachers use them as prompts for student writing or art.

We recognize books that reach into high school interest areas (particularly fiction) appeal to many seventh and eighth graders. We read and liked many of the books that fit this age range, but chose to include only a limited number. We opted instead to focus on titles more suited for a broader middle school audience. Informational (nonfiction) books were a bit trickier. We included a few nonfiction titles that would be appropriate for a middle school library reference collection; students might not read the entire volume, but could use it as a source for reports.

Review Style

We chose to write our reviews in a booktalk review style that includes both a summary and an evaluation. Why? Because we know teachers and librarians can't possibly remember (we often don't!) the details of a book or story at the very moment of need. Usually, these moments involve selling a book to a student or collecting titles for a curricular unit. Although shorter reviews are great for the book selection process, they don't give much to go on for a one-minute booktalk. Also, we wanted to give enough detail about a book to allow teachers or librarians to see how the title might fit into their curricular units.

We followed standard reviewing procedures in evaluating the format of each book. Are the typeset, font, and spacing appropriate for grades 5–8? Do the photographs and illustrations complement the text on the page? Do text boxes work with the overall layout, or are they distracting? Are the pages easy to digest, or overly busy in their graphic layout? We considered these questions when choosing titles. Also, because so many art teachers collaborate with other content area teachers, we have noted or identified the style of art in many titles. In this manner, both art and subject teachers can readily mesh the book with other curricula.

Content Area Standards

We chose to identify and review books in the major curricular areas most U.S. middle schools offer: health, language arts, performing arts (dance, music, and theater), physical education, science and mathematics, social studies, and visual arts. Using 2011 national content standards (see appendix A for organizations, websites, and standards), we aligned each title to applicable curricular areas and standards. A title's major curricular area might be visual arts, but the book could also fulfill standards in language arts or social studies. For example, the full annotation and review for *Sweethearts of Rhythm: The Story of the Greatest*

All-Girl Swing Band in the World by Marilyn Nelson is in "Performing Arts," chapter 3. However, because the book is written using individual poems and focuses on a specific time period in U.S. history, it would be appropriate in either the language arts or social studies classroom. Thus, it is important to consult the index by subject; by using the index, teachers and librarians can find *all* applicable titles related to a subject, no matter where the full annotation and review might appear.

A word about format of the content area standards: each national association makes its own choice between numbering its standards with Roman numerals and cardinal numbers (for example, LA1 or SSIV). We follow the format used by the associations. Some associations provide abbreviated lists of their standards; others give detailed descriptions for each of theirs. Again, our list of standards in the appendix reflects the work of the associations.

We are aware of the Partnership for 21st Century Skills (P21)[2] and the Common Core State Standards[3] initiatives. Most states have formally adopted these initiatives and are incorporating them into their curriculum. Organizations and associations that produce content area standards are working to mesh P21 and the Common Core State Standards with their standards. This is a time of flux for educational standards; however, we are confident the books we include readily meet many of these standards and will help students achieve learning objectives set forth by their school districts.

Cultures

Early in our research and reading, we focused on ethnic groups in the United States. However, we realized by doing so we weren't including books related to middle school world history topics or areas of interest, such as current issues, mythology, or world folktales. We then expanded our reading to incorporate a variety of historical periods and countries. The question became, Where do we draw the line? We decided to include books that focus on major areas of conflict between ethnic groups around the world. These conflicts are an important part of the social studies curriculum.

We also have included informational books that present what we term an *awareness of diversity* (AOD). Although these books are not truly multicultural, their inclusion of multiethnic characters or photographs of multiethnic people is better than the image of a "white world" that we have unfortunately discovered in many middle grade science, math, and series books. We hope editors and publishers will note this omission and take steps to correct it. We're heartened by the number of fiction titles that feature protagonists from a variety of cultures; we could not find many of these ten years ago.

To denote specific cultures we have done the following. Where possible, we've noted specific American Indian groups. We've chosen to use *Latino* rather than *Hispanic Americans*, and *Muslims* rather than *Moslems*. Within our reviews we use the term that the book's author used. We have chosen not to hyphenate cultural groups, because we see hyphenation as a means of diminishing the status of a group. For titles that cover ethnic groups around the world, we have used the term *Global*.

Keywords
We adapted most of the keywords from Library of Congress Cataloging-In-Publication information on the MARC record. We omitted words such as *juvenile, schools,* or *friendship* because these could apply to many titles.

Graphic Novels and Picture Books
Many multiethnic picture books, graphic novels, and folktale books not only express art from their respective cultures, they also showcase a specific artistic style.

WHAT'S NOT HERE
Despite our best efforts, we realize we have missed some great titles. We consulted numerous bibliographies, databases, review sources, and award lists during the course of our research. We considered diverse audiences, from rural to suburban to urban, realizing while one title might not be appropriate for one audience, it might fit the needs of others.

We read some books with excellent content, but we eliminated them based on the layout or format. If we struggled with reading the books, we felt students in these grades would not read them, even with encouragement.

HOW TO USE THIS BOOK
Readers will find books in one of several ways: by looking in a specific curricular area and by consulting the index by subject, keyword, or title. Each full entry for a title is annotated as below:

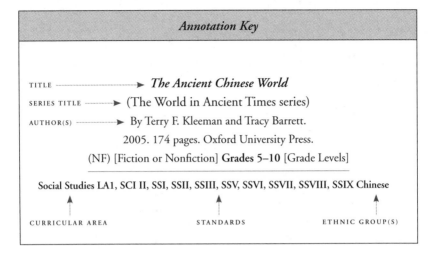

Annotation Key

TITLE ············▶ *The Ancient Chinese World*

SERIES TITLE ··········▶ (The World in Ancient Times series)

AUTHOR(S) ··········▶ By Terry F. Kleeman and Tracy Barrett.

2005. 174 pages. Oxford University Press.

(NF) [Fiction or Nonfiction] **Grades 5–10** [Grade Levels]

Social Studies LA1, SCI II, SSI, SSII, SSIII, SSV, SSVI, SSVII, SSVIII, SSIX Chinese

CURRICULAR AREA   STANDARDS   ETHNIC GROUP(S)

NOTES

1. Junko Yokota, "Issues in Selecting Multicultural Children's Literature," Language Arts vol. 70 (March 1993): 159–60.
2. See the Partnership for Learning 21st Century Skills website, www.p21.org. For a quick overview, see "P21 Framework Definitions," www.p21.org/documents/P21_Framework_Definitions.pdf (accessed August 29, 2012).
3. See the Common Core State Standards Initiative website, www.corestandards.org (accessed August 29, 2012).

1 HEALTH

~~~~~~~~~~~

In the context of health class, students discuss a host of issues, including peer pressure, family issues, clash of cultures, substance abuse, physical abuse, gender roles, sexual identity, bullying, lying, diseases, and more. Many contemporary fiction problem novels address these issues. We organized this chapter around these topics because the books are appropriate for health classes. School counselors who work with individual students or student groups will also find these titles helpful.

DECISION MAKING
(DRUGS, LYING, FAMILY ISSUES, GRIEF)

The Absolutely True Diary of a Part-Time Indian
By Sherman Alexie. 2007. 229 pages. Little, Brown. (F) **Grades 7–12**

Alexie pulls no punches as he describes Arnold, aka Junior, a bright kid who begins life with several strikes against him. Born with hydrocephalus (water on the brain) and getting poor care at the Indian Health Service, growing up on the Spokane Indian Reservation with poor parents, attending an inadequate reservation school, and being teased every day almost defeat him. Yet he perseveres. At 14, he transfers to the all-white Reardan High School off the reservation and feels like he becomes a part-time Indian. Some days he wonders how he'll get to or from school. Some days he wonders why he left the reservation and lost his best friend, Rowdy. However, attending Reardan means meeting his first girlfriend, making the basketball team, making friends, and having opportunities for college. Told in first-person in Junior's voice and illustrated with cartoonlike drawings (with captions that sound like they come from a 14-year-old), the book is definitely for older middle school readers.   Health, Language Arts H2, H5, H6, LA1, SSII, SSIII, SSIV, SSV, VA1, VA4, VA6
American Indians, Spokanes

Bird

By Zetta Elliott. 2008. Illus. No page numbers. Lee & Low. (F) **Grades 4–7**

Mehkai has a talent for drawing. He draws to escape his grief about his older brother's drug addiction and death and his grandfather's death. He and Uncle Son, his grandfather's friend, spend many hours after school in the park where Mehkai identifies and draws birds. Using free verse, color illustrations, and pen-and-ink drawings, Elliott and illustrator Shadra Strickland take the reader into Mehkai's confusion and sadness as he comes to peace with the losses of two people he truly loved. The book is short but powerful in its expression of despair and hope for the future.   Health, Visual Arts H2, H5, LA1, SSIV, VA4, VA5, VA6 **African Americans**

Blessing's Bead

By Debby Dahl Edwardson.
2009. 178 pages. Farrar, Straus and Giroux. (F) **Grades 6–9**

Based on true events, this book alternates between the early-1900s story of Nutaaq and the late-1980s tale of her great-granddaughter, Blessing. When Nutaaq's family goes to the annual trade fair on mainland Alaska, Nutaaq is heartbroken when her sister, Aaluk, marries a handsome Siberian and goes to live in his country. The next year, Nutaaq's village is ravaged by the 1918 influenza epidemic, and her life takes a drastic turn. The book then moves to 1989 and the story of Nutaaq's great-granddaughter, Blessing. Blessing's alcoholic mother is undergoing treatment, and Blessing and her brother are taken in by relatives. Fitting in is not easy, but as she learns about her family's fractured past she finds her own place in this new world and begins to heal. First-person narrative filled with dialect and the smooth insertion of Iñupiak history and customs adeptly bring the reader into both stories.   Health H1, H2, H4, H5, LA1, LA9, SSII, SSIII, SSIV, SSV, SSIX **American Indians, Inupiats**

The Broken Bike Boy and the Queen of 33rd Street

By Sharon Flake. 2007. 132 pages. Jump at the Sun/Hyperion. (F) **Grades 4–6**

Fifth-grader Queenie reveals her own foibles as she tells the story of the new boy, Leroy, who smells bad, rides a broken old bike, and tells his classmates he's a prince from Senegal. Her mean-spirited comments, which she interprets as "telling the truth," ensure that she has no friends at school. Queenie is an adept liar, can usually manipulate her parents, and is determined to prove that Leroy is a fake. When she sneakily learns that he is helping an old man, Queenie begins to see that truth can be interpreted in a number of different ways. Queenie's realistic view of how others see her may help readers better analyze their own relationships.   Health H2, HE4, H5, H6, LA1, LA9, SSIII, SSIV, SSV African Americans

Confessions of a Closet Catholic
By Sarah Littman. 2005. 193 pages. Dutton. (F) **Grades 6–8**

Justine Silver is Jewish, and a middle child who thinks her parents love her less than they do her siblings. The family has just moved; Justine's new best friend, Mary Catherine, is Catholic, so Justine decides she wants to be Catholic, too. She searches for her identity, her religion, and her place in her family, all while dealing with the death of her beloved grandmother. When she goes to confession at Mary Catherine's church, she is surprised when the wise priest suggests she explore her own Jewish faith. In this funny yet serious novel, Littman addresses one of the important issues preteens and teens face—how, or if, they will follow in the religious traditions of their parents. She provides the venue for readers to explore their own feelings about several issues: growing up, a sense of insecurity, death, and relationships with boys.   Health HE2, HE5, LA1, SSIV Jewish Americans

Ethan, Suspended
By Pamela Ehrenberg. 2007. 266 pages. Eerdmans. (F) **Grades 5–8**

When he is sent to stay with his old-fashioned, frugal grandparents in Washington, DC, eighth-grader Ethan Oppenheimer has no idea he will actually live with them and go to the nearby inner-city school. He's been suspended from his affluent suburban school, and his divorcing parents simply can't cope. Now Ethan faces new challenges as the sole Jewish kid among street-savvy black and Hispanic groups at Parker Junior High. Slowly, he finds his place with the help of new friends and the jazz band teacher, Mr. Harper. He also discovers more about his mom's family and how the 1968 race riots affected them. The first-person narrative is packed with dialogue and underscores Ethan's confusion and small joys as he matures.   Health, Social Studies H2, H5, LA1, LA9, SSIII, SSIV African Americans, Jewish Americans, Latinos

Finding Family

By Tonya Bolden. 2010. 181 pages. Bloomsbury. (F) **Grades 4–8**

Twelve-year-old Delana has lived with her wealthy grandpa and great aunt Tilley since her mother's death after childbirth. She memorizes stories about her extended family as she and her aunt line up family photos and talk about each person's character and life. When her mysterious cousin Ambertine secretly visits her, Delana is stunned to learn most of the stories aren't true. As she uncovers the truth about her mother—and missing father—Delana must decide if she's strong enough to break free from her sheltered, highly controlled existence. Inspired by the faces on old photographs in her personal collection, Bolden spins an intriguing tale set at the turn of the century in Charleston, West Virginia. Delana's first-person narrative adds to the mystery of the story. Health H2, H5, LA1, SSII, SSIII, SSIV African Americans

Freshman Focus

By Carla R. Sarratt. 2007. 292 pages. Outskirts Press. (F) **Grades 7–10**

Freshmen Kendra, Lamar, Destiny, and Steven are all excited to start school at Carter G. Woodson High in Charlotte, North Carolina. Reflecting the author's experiences in a predominantly black high school in suburban Cleveland, the story is a tribute to the Sweet Valley High series she loved as a girl. Readers follow Kendra's experiences as she and Destiny (whom she can't stand) are courted by older girls to join an exclusive, secret club. At the same time, popular class clown Lamar is having difficulty buckling down regarding the rigors of high school academics, and Steven, new to the school, is adjusting to a foster family while he attempts to distance himself from his past. Filled with believable dialogue, warm family interactions, and detailed descriptions of the freshman experience, this is a highly readable novel, if at times somewhat choppily written. Readers will look forward to hearing more about the characters in *Just Be* (2008). Health HE2, HE5, LA1, SSIII, SSIV, SSV African Americans

Jimi & Me

By Jaime Adoff. 2005. 329 pages. Jump at the Sun/Hyperion. (F) **Grades 7–9**

When his father dies in a convenience store shooting, Keith James thinks this is the worst thing that could ever happen. However, his life is uprooted even more when he and his mother move from Brooklyn, New York, to Hollow Falls, Ohio, to live with his aunt. They have no money; Keith is the only biracial guy in his school; and he can't figure out why his mother is so sad all the time. He especially misses playing Jimi Hendrix tunes with his father. He isn't prepared for the unexpected turn of events that leads him on an angry search for a family member he never knew existed. Adoff's free verse, short sections, and use of first person bring Keith's personality to life. The book may sound depressing, and it is—and it isn't. **Health H2, H5, LA1, LA9, SSII, SSIII, SSIV African Americans, Mixed-Race Americans**

Keeping the Night Watch

By Hope Anita Smith and Earl B. Lewis. 2008. 73 pages. Holt. (F) **Grades 5–9**

In this sequel to *The Way a Door Closes* (2003) readers again meet 15-year-old C. J. His family is dealing with raw emotions as they adjust to the father's reappearance. Their trust was broken when he left; now each must come to terms with his return. The family pretends everything is fine; but, individually that isn't the case. C. J. in particular is angry at his father and doesn't want to be hurt again. As he lets go of his anger, readers find hope that father and son will rebuild their relationship. Smith's powerful free verse poems and Earl B. Lewis's illustrations portray a family rebuilding itself. **Health H2, H5, LA1, SSIII, SSIV African Americans**

Little Divas

By Philana Marie Boles. 2006. 164 pages. HarperCollins/Amistad. (F) **Grades 5–7**

With her mother in Ghana for a year, 12-year-old Cassidy lives with her father and spends her time with her bossy cousin, Rikki. Both girls can't wait for seventh grade to begin, but when Cassidy discovers her divorced parents plan to send her to a snooty private school, the summer seems ruined. Worse, class cutup Travis Jones simply won't leave her alone. She's been mad at him for ages, but he's gotten really cute; what if he really does like her? Guided by Mary, Rikki's sister, who regularly sneaks out to see her boyfriend, the girls plan to attend a forbidden pool party where they hope to set their new reputations as divas—cool girls who are also nice. The first-person narrative is full of dialogue and flows smoothly. Strong family connections, a positive depiction of contemporary African American life and language, and details involving fashion, boys, and a girl's place in the world make this a great read. **Health H2, H5, LA1, LA9, SSIII, SSIV African Americans**

The Other Half of My Heart
By Sundee T. Frazier. 2010. 296 pages. Delacorte. (F) **Grades 4–7**

Everyone in their town knows 11-year-olds Keira and Minni are twins—despite the fact that Keira is cinnamon brown with dark, curly hair and Minni is pale white with reddish blond hair. Minni has noticed racist attitudes toward her sister but has pushed aside her worries. Then her grandmother Minerva enters the girls in the "Miss Black Pearl Preteen" beauty pageant in North Carolina, and Minni experiences, for the first time, what it is like to stand out because of skin color. She realizes this is what Keira faces at home, and bristles when her prickly grandmother tries to make her sister appear more "white" for the pageant. When Keira accuses Minni of feeling superior to her, Minni's worst fear seems about to come true. Exploring issues of race, prejudice, and self-concept with a compelling plot and a deft, sometimes humorous touch, this is a solid tale.   Health H2, H5, LA1, SSIII, SSIV African Americans

Outside Beauty
By Cynthia Kadohata. 2008. 265 pages. Atheneum. (F) **Grades 7–12**

Thirteen-year-old Shelby and her three sisters adore their mother, Helen. She has given them a strong sense of independence while teaching them all the ways they can use their looks to attract a rich man. The sisters have developed close bonds as they cope with their mother's narcissistic personality and peripatetic lifestyle. When Helen must recover from a car accident, the girls are sent to their respective fathers. Shelby goes to Arkansas, where her dad runs a gum company. She misses her city lifestyle, but as she gets to know her father, she begins to appreciate this new parent. When she discovers her younger sister, Maddy, is in trouble, it takes the power of all the sisters to figure out how to reunite their family. Shelby's first-person narrative tells a thought-provoking and fast-paced tale.   Health H2, H5, H8, LA1, SSIV, SSVII Japanese Americans, Mixed-Race Americans

The Road to Paris
By Nikki Grimes. 2006. 153 pages. Putnam. (F) **Grades 4–7**

Paris Richmond and her brother, Malcolm, flee their alcoholic mother's abuse and are placed in foster care. Malcolm ends up in a home for boys, and Paris is sent to live with the Lincolns, a white middle-class family. She becomes friends with a white girl in the neighborhood. However, in a cruel outburst about Paris's ethnicity, the girl's father forbids his daughter from seeing her. Although she loves the Lincolns, Paris misses Malcolm. In a too-tidy ending, Paris and Malcolm are reunited with their mother, who has successfully completed a rehabilitation program. Despite its choppy nature, the book presents a positive picture of a foster family. It would mesh nicely with a study of individual growth or interaction of individuals and groups.   Health H2, H5, LA1, SSIII, SSIV, SSV African Americans, Mixed-Race Americans

Secret Saturdays
By Torrey Maldonado. 2010. 195 pages. Putnam. (F) **Grades 5–8**

Middle schoolers Justin and Sean have always been close friends. They live in the same building in the rough Red Hook projects in Brooklyn. Sean's mother frequently reminds him to fight with words, not fists. Now Sean has become a bully; when he disses other students, his words are hurtful; and his fists become active as well. His grades suffer, and he begins hanging with the wrong crowd. Justin is worried—particularly when he sees Sean and his mother leave the building very early on Saturday mornings. Where do they go? With urban dialect and rapping, Justin tells the story from his perspective. Having grown up in the Red Hook projects, Maldonado applies his "firsthand knowledge of youth, fatherlessness, and poverty" to create the story.   Health H2, H5, H8, LA1, LA9, SSIII, SSIV African Americans

Shanghai Messenger
By Andrea Cheng. 2005. Illus. No page numbers. Lee & Low. (F) **Grades 4–7**

Visiting her relatives in China for the first time, Xiao Mei doesn't understand Chinese ways and feels just as out-of-place with her mixed-race heritage in China as she does in America. But many aspects of China touch and charm her, from the warm acceptance of her grandmother Nai Nai's extended family to participating in tai chi exercises with the ladies in the park. Each page is framed by strong, orange-red patterns resembling gates, giving the perception of entering another world. The free-verse format is offset by Ed Young's soft pastel, ink, dye, charcoal, and crayon illustrations, bringing to life the experiences—and decisions—of Xiao Mei. A pronunciation glossary is included at the beginning of the book. **Health H2, H5, LA1, LA9, SSIII, SSIV, VA1, VA4, VA6 Chinese Americans, Mixed-Race Americans**

Sweet Thang
By Allison Whittenberg. 2006. 149 pages. Delacorte. (F) **Grades 5–7**

Life changed drastically for 11-year-old Charmaine Upshaw when her Aunt Karyn died, leaving her 3-year old son, Tracy John. Devastated by her favorite aunt's death, Charmaine worried about Tracy John's fate. Now, at 14, Charmaine knows where Tracy John lives—with her family. As she tells her own story, readers understand the sense of injustice she has felt. Charmaine shares her room with Tracy John and thinks it's unfair. Her family dotes on Tracy John, as do strangers on the street. However, Charmaine stews with frustration bordering on anger until she babysits him. Slowly she realizes she, too, loves the spoiled little boy, nicknamed "Sweet Thang." In this coming-of-age novel, Whittenberg explores the feelings of younger adolescent girls who often say, "Life isn't fair." The fully developed characters could almost be the family next door. **Health HE2, HE5, LA1, LA9, SSIII, SSIV African Americans**

The Trouble with Tessa
By Ofelia Dumas Lachtman.
2005. 122 pages. Piñata Books/Arte Público. (F) **Grades 4–6**

Eleven-year-old Tessa del Campo is surrounded by her family, including a lively group of extended relatives. As she tries to make her way through a boring summer, she finds yellowing pages in the bottom of a junky trunk and thinks she has found directions for magic spells. She begins her "magic" by casting a spell to prevent her little sister from calling her "Tess"—and can't believe her luck when the magic spell seems to work. Tessa's belief in her developing powers hits a major roadblock when she thinks she has cast a spell that will cause her parents to divorce. Suddenly, everything is changing. Short diary entries accompany the third-person singular narrative, giving insight as to Tessa's motives and adding interest to the text. A sprinkling of Spanish words and details about Tessa's extended family let readers know about her Latino heritage, but the focus stays on Tessa's highly imaginative view of the world. **Health, Language Arts HE2, HE5, LA1, SSII, SSIII, SSIV Latinos**

We Beat the Street: How a Friendship Pact Helped Us Succeed
By Sampson Davis, George Jenkins, and Rameck Hunt.
2005. 194 pages. Dutton. (NF) **Grades 7–12**

Three eleventh-grade boys make a pact to help one another become doctors. In alternating chapters, they relate their stories of growing up in the tough neighborhoods of Newark, New Jersey. Each chapter ends with a short "conversation with" section in which the adult doctor reflects on that section of his life. ("Let me tell you about the boys I used to hang out with. Two of them were murdered. Two of them are strung out on drugs.") Drugs, gangs, and life in the projects often come close to claiming the boys' future, but each manages to make it to the next step on the way to becoming a physician. The matter-of-fact tone makes this all the more inspirational.   Health H2, H5, LA1, LA9, SSIII, SSIV, SSV, SSVI African Americans

We Could Be Brothers
By Derrick Barnes. 2010. 164 pages. Scholastic. (F) **Grades 5–8**

On Monday, Robeson and Pacino are strangers in afterschool suspension at Alain Locke Middle School. Robeson's family lives in an upscale gated community; Pacino's family lives in the projects—just ten minutes away. Robeson always wears preppy clothes, and Pacino most often wears low-slung jeans and rumpled shirts. However, Pacino is the straight-A student, while Robeson does well to make Bs. As the week progresses, the two discover just how different their home lives are. Pacino takes care of his younger twin sisters on the nights his mother works; Robeson has few responsibilities. On Friday afternoon, when Robeson learns Pacino is in danger of being shot, he runs to protect his friend. From their tenuous beginning on Monday to midday Saturday, the boys learn "what makes the other tick," and they feel they are truly brothers. Health H2, H5, LA1, SSIII, SSIV African Americans

What I Meant
By Marie Lamba. 2007. 310 pages. Random House. (F) **Grades 7–10**

Fifteen-year-old Sang remembers a lot of laughter in her family before her mean-spirited Aunt Chachi arrived. Now the straight-A student can do nothing right; her parents always seem to take Aunt Chachi's side. Sang can weather anything with her friend Gina's support, but Gina seems to be slipping away from her. To make things worse, the cutest boy in her class has asked her out—and she's not allowed to date! Both funny and suspenseful mishaps escalate as Sang tries to negotiate these obstacles (without really lying), expose her aunt's erratic behavior, and solidify new friendships at school. Sang's breezy first-person narrative gives a heartfelt look at life with a Sikh father, an American mother, and a mentally ill aunt.   Health H4, H5, LA1, SSIV East Indian Americans, Mixed-Race Americans

You Don't Even Know Me
By Sharon Flake. 2010. 195 pages. Jump at the Sun. (F) **Grades 7–9**

While some middle school readers will recognize the urban world of the twenty-four boys featured in these short stories, others will mostly only relate to the boys' feelings. All struggle with issues familiar to most preteens and teens, such as a first kiss, love against the odds, and breaking away from parental control. Other topics reveal more troubling pressures: early pregnancy and marriage, AIDS, a beloved grandfather's unsolved murder, homelessness, a twin's suicide. Poems, stories, and diary entries reveal each boy's, doubts, failures, and triumphs. Although some of the topics might be for more mature tweens, the lack of explicit detail makes this appropriate for seventh and eighth graders.   Health, H2, H5, LA1, SSIII, SSIV African Americans

Zen and the Art of Faking It
By Jordan Sonnenblick. 2007. 264 pages. Scholastic. (F) **Grades 5–8**

For 14-year-old San Lee, nothing is worse than moving to a new town and a new school in the middle of the school year. He should know; he's done it often enough. Because his father is in prison in Texas and his mother spent most of their money for the lawyer, San and his mother have moved to Harrisonville, Pennsylvania. Each other time San has moved he's had to reinvent himself to fit in at the new school; this time, he becomes an "expert" on Zen Buddhism. What he doesn't realize is one of his teachers has studied Zen Buddhism. Coming to the end of the year, San is caught in his lies, and must set about making things right with everyone, including his father. More a book about adjusting and finding a place for oneself than a book about an ethnic group, yet ethnicity plays a part.   Health HE2, HE5, LA1, SSIII, SSIV Chinese Americans

DISEASES AND DISEASE PREVENTION

The Happiness of Kati
By Ngamphan Vejjajiva. 2006. 139 pages. Atheneum. (F) **Grades 4–7**

Nine-year-old Kati has always lived with her grandparents, but she often dreams about her mother, whom she has not seen for five years. Her grandmother finally explains her mother's illness (amyotrophic lateral scleroses, or ALS) and asks Kati if she would like to visit her mother before she dies. Kati finds her mother bedridden and weak, but her mother explains why she gave Kati to her grandparents to raise. She also tells Kati all of the things that she has set aside for her future. When her mother dies, Kati receives an envelope containing information about the father she has never known, and she must choose to live with him or return to her grandparents. Although set in Thailand and filled with lush flowers and natural beauty, the story could have taken place anywhere in the world. It has a beautiful message of love and belonging.   **Health HE1, HE2, LA1, SSIII, SSIV Thais**

Next to Mexico
By Jennifer Nails. 2008. 235 pages. Houghton Mifflin Harcourt. (NF) **Grades 4–6**

When she enters sixth grade, Lylice is assigned as "English buddy" to the new girl, Mexico Mendoza. Mexico has diabetes and lives with her aunt in Arizona while her father works as a taxi driver in Nogales, Mexico. As Lylice navigates the treacherous waters of middle school betrayals, she rebels against various injustices and learns that the boy she likes can't stand up to his friends. She also tries to help Mexico's family in their struggle to stay in the U.S. legally so they can treat Mexico's diabetes. This book personalizes the challenges of immigration. Notes and newspaper articles add to Lylice's lively and entertaining first-person narrative.   **Health, Social Studies H1, H2, LA1, LA9, SSIII, SSIV, SSV, SSVI Latinos**

Out of My Mind
By Sharon Draper. 2010. 295 pages. Atheneum. (F) **Grades 4–6**

When Melody was born, her parents were told she should be institutionalized. They refused. Melody remembers *everything* anyone has said around her for all her eleven years. Until now, the words were only in her mind. When her new aide, Catherine, finds a computer that allows her to talk, all those words tumble out. She answers questions at school and even wins a spot on the quiz bowl team. Fifth grade is tumultuous for a girl with severe cerebral palsy, but as she tells her story through first-person narrative, readers share her joys, frustrations, pains, and endurance. Draper's fluid, poetic prose flows in this story.   Health, H2, H3, LA1, SSIV, SSVIII African Americans

Sickle Cell Disease (Diseases & Disorders series)
By Lizabeth Peak. 2008. Illus. 112 pages. Lucent. (NF) **Grades 7–12**

Sickle cell disease takes various forms, depending on dominant or recessive genes and the mutation of only one cell. The disease can be mild to deadly and affects 8 to 10 percent of African Americans. People of Middle Eastern, Italian, Caribbean, Indian, or Hispanic descent also can be affected. This densely written scientific report book is informative and fills a real niche for health studies but requires attentive reading. The twenty pages of back matter make it more valuable: chapter notes; an extensive glossary; lists of organizations to contact, related books and websites; and a detailed index.   Health HE1, HE3, HE7, HE9, LA1, SCIV, SCVII, SCVII African Americans, AOD

Sparrow
By Sherri L. Smith. 2006. 184 pages. Delacorte. (F) **Grades 7–11**

Raised by her grandmother, Kendall has always been taught that family is everything. But G'ma isn't doing well, and Kendall struggles to be student and caregiver with minimal funds and no outside help. When G'ma dies, Kendall heads to New Orleans, where her aunt lives. Unfortunately, her aunt has moved, but the landlady lets Kendall stay in the duplex, asking only that she keep her daughter, Evie, company. Evie has muscular dystrophy and is in a wheelchair. She is grouchy and temperamental, but needs someone to help her while her mother works. As Kendall searches for her elusive aunt, she comes to realize that while sometimes your family lets you down, you can still create a family of your own.   Health H2, HE3, H5, LA1, SSIII, SSIV, SSV African Americans

GANGS AND BULLYING

Call Me Henri
By Lorraine López. 2006. 237 pages. Curbstone Press. (F) **Grades 6–9**

Enrique wants to learn French, but at Peralta Middle School the rule requires him to successfully complete two years of ESL before starting a foreign language. When Monsieur Nassour offers to let Enrique join the French club, he jumps at the chance. Unfortunately, outside of school his life is full of complications. He goes home every day to care for his triplet baby brothers. He can handle the teasing and girl troubles at school, his best friend's new activity in the White Fence gang, and even his stepdad's escalating abuse; but can Enrique confront gang members after he witnesses a shooting? López presents a warm yet realistic portrayal of the many complicated relationships within a rough-and-tumble barrio middle school. **Health H4, H5, H7, LA1, SSIV, SSV, SSVI Latinos**

The Liberation of Gabriel King
By K. L. Going. 2005. 151 pages. Putnam's. (F) **Grades 4–6**

On the last day of fourth grade, Gabe is missing from the "Moving Up" ceremony at school. After his friend Frita discovers him tied up under a picnic table, she finds the bully responsible—Duke Evans—and gives Duke a good fist to the nose. Although it is 1976, racism in the South is still rampant, and Duke's father threatens them with a visit from the Ku Klux Klan.

Gabe and Frita decide they both have too many fears and agree to spend the summer eliminating them. As they cross items off their lists, they realize that one item will require help from their parents. Biracial friendships in the 1970s South took courage, and Going's characterization of Gabriel and Frita makes them great examples of how friends strengthen each other and spread friendship outward. **Health, Social Studies H2, H5, LA1, SSII, SSIII, SSIV, SSV, SSVI African Americans**

Standing against the Wind
By Traci L. Jones. 2006. 184 pages. Farrar, Straus and Giroux. (F) **Grades 5–8**

Patrice Williams faces many changes when, under false pretenses, her mother takes her from the warm love of her grandmother's home in Georgia and brings her to Chicago. Not two weeks later, Patrice's mother lands in jail, leaving Patrice with Aunt Mae, where Patrice cooks, cleans, and watches her two young cousins. Two things distinguish Patrice from the other eighth graders in Martin Luther King Jr. Middle School—her unruly hair and her intelligence. The thing she dreads most is walking to school and being bullied and taunted by a group of boys. When the leader of the group, Monty, starts walking with Patrice, they become friends. Monty asks Patrice to tutor his little brother; she agrees, and soon, Monty and Michael join Patrice and her cousins in afterschool study sessions. Monty's grades improve substantially as a result. In this realistic school story, readers see Patrice's dedication to improving her life despite the obstacles she faces each day. Believable dialogue reflecting her inner-city neighborhood helps moves the story along. **Health HE2, HE5, LA1, LA9, SSIII, SSIV, SSV, SSVI, African Americans**

SEXUALITY AND SEX ROLES

Accidental Love
By Gary Soto. 2006. 179 pages. Harcourt. (F) **Grades 6–10**

When they meet to exchange mixed-up cell phones, 14-year-old Marisa is amazed at how nerdy Rene is. Why is she so attracted to him? In her gritty world she gets into fistfights and has a hard time controlling her anger. When she switches to Rene's school, ritzy Hamilton Magnet High, Marisa is amazed to learn the world can work differently than she'd thought. Soon she is involved in the school play, making friends, doing well with her schoolwork, and spending every free minute with Rene. But Rene's mom doesn't like her, and Marisa discovers Rene may have a reason to act wimpy around his custodial parent. Refreshingly real dialogue, Marisa's inner conversations, and text peppered with Spanish give readers one version of life in the barrio. **Health H2, H5, LA1, LA9, SSIII, SSIV, SSV Latinos**

After Tupac and D Foster
By Jacqueline Woodson. 2008. 153 pages. Putnam. (F) **Grades 5–9**

Through the first-person account of her unnamed narrator, Woodson places the reader in the heart of Queens in the late 1990s. Two 11-year-old girls have grown up as sisters in their "boring and quiet" neighborhood. When D walks into their lives, they become a threesome, each looking for the "Big Purpose" of her life. The girls envy D's independence; a foster child, D takes the bus wherever she likes and seems to know much more about life than they. D connects with the songs the rapper Tupac sings: "When I see him on TV, I be thinking about the way his life was all crazy. And my life is all crazy. And we both all sad about it and stuff." Each girl has her troubles. The narrator has never known her dad; Neeka's large family includes a "swishy" older brother who is wrongly jailed after being duped and beaten by a gay-basher; and D longs for a mother who isn't there. Their friendship is strong, and the story is full of hope, even as it moves toward the girls' inevitable parting. Woodson's deft portrayal of their community adds great depth to this story of growing up and moving on.   Health, Music H2, H5, LA1, LA9, MU8, MU9, SSIII, SSIV, SSVI African Americans

The Fold
By An Na. 2008. 280 pages. Putnam. (F) **Grades 7–10**

Joyce thinks John Ford Kang is perfect: he's totally gorgeous and the most popular boy at school. How will she ever get him to look at her? The answer appears when her great-aunt Gomo decides to pay for surgery to put a crease in Joyce's eyelids to make her eyes appear round. Joyce is sure this popular look will improve her life. Before the surgery, she spends her summer working at her parents' restaurant, hanging out with her best friend, Gina, and watching her faultless older sister, Helen, charm everyone in sight. In this multilayered novel, Na explores themes of self-acceptance and fitting in as she takes a hard look at beauty, sexuality, and cultural mores. She leads the reader into the heart of one Korean American community, where reputation is everything and lesbianism is not acceptable.   Health H2, LA1, LA9, SSIII, SSIV Korean Americans

The God Box
By Alex Sanchez. 2007. 248 pages. Simon & Schuster. (F) **Grades 8–12**

Deeply immersed in his fundamentalist Christian group, Paul's church has been the center of his life. He's dated Angie since middle school; they've been best friends since he moved from Mexico to Texas. Then Manuel transfers to their school. Cute, openly gay, with a broad knowledge of the Bible and a firm Christian faith of his own, Manuel challenges Paul to look beyond the boundaries his church has set. Highly attracted to Manuel, Paul tries to keep his feelings at bay. Then Manuel is badly beaten; Paul has to make a choice. The first-person narrative brings Paul and his questioning to life; the theological explorations will give readers much food for thought   Health H4, H6, LA1, SSIV, SSV Latinos

Koyal Dark, Mango Sweet
By Kashmira Sheth. 2006. 250 pages. Hyperion. (F) **Grades 7–10**

Sixteen-year-old Jeeta is relieved her mother has two older daughters to marry off before her. Constant talk of prospective grooms annoys her, and when her new friend Sarina introduces her to a world in which Indian women have professional careers, she begins to see other possibilities for her life. Jeeta lives in Mumbai, where her middle-class family struggles with the cultural change in modern India. Her father seems to accept the changing times and new role of women, but her domineering mother handles family issues. When Jeeta's budding romance with Neel is exposed, her father stands up for her. And when her older sister, Mohindi, is abused by her new husband, she writes Jeeta for help. Richly detailed with a strong sense of place, this brings readers into the heart of city life in Mumbai. Although a few of the plot turns seem a bit pat, the pace is good, and Jeeta's feisty voice and dissatisfaction with the status quo will resonate with teen readers.   Health, Social Studies H5, LA1, SSII, SSIII, SSIV, SSV East Indians

No Girls Allowed:
Tales of Daring Women Dressed as Men for Love, Freedom and Adventure
By Susan Hughes. 2008. Illus. 80 pages. Kids Can. (NF) **Grades 4–8**

Hatshepsut, Mulan, Alfhild, Esther Brandeau, James Barry, Ellen Craft, and Sarah Rosetta Wakeman—these women span the ages but have one thing in common: all "passed" as men in order to further their own ambition or the fortunes of their families. This graphic novel presents each woman's story in easy-to-read prose accompanied by bold, sharp, black-and-white graphic illustrations. An afterword discusses gender issues in modern times, and a list of further reading leads to other works about these women's interesting lives.   Health H2, LA1, SSII, SSIII, SSV, SSVI African Americans; Chinese, Egyptians, Jewish French, Norwegians, Scots

Strong, Beautiful Girls
(Essential Health series)
By Ashley Rae Harris. 2009. Illus. Approx. 112 pages. Advance. (NF) **Grades 6–9**

The books in this series address issues of self-concept that most teenage girls face at one time or another. At the beginning of each book the reader meets Dr. Vicki Panaccione, a licensed psychologist who specializes in issues with teens, children, and families. The author, Ashley Rae Harris, also introduces herself and gives a short depiction of her own struggles as a teenager. Each volume in the series contains nine or ten chapters that focus on that volume's theme; themes range from physical changes to relating to relatives, making healthy dating decisions, and school cliques. Each chapter introduces a problem and gives a real-life scenario of one girl's struggles with that issue. Questions designed to foster discussion are placed in text boxes. At the end of each chapter, Dr. Vicki gives specific advice directly to the reader. She and the author comment on ways to handle each situation. The graphic layout is accessible and, with its purple and floral design, is crafted to appeal to girls. The contemporary photographs consistently depict girls from a variety of ethnicities. Racial issues are not predominant, but are included at times. The reassuring tone and direct writing style make these books suitable for both individual and group reading. We recommend all titles in this series for middle school collections.   Health H2, H3, H5, LA1, SSIV AOD

Tofu Quilt
By Ching Yeung Russell. 2009. 125 pages. Lee & Low Books. (F) **Grades 5–8**

Girls growing up in 1960s Hong Kong weren't supposed to have much education. Their purpose in life was to marry and care for the family. Careers, particularly those requiring extended education, were reserved for men, so when Yeung Ying decides to become a writer she faces a number of obstacles and has little support from those around her. However, her mother supports the changing roles for women. She insists on educating Yeung Ying despite the fierce opposition she faces from Yeung Ying's uncles. Yeung Ying loves to write. Unbeknownst to her family and using a pen name, she submits a story, "The Tofu Quilt," to a weekly youth newspaper. Three months later, a classmate shows the story to Yeung Ying, having no idea she is the author. This encourages her to pursue her dream and prove her uncles wrong. In her author's note, Russell explains that her novel-length free verse fictional poem traces her own path to becoming a writer.   **Health, Social Studies H2, LA1, SSII, SSIII, SSIV, SSV, SSVI, SSIX Chinese, Chinese Americans**

Your Sexuality
(Ripped from the Headlines series)
By Kris Hirschmann. 2007. Illus. 64 pages. Erickson Press. (NF) **Grades 6–11**

Using simple language, statistics, illustrations, and photographs showing teens from a variety of ethnicities, this book presents basic information on the physical and emotional changes teenagers may experience as they mature. Wide margins and well-spaced text are interspersed with large graphics and text boxes that give facts such as "What Teens Really Think about Condoms." The tone is neutral, with a matter-of-fact presentation of sensitive topics such as setting boundaries on sexual conduct; realizing one is gay, lesbian, or bisexual; and teen pregnancy. A well-documented resource that includes chapter source notes; a glossary; a bibliography of books and websites; a complete index; picture credits; and author information.   **Health H2, H3, H5, LA1, AOD**

2 LANGUAGE ARTS

Every book in the bibliography has at least one language arts standard because each can provide a reading enrichment experience. This chapter, however, contains titles specific to language arts. Biographies of writers and television personalities are here. Various genres and formats, such as fantasy and short stories, are here. Speeches are here. Folklore is here. We know teachers and librarians use folklore to introduce or enhance a study of a particular culture or country, as well as to compare cultures. Poetry books were tricky. Where form is dominant, the entry is included in language arts. Narrative poetry titles, however, are found in their curricular areas. Readers are encouraged to use the index to find all poetry titles. Diaries, journals, letters, and memoirs are here as well; we know many middle school students gravitate toward them.

LITERATURE

AUTHORS AND POETS

Always an Olivia: A Remarkable Family History
By Carolivia Herron. 2007. Illus. 30 pages. Kar-Ben. (NF) **Grades 2–6**

When Carol Olivia visits her great-grandmother, she learns about her family's history. "Hundreds of years ago there was a Jewish family living in Spain near the sea. Spain was a dangerous place for Jews . . . It was a terrible time." The family sails to Portugal and settles in the village of Almansil, keeping their religion behind closed shutters. Later, the family is forced to move to Venice. Young Sarah is kidnapped, but a dashing pirate rescues her, and the two end up in the Georgia Sea Islands. Here they are embraced by the Geechees, who originally came from West Africa. This exploration of one family's African American and Jewish heritage leaves many questions for the inquiring student, making it a fine introduction to a number of cultural discussions. A note on "Jews and Racial Designation" gives further background on historical perceptions of race. Large, richly colored illustrations give snapshots of the family throughout the centuries. The bibliography contains only adult references; however, these might be of interest to teachers and advanced students. Social Studies LA1, SSIII, SSV Jewish African Americans

Maya Angelou (Just the Facts Biographies series)
By L. Patricia Kite. 2006. Illus. 112 pages. Lerner. (NF) **Grades 7–12**

Born in St. Louis, Missouri, in 1928, Maya Angelou and her brother were bounced between their mother and their paternal grandparents throughout their childhood; when their parents divorced, their father sent the very young children alone by train to Stamps, Arkansas, to live with their grandparents. Maya's stepfather raped her when she was 8, and by 17 she had lived on the streets, become a streetcar driver in San Francisco, and had a son. Despite the segregation and racism in Stamps, from time to time she returned when she most needed family and a sense of belonging. While living in Harlem, Maya was encouraged to write and to tell the story of her childhood—the basis of her book *I Know Why the Caged Bird Sings*. This biography's clear, engaging text, uncluttered format, photographs, source notes, further readings, websites, and index make it more than a report book. Language Arts LA1, SSII, SSIII, SSIV, SSV African Americans

Oprah Winfrey: A Twentieth-Century Life (Up Close series)
By Ilene Cooper. 2007. Illus. 204 pages. Viking. (NF) **Grades 5–9**

Cooper has taken the very public life of megastar and author Oprah Winfrey and personalized it in this smoothly written, intimate biography. Winfrey spent her early years on her strict grandmother's Mississippi farm. At age 6, she began to be shuttled between her mother's apartment in Milwaukee and her father's more stable and secure home in Nashville. The book tells of Winfrey's sexual abuse at her mother's house, her subsequent promiscuity, and her secret pregnancy (her premature son died after two weeks). Always an excellent and eager student, Winfrey's ability to connect with people led to her meteoric rise in radio and then television. The book's small size is appealing, but the text is rarely relieved by photographs. The narrative flows quickly, however, and the book is well documented, with source notes, an extensive bibliography, an index, and photo credits. Language Arts LA1, H2, SSIV, SSV, SSVII African Americans

Zora and Me

By Victoria Bond and T. R. Simon. 2010. 170 pages. Candlewick. (F) **Grades 5–9**

Even as a child, Zora Neale Hurston had a vivid imagination. Did she or didn't she actually see a "gator man"? She swears she did, and as unexplained sightings, deaths, and injuries become more common, people in her all-black hometown raise questions. Even though insulated from white Jim Crow mentality, life in Eatonville, Florida, in the early 1900s isn't free of racial tensions. Using Hurston's own writings as the basis of their fictional work, the authors weave a lively, suspenseful, funny story told by Zora's best friend, Carrie. Children in her school want to believe Zora's "gator man" story, but adults wonder. Determined to prove she is correct, tenacious Zora doesn't stop her investigation. The surprise ending makes readers want more! Engaged in the children's escapades, readers forget that the girls and their friend, Teddy, are only fourth graders. The authors include a timeline of Hurston's life, as well as a bibliography of her works and children's books based on her adult works.   Language Arts LA1, LA9, SSII, SSIII, SSIV, SSV African Americans

FANTASY

47

By Walter Mosley. 2005. 232 pages. Little, Brown. (F) **Grades 7–12**

Field slaves on the Corinthian Plantation have only numbers for names. Number 47 is most likely 14 years old, but, as he says, slaves don't have birthdays. He tells how Tall John comes into his life as a runaway slave from a nearby plantation. From his first day, it is evident that Tall John has a mysterious side. He is centuries old and is not from this planet; he is gifted with powers to fight Wall, the evil one who can disguise himself as a human. Tall John tells 47 he has been seeking him all his life. It seems 47 has a special gift that will allow him to carry on Tall John's work. In this gripping historical fantasy, Mosley takes the reader on wild rides through time and space. He uses the n-word frequently, yet it is always in context of conversation. By using first-person narrative from the viewpoint of Number 47, readers can feel the pain and fear the slaves endured.   Language Arts, Social Studies LA1, LA9, SSII, SSIII, SSIV, SSV, SSVI, SSVII African Americans

Archer's Quest

By Linda Sue Park. 2006. 167 pages. Clarion. (F) **Grades 6–8**

Twelve-year-old Kevin Kim wishes he'd listened when his grandparents told him about his Korean heritage. A strange man with a wickedly accurate bow and arrow has appeared in his house and seems to think Kevin is his mortal enemy. Italicized dialogue reveals Kevin's thoughts as he progresses through an adventurous day with the stranger, whom he names Archie (for *archer*). He comes to realize Archie is really the legendary Chu-mong, a king of ancient Korea who has somehow ended up in the wrong place and time. It is up to Kevin to figure out why Chu-mong is at his house—and how to get him back so he can save his people. Using the Chinese calendar and zodiac, Kevin must put his math skills to work in order to help Archie in this intriguing fantasy. Chu-mong slowly reveals his story as the two pursue a means of returning him to his home. **Language Arts, Mathematics LA1, M5, SSII, SSIII Korean Americans**

The Arrival

By Shaun Tan. 2006. Illus. No page numbers. Lothian Books. (F) **Grades 5–12**

In this powerful and thoughtful wordless graphic novel, a man leaves his wife and child to go to another country in search of a better life for his family. This man could be any man from any time. Illustrations produced with graphite pencil on cartridge paper depict a surrealistic, timeless city into whose midst the man is placed. Still, premoving picture frames, sometimes nine to a page, are interspersed with historical photographs and one- or two-page drawings. These create a magical, yet emotion-packed experience for readers, who feel the wonder, the fear, and the excitement of the characters. This book deserves multiple readings and viewings. **Language Arts, Visual Arts LA1, LA9, LA10, SSII, SSIII, SSIV, SSV, SSVI, SSIX, VA1, VA4, VA6 Global, AOD**

The Black Canary

By Jane Louise Curry. 2005. 279 pages. Margaret K. McElderry. (F) **Grades 5–8**

Twelve-year-old James hides his incredible voice because he is tired of his family's obsession with music. His mother is a famous black jazz singer and his father is a white jazz piano player. James feels like he lives in three cultures: black, white, and mixed-up- in-between. He reluctantly accompanies his parents on a performing trip to London, where he slips through a wormhole into seventeenth-century London. James is a curiosity to everyone he meets but soon discovers a boy with a wonderful voice can get both food and shelter. He becomes known as "the black canary"; his ethnicity becomes his strength. He loses track of time and is swept up in preparing a solo for the queen. The tension between James's increasing involvement in the early 1600s and finding his way back to the present keeps this a fast-paced, highly involving story.   **Language Arts, Music LA1, MU8, MU9, SSII, SSIV, SSV Mixed-Race Americans**

Come Fall
By A. C. E. Bauer. 2010. 231 pages. Random House. (F) **Grades 5–8**

Imagine being in eleven schools in nine years *and* being held back twice. At 15, Salman begins seventh grade in a new school. He knows his skin color sets him apart but hopes things might be different in Springfalls Junior High. Those hopes are dashed the first day as Crow appears and swoops down to take a shiny object from Salman's hand. Rumors fly fast, and the other students begin to call Salman "Crow" and hurl cruel remarks at him. Salman can't really explain the bird's presence; readers, however, understand Crow is connected to the fairy queen who had promised Salman's human mother she'd protect him. Bauer's use of the fairy folk from Shakespeare's *Midsummer Night's Dream* adds an other-world fantasy dimension to the story. Salman's East Indian ethnicity isn't central here, but it adds another layer to reasons students think him different. **Language Arts LA1, LA9 AOD, East Indians**

Hannah's Winter
By Kierin Meehan. 2009. 212 pages. Kane/Miller. (F) **Grades 5–8**

Thirteen-year-old Hannah's mother insists that Hannah accompany her to Japan while she researches her latest book. Hannah stays with the Maekawa family in their quarters above their stationery shop. She and Miki (age 14) become friends. The girls find an old box with an assortment of odd things, including a creased square of paper covered with old Japanese calligraphy. As strange things begin to happen—in the shop and in Hannah's room—the family gets involved in solving the mystery of the poem on the old paper. Hannah's stay suddenly becomes more than she bargained for. Japanese culture is woven throughout and adds interest to a good ghost story.   Language Arts, Social Studies LA1, SSIII, SSIV, VA4 Japanese

Hereville: How Mirka Got Her Sword
By Barry Deutsch. 2010. Illus. 144 pages. Abrams. (F) **Grades 4–7**

Spunky 11-year-old Mirka Hirschberg doesn't want to become a proper girl and learn to knit or find a husband; she *does* want to fight dragons. She has one problem—she doesn't have a sword! Going in search of a sword, Mirka outwits her two older bullying brothers and ends up in front of a deserted-looking rickety old house. It isn't deserted—its witch owner is floating in the air! Her siblings don't believe Mirka, of course, so she takes them to see it. No witch, but they do find a superpig! Now what's an Orthodox Jewish girl to do when she sees something she's never seen? Run or climb a tree? Her adventures are just beginning as she tries to solve the witch's riddle and acquire her sword. This hilarious comic-strip graphic novel is a quick read filled with action, dialogue, and lots of Yiddish and Hebrew words and sayings. Deutsch used Photoshop and a Cintiq tablet for the black-and-white artwork; Jake Richmond used Photoshop to digitally add color.   Language Arts, Visual Arts LA1, LA9, VA1, VA4, VA6 Jews

Hiroshima Dreams
By Kelly Easton. 2007. 198 pages. Dutton. (F) **Grades 7–10**

Lin is a quiet child who watches the world around her but rarely enters into the bustling activities and friendships her sister loves. Their grandmother moves in when Lin is 5; the close bond between Obaachan and Lin—and the psychic ability they share—is at the heart of this lyrically written fantasy. Obaachan is full of koans—Buddhist riddles—and Lin includes these as she recounts the daily happenings of her life from kindergarten to high school. Readers see her master the cello, join a private school, and make her first friend, an African American student who welcomes Lin into her family. Lin struggles with her psychic visions, and as Obaachan weakens, she finally learns about the mysterious box labeled HIROSHIMA in her grandmother's room.   Language Arts, Social Studies LA1, LA9, SSIII, SSIV, SSV, SSVI African Americans, Mixed-Race Americans, Japanese, Japanese Americans

The House of Djinn
By Suzanne Fisher Staples. 2008.
207 pages. Farrar, Straus and Giroux. (F) **Grades 7–12**

Bringing the story of Shabanu (*Shabanu, Daughter of the Wind*, 1989) full circle, this explores the complex relationships within the extended family of a powerful tribal leader. Fifteen-year-old Mumtaz, or Muti, lives with her Uncle Omar, her hateful Aunt Leyla, and her fun-loving, modernist grandfather Baba, the Amirzai tribe's patriarch. Well educated and living a modern lifestyle in the wealthy section of Lahore, Muti seemingly lacks for nothing. Muti's best friend is her cousin Jameel, who visits every summer from San Francisco. This summer, Baba falls gravely ill, and suddenly the future of Jameel and Mumtaz changes radically. Told in alternating chapters from multiple viewpoints, this plunges the reader into a modern-day Pakistan that still cherishes tradition. Exceptionally well written, the fast pace, suspense, and romantic and supernatural elements make this book hard to put down.   Language Arts, Social Studies LA1, SSIII, SSIV, SSV Pakistani Americans, Pakistanis

Ninth Ward
By Jewell Parker Rhodes. 2010. 217 pages. Little, Brown. (F) **Grades 4–7**

Lanesha, 12, sees ghosts. This is why her rich relatives are afraid of her and allow Mama Ya-Ya, the midwife who birthed her but was unable to save her teenage mother, to rear her. In fact, Lanesha can see her mother on Mama Ya-Ya's bed at times—still pregnant and never really turning her gaze to Lanesha. In this first-person account, Lanesha worries about her 82-year-old guardian as Hurricane Katrina heads towards New Orleans. Mama Ya-Ya has seen the signs, and with her help—and the help of Lanesha's mother—this smart, feisty girl puts her inner resources to the test. Descriptions of the neighborhood, the reactions people have to the impending disaster, the truly horrific power of Katrina, and the ensuing flood give a clear account of this historic event. Lanesha's hopeful spirit carries the action-packed yet mysterious story. Language Arts, Social Studies LA1, LA9, SSIV, SSV African Americans

The Old African
By Julius Lester. 2005. Illus. 79 pages. Dial. (F) **Grades 6–10**

Lester bases his story on a legend about an African man, Jaja, brought to this country in chains, who led his Ybo people out of slavery and back home to Africa. It begins with the old African man watching a boy being whipped. Through his magical powers, the man assumes the boy's pain so the boy does not cry out. Jaja sits with the boy and falls asleep, remembering the time when he and his wife, Ola, were captured; Lester recounts that voyage and its accompanying horrible acts. From the time Jaja saw his wife, Ola, jump overboard, he never speaks again. Yet he has powers that allow him to see into the minds of others. He decides to lead his people away from the plantation and back to Africa. Descriptive text and Jerry Pinkney's vivid illustrations—in graphite, gouache, pastel, and watercolor on paper—transport the reader. The serious tone and graphic depictions make this appropriate for grade 6 and above. Language Arts, Visual Arts LA1, LA9, SSII, SSIV, SSV, SSIX, VA1, VA4, VA6 Africans, African Americans, Ybo

Pemba's Song: A Ghost Story
By Tonya Hegamin and Marilyn Nelson. 2008. 110 pages. Scholastic. (F) **Grades 6–9**

Fourteen-year-old Pemba does not want to leave her homegirls in Brooklyn, much less her new boyfriend, Malik. But her mother has a new teaching job in Colchester, Connecticut, and now they're trying to settle into a creaky, creepy old house. When the dreams—and daydreams followed by horrible headaches—begin, Pemba isn't sure what to think. Someone is scared, upset, and talking about living "in the home of this wicked man." By talking to Abraham, an eccentric who is researching the history of the area's African American community, Pemba learns about the town's history and the story of the mysterious ghost she now occasionally sees in the house. Alternating between first-person prose and verse sections, this fast-paced mystery is a solid read. Language Arts LA1, LA9, SSIII, SSIV, SSVI African Americans

Seer of Shadows
By Avi. 2008. 202 pages. HarperCollins. (F) **Grades 5–8**

Fourteen-year-old Horace, an apprentice to a lazy photographer, Mr. Middleditch, finds himself in a predicament when Mr. Middleditch gets a wealthy client. The seemingly bereft Mrs. Von Macht requests a photograph of herself to put on the grave of her recently deceased daughter, Eleanora. Seeing an opportunity, Middleditch sets out to "enhance" the photograph by superimposing a photograph of Eleanora onto the picture of her mother. As Horace searches the house for photographs of Eleanora, he gets acquainted with Peg, the servant girl who was like a sister to Eleanora. He learns Mrs. Von Macht's story is quite different from the truth. As he takes and develops the photographs, Horace realizes he has brought Eleanora's ghost "to life." Peg's and his urgent mission now is to capture and put the ghost away before she does more terrible harm. Avi brings 1872 New York City to life as he weaves a suspenseful ghost story into a historically accurate setting. **Language Arts LA1, SSIV African Americans**

Sisters of the Sword
By Maya Snow. 2008. 275 pages. HarperCollins. (F) **Grades 6–9**

Kimi and Hana are caught in the chaos when their uncle and his samurai warriors turn a celebration into a slaughter. Having watched their father and brother die, along with most others in the household, the girls flee for their lives. Disguised as peasant boys, they arrive at a dojo, a samurai training school, where they are taken in as servants. They must always maintain their station in life, despite Kimi's strong wishes to identify herself and take revenge on their cousin. As the girls work and train alongside the other servants, they grow stronger and more poised in their fighting techniques. Snow, an excellent storyteller, weaves the traditions of feudal Japan into a thrilling tale of samurai skills and grace. As the days of the dojo tournament approach, readers feel the tension and excitement. Will Kimi get her chance to avenge her father's murder? Snow adds twists to the plot, keeping readers guessing right to the end. Equally exciting sequels to this story are *Chasing the Secret* (2009) and *Journey through Fire* (2009). **Language Arts, Social Studies LA1, LA9, SSI, SSIII, SSIV Japanese**

Stormwitch
By Susan Vaught. 2005. 208 pages. Bloomsbury. (F) **Grades 5–9**

In Pass Christian, Mississippi, Ruba Jones is a misfit. After her maternal grand-mother's death in Haiti, Ruba has come to Pass Christian to live with her pater-nal grandmother. The two grandmothers are polar opposites—Ba had taught Ruba about their family history back to the ancient African Amazon women; Grandmother Jones teaches Ruba that the "spells" she learned in Haiti aren't appropriate for Mississippi and makes her attend church. In the days leading up to Hurricane Camille (1969), Ruba learns what it means to be black in southern Mississippi. She also learns she must hide her bag of herbs and ritual attire from her grandmother. Ruba senses the oncoming storm, hears the voice from the storm, and knows she must face the stormwitch and protect her family from destruction. Vaught has created an atmosphere of intrigue in a historical fantasy that addresses native Haitian cultures and the struggle for civil rights in southern Mississippi.   Language Arts LA1, LA9, SSII, SSIII, SSIV, SSV, SSIX **Haitian Americans**

The Third Eye
By Mahtab Narsimhan. 2007. 240 pages. Dundurn. (F) **Grades 6–9**

Ever since their mother and grandfather left, Tara and her little brother, Suraj, have suffered the cruelty of their stepmother. Their father has a vacant look and seems not to notice his children's distress. When an evil healer comes to Morni, the villagers are mesmerized, and only Tara makes the connection between the healer and the Vetalas—the strange, zombielike creatures who attack people in the forest. Braving the forest, Tara escapes with Suraj to search for her mother and grandfather who she knows can save their village. Helped by Lord Ganesh and Lord Yama, Tara is tested by the supernatural. With lots of dialogue and a chilling plot, this fantasy begins slowly but works into a satisfying conclusion.
Language Arts LA1, SSIII, SSIV, SSV, SSVI **East Indians**

FOLKLORE

Around the World in 80 Tales
By Saviour Pirotta. 2007. Illus. 176 pages. Kingfisher. (NF) **Grades 3–12**

What a collection of tales! They do indeed span the globe—including tales from North America, South America, Europe, Africa, Asia, and Australasia. Some are short, others are long; some are familiar, others are not. As is typical, these tales range from funny to cautionary to wise to pourquoi. A banner representing each continent runs across the top of each two-page spread in that section. Not all tales have accompanying illustrations, but those that do are bright and engaging.
Language Arts LA1, LA9, SSI, SSII Global

Dibé yázhí táá'go baa hane' (The three little sheep)
By Seraphine G.Yazzie. Trans. by Peter A. Thomas. 2006. Illus.
No page numbers. Salina Bookshelf. (NF) **Grades 2–6**

Bright purple, orange, green, blue, and red colors make the large, cartoonlike sheep and wolf spring off the page in this Navajo version of "The Three Little Pigs," written in a true fractured-fairy-tale style that reflects Navajo philosophy. When three brothers leave home, their mother tells them, "If one of you gets into trouble, go to your brothers for help. You must take care of each other." Each double-page spread includes a paragraph in both Navajo and English. The narrative is well suited for storytellers; it moves quickly and includes enough dialogue to make the brothers come alive. End flaps include author and illustrator information.   **Language Arts, LA1, SSII, SSIII American Indians, Navajos**

Dybbuk: A Version
By Barbara Rogasky. 2005. Illus. 64 pages. Holiday House. (NF) **Grades 5–9**

Sender, the richest man in Brinitz, wants to find a rich scholar to marry his daughter, Leah. Enter Konin, a starving scholar. He and Leah know they are destined to be together, but how that will happen isn't clear. Konin spends days each week studying the Kabbalah trying to find a way to marry Leah, to no avail. The story involves a dybbuk, a staple in stories of Jewish culture: "simply put . . . the personality, spirit, or soul of someone who has died that enters the body of someone who is alive." Rogasky's gift of storytelling and Leonard Everett Fisher's stark, dramatic sepia drawings make this an appealing, though tragic, read-aloud. The multiple voices make this a strong candidate for a reader's theater production.   Language Arts LA1, LA9, SSII, SSV Jews, European Jews

The Ghost Catcher: A Bengali Folktale
By Martha Hamilton and Mitch Weiss. 2008. Illus. No page numbers.
August House. (NF) **Grades K–6**

Sent out to earn money by his frustrated and hungry wife, an overly generous barber decides to ply his trade in the next village, where it would be "easier to accept money from strangers" than to succumb to his neighbors' litanies of woes. He settles under a banyan tree for the night and ends up tricking a ghost into believing that he is a ghost catcher by reflecting its image in his mirror. Kristen Balouch's illustrations are hilarious: the barber's blue eyeglasses and characters' snazzy clothing combine with sleek, bright colors to make this traditional tale fit right in with today's world. Clever endpapers include captioned portraits of the story's characters; glossy pages add to the appeal. An afterword tells about barbers in India and about some traditional characters in Indian tales—including the rakshasa demon "ghosts" of this story. Sources provided.   Language Arts LA1, LA9, SSII, SSIII, SSVII Bengalis, East Indians

Girl from Chimel
By Rigoberta Menchú . 2005. Illus. 54 pages. Groundwood. (F) **Grades 4–12**

Rigoberta Menchú tells about her life in Chimel, her Guatemalan hometown, with a voice that is direct, unsentimental, and very much in the here-and-now. The book is a series of short chapters, each a story that might contain other tales, often from the Mayan tradition. Woven throughout are explanations of some of the traditions and religious beliefs of the Maya. Menchú begins with the story of how her grandfather carried off her willing grandmother on a "beautiful brown stallion with a golden mane." The book is richly illustrated in deep, vivid colors by native Mexican artist Domi. It gives a warm picture of life in Guatemala before the conflict and brutal genocide that set Menchú on the path of activism that would eventually win her the Nobel Peace Prize.   Language Arts LA1, LA9, SSII, SSIII, VA4, VA6 Guatemalans, Maya

The Girl Who Helped Thunder and Other Native American Folktales
By James Bruchac and Joseph Bruchac, retellers. 2008.
Illus. 96 pages. Sterling. (NF) **Grades 3–8**

James Bruchac joins his father, Joseph, and artist Stefano Vitale to create an engaging collection of twenty-four American Indian tales. They present the tales with a one-page description of a region of the United States, followed by one tale from each cultural group that lives in the region. The stories vary from humorous accounts of the underdog to creation myths to cautionary tales that beg to be told or read aloud with expression. Stefano Vitale's naive oil-and-tempera paintings on wood are captivating and representative of aspects of each story.   Language Arts, Visual Arts LA1, LA9, SSI, SSII, SSIII, SSV, SSVI, VA1, VA4, VA6 American Indians

Glass Slipper, Gold Sandal: A Worldwide Cinderella
By Paul Fleischman. 2007. Illus. 32 pages. Henry Holt. (NF) **Grades 3–12**

In this intriguing look at the global reach of the Cinderella story, Fleischman has put together a retelling that includes elements of the tale from Appalachia, China, France, Germany, India, Indonesia, Iran, Iraq, Ireland, Japan, Korea, Laos, Mexico, Poland, Russia, the West Indies, and Zimbabwe. French glass slippers can be diamond anklets or sandals of gold, the prince becomes the headman's son, and the wedding feast consists of everything from mangoes and melons to anise cookies and custards. The real draw to the story lies in Julie Paschkis' fantastic folk art illustrations created with Winsor & Newton gouaches; these saturate every page with color and capture each culture's traditional dress. Inspired by the textiles of the cultures, Pashchkis has placed her multicolored scenarios against painted, fabriclike backgrounds filled with images of the country depicted.   Language Arts, Visual Arts LA1, LA9, SSI, SSII, SSV, SSVI, VA1, VA4, VA6 Appalachians, Mexicans, West Indians, Irish, Germans, French, Poles, Russians, Iraqis, Iranians, Zimbabweans, East Indians, Chinese, Laotians, Indonesians, Koreans, Japanese

Hindu Stories: Traditional Religious Tales
By Anita Ganeri. 2006. Illus. 32 pages. Picture Window. (NF) **Grades 2–7**

Gathered from the Hindu scriptures, these tales describe the creation of the world, as well as incidents in the lives of Hindu gods and goddesses. Interesting insets entitled "Did you know?" highlight the connection between these stories and aspects of Hindu culture, including festivals such as Holi, Diwali, Ganesh Chaturthi, and Durga Puja. Bright illustrations, well-spaced text, glossary, index, and a resource page add to the usefulness of this collection.   Language Arts LA1, LA9, SSI, SSII, SSIII, SSV, SSVI East Indians, Hindus

Indian Children's Favourite Stories
By Rosemarie Somaiah. 2006. Illus. 80 pages. Tuttle. (NF) Grades 3–7

The strength of this collection lies in the author's clear retelling of major Hindu tales. Krishna's birth and his exploits as well as the complicated events in Rama's life are easy to follow despite the large cast of characters involved. Children feature heavily here as well: young Munna outwits the Raja in "One Grain of Rice," and scrawny Raman causes even the fearsome goddess Kali to laugh. Colorful pencil-and-watercolor illustrations in a traditional style fill each page and add to every story. The introductory notes give readers some basic information to help them better understand the tales and their characters. A short glossary is appended, although storytellers will have to search for sources of individual tales.   Language Arts LA1, LA9, SSI, SSIII, SSIV, SSVI East Indians, Hindus

Indian Tales
By Shenaaz Nanji. 2007. Illus. 96 pages. Barefoot Books. (NF) Grades 4–8

This collection presents stories told in simple, descriptive language that effortlessly incorporates Indian words. Clear dialogue and a fast pace make the tales easy to learn and tell. Some come from traditional sources such as the *Ramayana*; others are told worldwide. Nanji begins with a brief introduction to Indian history. A well-marked map outlines the regions of the country. Each tale comes from a different area and is prefaced by cultural information. Christopher Corr's wonderfully bright, bold, naive-style acrylic-and-gouache illustrations and borders depict the characters, flora, fauna, and buildings featured within each tale. The book ends with a resource list of articles and websites for further study of the regions and stories.   Language Arts, Visual Arts LA1, LA9, SSI, SSIII, VA1, VA4, VA6 East Indians

Karna: The Greatest Archer in the World
By Vatsala Sperling. 2007. Illus. 28 pages. Bear Cub Books. (NF) **Grades 6–8**

Part of the *Mahabharata*, this intricate story of Karna follows his adoption by commoners, his subsequent studies, his mastery of archery, and his introduction to his real family, the Pandava brothers and their parents. Unfortunately, Karna's great and continuing love for his adoptive parents, his generosity, and his skill as an archer cannot save him from the costly mistake of pledging loyalty to a deceitful despot. Full of interesting characters and situations, the story is preceded by a useful cast of characters to help readers keep track of Karna's adventures. Colorful, traditional illustrations by Sandeep Johari add to this long, detailed epic. **Language Arts LA1, LA9, SSI, SSII, SSV, SSVI East Indians, Hindus**

Kibitzers and Fools: Tales My Zayda (Grandfather) Told Me
By Simms Taback. 2005. Illus. No page numbers. Viking. (NF) **Grades 3–6**

Taback, the illustrator of *The Old Woman Who Swallowed a Fly* (1997), brings to life this hilarious collection of short Jewish tales about tricksters and fools. The book has broad audience appeal: among the younger set, only a few will get the dry humor; however, older children will certainly appreciate it. Using bright colors and comical characterization, Taback's book will endear itself to readers of all ages. **Language Arts LA1, LA9 Jewish Eastern Europeans**

The Legend of Hong Kil Dong, the Robin Hood of Korea
By Anne Sibley O'Brien. 2006. Illus. No page numbers.
Charlesbridge. (NF) **Grades 3–6**

Because Hong Kil Dong is the illegitimate son of Minister Hong, he cannot call him father. Kil Dong is bright and very studious, much more so than the minister's other son. However, Kil Dong gets no privileges—not even schooling. When he can no longer handle the daily humiliations, Kil Dong tells his mother he is going to study with the monks. On his way he meets some bandits who demand of him what they think is an impossible task. It isn't. Kil Dong becomes the leader of the group and trains the men to be great warriors who rob the rich to care for the poor. O'Brien grew up in South Korea and knows the language and the culture. She created her book in a graphic format using ink and watercolor and Arches paper—an appealing style for many middle grade readers. Language Arts, Visual Arts LA1, LA9, SSII, SSIII, SSIV, SSV, SSVI, SSIX, VA1, VA4, VA6 Koreans

The Magic Horse of Han Gan

By Jiang Hong Chen. Claudia Zoe Bedrick, trans. 2006. Illus.
No page numbers. Enchanted Lion. (NF) **Grades 3–7**

Han Gan loves to draw and paint, but his family is poor. He helps out financially by delivering meals for the innkeeper. One day, leaving the home of the painter Wang Wei, Han notices some beautiful horses and stops to sketch them in the sand. Wei sees promise in the young boy and provides him with paper, brushes, and paints—and gives him the freedom to paint anything he likes. Han is later invited by the emperor to study at the academy; there, Han paints only horses. Once, when asked why his horses are always tethered, he replies, "My horses are so alive they might leap right off the paper." A warrior asks Han to paint him a horse and bring the horse to life so he might ride the steed into battle. Han accomplishes the feat, and the warrior rides off. Years later, tired of relentless and unnecessary killings, the horse returns to Han Gan and reenters a painting. Han Gan lived in China over 1,200 years ago and is remembered for his exquisite depiction of horses, although the magic horse is a legend. Using a technique similar to that of Han Gan, Hong has created these lifelike paintings on silk. Language Arts, Visual Arts LA1, LA9, SSII, SSIII, SSIV, SSIX, VA4, VA6 Ancient Chinese

Myths of the World series

By Virginia Schomp. 2007–2010. Illus. Approx. 96 pages.
Marshall Cavendish Benchmark. (NF) **Grades 5–10**

Myths of ancient civilizations are presented in this series along with basic information about the cultural group from which they came. The first part of each book gives a brief look at the history, social structure, and beliefs of the culture. The second part contains myths central to the beliefs of the people, including creation myths and stories about key gods and goddesses. The illustrations jump off the well-designed pages, and maps are well-placed. The writing style is conversational and helpful for aspiring storytellers. Fortunately, pronunciation guides are included. A glossary, a description of sources, resources for further information, a thorough selected bibliography, notes on quotations, an index, illustration credits, and author information are all included. We have read and recommend the following titles in this series: *The Ancient Africans*, *The Ancient Chinese*, *The Ancient Egyptians*, *The Ancient Maya*, *The Ancient Mesopotamians*, *The Ancient Persians*, *The Aztecs*, and *The Native Americans*. **Language Arts LA1, LA9, SSI, SSIII, SSV, SSVI, SSVII, SSVIII Africans, Aztecs, Chinese, Egyptians, Maya, Mesopotamians, Native Americans, Persians**

Porch Lies: Tales of Slicksters, Tricksters, and Other Wily Characters

By Patricia C. McKissack. 2006. Illus. 146 pages. Schwartz & Wade. (F) **Grades 3–8**

In this collection, McKissack's nine original folktales are delightful and, as she says, "filled with tales of slicksters, tricksters, and other wily characters." In the introduction to each, she sets the tone and makes readers feel as if they are joining the circle of family and friends on the front porch to hear the stories. Each tale brings recollections of a different time and place in this country. Great for reading alone, reading aloud, reading straight through, or reading one at a time. **Language Arts LA1, LA9, SSII, SSIII, SSIV, SSV, SSVI African Americans**

Red Ridin' in the Hood: and Other Cuentos

By Patricia Santos Marcantonio. 2005. 185 pages.
Farrar, Straus and Giroux. (F) **Grades 5–9**

In these humorous retellings, Marcantonio takes familiar (and not so familiar) fairy tales and turns them into Latino tales. How about a basket filled with "chicken soup, heavy on cilantro, along with a jar of peppermint tea, peppers from our garden and a hunk of white goat cheese that smelled like Uncle José's feet"? That's what Red takes to her ailing grandma. But that's not what the two of them eat at the end of the story; they get takeout Chinese! The book contains eleven tales, all with Latino character names, places, and fun black-and-white illustrations by Renato Alarcão. Includes a pronouncing glossary of Latino terms and names. **Language Arts LA1, LA9, SSII, SSIII, SSIV, SSV, SSVI, SSIX Latinos**

The Six Fools

By Joyce Carol Thomas and Zora Neale Hurston. 2006.
Illus. 40 pages. HarperCollins. (NF) **Grades 4–7**

In this version of the worldwide "Three Sillies" tale, a young man asks his young woman to marry him. Her parents agree to the marriage, and her father sends his daughter to the cellar for some cider so they can celebrate. When she doesn't come back, her mother and then her father go looking for her; both end up sitting and thinking with her. All the while, the cider spigot flows, and the cellar is flooding with cider. When he discovers them, the young man says if he finds three more fools, he'll be back. This tale is all the funnier with Ann Tanksley's bright, exaggerated illustrations.   Language Arts LA1, LA9, SSIII, SSIV, VA4, VA6 African Americans

Stories from the Billabong

By James Vance Marshall. 2009. Illus. 64 pages. Frances Lincoln. (NF) **Grades 5–8**

These ten stories from Aboriginal Australia would be considered either pourquoi or creation tales from the Dreamtime. Frances Firebrace Jones, a member of an Aboriginal group, has illustrated the stories in acrylics using traditional colors and designs. At the end of each story is a factual explanation of the animal, plant, or place talked about in the story. Back matter includes descriptions and definitions of terms used in the book and Aboriginal symbols and their meanings. These stories beg to be told but would also be very effective if read aloud. They could be used in comparison with creation tales from other ethnic groups around the world. The book would also be useful in studying Aboriginal art.   Language Arts, Visual Arts LA1, LA9, SSI, SSIII, SSIX, VA1, VA4, VA6 Aboriginal Peoples–Australia

The Three Witches

By Joyce Carol Thomas and Zora Neale Hurston. 2006.
Illus. 32 pages. HarperCollins. (NF) **Grades 3–7**

Grandma leaves to "fetch" some food and tells her grandchildren she'll be back by dusk. Three witches come, and the children must find ways to outsmart them. Scary and funny at the same time, this is just the story to tell around a campfire, although in so doing, one would miss Faith Ringgold's creatively colored witches with their fangs and long fingernails. Part of Hurston's collection of African American folktales, this is a witty retelling perfectly illustrated by Ringgold's folk art technique.   Language Arts LA1, LA9, SSII, SSIII, SSV, VA4, VA6 African Americans

Trick of the Tale: A Collection of Trickster Tales
By John Matthews and Caitlin Matthews. 2008. Illus.
85 pages. Candlewick. (NF) **Grades 4–8**

The writing style in this sampling of trickster tales makes it an excellent choice for middle school students and aspiring storytellers. Sparse, simple language propels each story forward, and rich dialogue gives good insight into the characters' personalities. Most of the tales are short and to the point. This collection serves as an introduction to the sly humor of this genre. Tomislav Tomi 's beautifully executed pen-and-ink illustrations and occasional watercolor wash borders add a timeless quality to the book. Not all continents are covered, but the country or region of origin is given for each tale. Although not a book that many middlers would pick up on their own, each story is one that would engage them from the very first.   Language Arts, Visual Arts LA1, LA9, SSII, SSIII, SSIV, VA1, VA4, VA6 Global

Where the Mountain Meets the Moon
By Grace Lin. 2009. 278 pages. Little, Brown. (F) **Grades 4–8**

Minli's family lives in a village where the Jade River meets Fruitless Mountain. Everything around them is bleak and brown; but Minli, whose name means "quick thinking," isn't deterred by the bleakness. One day she impulsively uses one of her coins to purchase a goldfish. Her mother complains about having to feed the fish. Minli makes a decision—she will take the fish to the Jade River and let it go; then she will search for the Old Man of the Moon to ask him to give her family good fortune. Interwoven in the book are numerous Chinese tales, each connected to the journey of Minli, and each accompanied by a full-page colored illustration by the author.   Language Arts LA1, LA9, SSII, SSIII, SSIV, SSIX, VA4, VA6 Chinese

Why Monkeys Live in Trees and Other Stories from Benin
By Raouf Mama. 2006. Illus. 84 pages. Curbstone. (NF) **Grades 4–9**

In his second collection of stories from Benin, Mama presents tales from several ethnic groups. In his first collection, *Why Goats Smell Bad and Other Stories from Benin* (Linnet, 1998), all the tales came from the Fon people. In both collections, Mama's retelling is authentic, with a storyteller's voice that makes the tales adaptable for a wide range of audiences. Stories include fantasy, wisdom, and tricksters as they portray the reality of human nature at its best and worst. Jones's drawings add interest.   **LA1, LA9, SSI, SSIII Beninians, Africans**

REALISTIC FICTION

Bindi Babes
By Narinder Dhami. 2005. 184 pages. Yearling. (F) **Grades 5–8**

Irrepressible sisters Geena, Amber, and Jazz are the icons of fashion at their private school in England—popular with classmates and the darlings of their teachers. Because they have recently lost their mother, their father invites his sister from India to come care for the family, and an all-out war is quietly set into motion. Auntie seems determined to put a stop to the girls' "spoiled" ways, and the sisters' only hope is to marry her off to their favorite teacher. The story is firmly set in the world of the Indian immigrant, but the plot centers on the girls' many hilarious attempts to circumvent Auntie. Amber's first-person narrative has plenty of zippy dialogue to keep the story bustling along. Readers will enjoy the two sequels, *Bollywood Babes* (2005) and *Bhangra Babes* (2007).   **LA1, LA2, LA9, SSI, SSIII, SSIV, SSV East Indian British, East Indians**

Confetti Girl
By Diana López. 2009. 198 pages. Little, Brown. (F) **Grades 5–8**

Two girls, best friends and neighbors, each with parent problems: Lina Flores's mother has died; Vanessa Cantu's father has left. Lina loves funky socks, sports, and science, but hates English; her English-teacher father keeps his nose in a book. Lina loses her eligibility for sports because her creative answers to each quiz don't get her by. Yet her "creative" writing catches the attention of her English teacher and the school counselor. Vanessa, on the other hand, is very interested in boys—well, Carlos in particular. She finds ways to meet him while her mother sits at home making *cascarones,* confetti-filled eggs. The *cascarones* tie this story of friendship, school, and healing together, as the girls and even Mr. Flores begin to help make them. Although Lina is the protagonist, her father, Vanessa, and Ms. Cantu are crucial, fully developed characters. Humor, sadness, jealousy, love, and forgiveness make this a warm, satisfying read.   **Language Arts LA1, LA9, SSIII, SSIV, SSV Latinos**

Estrella's Quinceañera
By Malín Alegría. 2006. 260 pages. Simon & Schuster. (F) **Grades 5–9**

Caught between two worlds, Estrella Alvarez does not want her mother to plan a *quinceañera,* the traditional 15-year-old "coming out" party. She'd much rather celebrate at a sophisticated party like those of her private school friends, Sheila and Christie. Embarrassed by her mother; attracted to a street boy her father emphatically dislikes; feeling separated from her family, old friends in her barrio, and new friends in her school, 14-year-old Estrella flounders trying to discover who she really is. The first-person narrative gives an in-depth look at Estrella and her feelings. Peppered with Spanish words (explained in a glossary), Alegría uses realistic dialogue keeping the pace moving. This whirlwind tour of Estrella's warm yet strained family life, her barrio, and the world of her private school friends gives a realistic glimpse of how hard it can be to straddle two cultures.   **Language Arts LA1, LA9, SSIII, SSIV, SSV Latinos**

Facts of Life: Stories
By Gary Soto. 2008. 176 pages. Harcourt. (F) **Grades 5–8**

Life happens—and kids experience it. In this collection of stories, Soto introduces readers to ten Latino tweens and teens and their ordinary, or not-so-ordinary, lives. They find themselves in myriad situations—some funny, some scary, some poignant, and some hopeful. Real kids in real situations.   **Language Arts LA1, LA9, SSIII, SSIV Latinos**

Famous: The Awesome Life of David Mortimore Baxter
By Karen Tayleur. 2009. 81 pages. Stone Arch. (F) **Grades 4–6**

When his parents agree to be on the television reality show *Trading Moms*, David isn't thrilled. The mother of his archenemy, Rose Thornton, is going to switch roles for a week with his mom! David is certain the show will be a disaster—and it is. David's humorous look at his world includes hand-drawn cartoon illustrations showing both characters and objects (a brown lunch bag, a house key, a piece of cake) relevant to the story. Written on a third-to-fourth-grade level, the cover and characters' ages will attract the target audience of middle school readers. This joins the ranks of light-reading books that do not focus on multicultural issues but have a nonwhite protagonist who struggles with universal questions. **Language Arts, Visual Arts LA1, SSIII, SSIV, SSVIII, VA4, VA6 African Australians, AOD**

First Daughter: White House Rules
By Mitali Perkins. 2008. 216 pages. Dutton. (F) **Grades 7–10**

Lifestyles of the rich and famous combine with political awareness in this fast-paced, teen-centered view of life in the White House, moving it a step beyond chick lit. As the president's daughter, Sameera—Sparrow—is busier than ever. She enthusiastically embraces formal dances, her cousin Miranda's new interest in videotaping every activity, and matchmaking for Tara, the First Lady's secretary. Her warm, chatty entries on "Sparrowblog" not only give glimpses of daily life in the First Family, but introduce issues of race and privilege as Sparrow is challenged to examine her upper-class lifestyle. However, foremost on her mind is her relationship with Bobby Ghosh, an East Indian American student whose parents are worried his Hindu grandfather will disapprove of a relationship with a Muslim-born, adopted Pakistani. Can Bobby convince them to let him date Sparrow? **Language Arts LA1, SSIV, SSV East Indian Americans, Pakistani Americans**

Hot, Sour, Salty, Sweet
By Sherri L. Smith. 2008. 167 pages. Delacorte. (F) **Grades 5–8**

Ana Shen knows just how she wants her graduation day to unfold. Unfortunately, nothing goes according to plan! She never gets to give her salutatorian speech, because the water main in the gym bursts. There go her dreams of kissing her secret crush, Jamie Tabata, at the graduation dance. Now, instead of going out to eat—a safe move with her two grandmothers always at odds—Jamie and his family are coming for dinner. Ana fervently hopes her Chinese and African American grandmothers can get along long enough to help her pull this off. Through the afternoon of frantic, and at times hilarious, preparation, readers see how love and exasperation combine to make Ana's family one of a kind. Stories about her grandparents' lives reveal the prejudice they've encountered. This fast-paced story has humor, strong characterization, and a likeable, if harried, protagonist.   Language Arts LA1, LA9, SSIII, SSIV African Americans, Japanese, Japanese Americans, Mixed-Race Americans, Taiwanese, Taiwanese Americans

Home Is East
By Many Ly. 2005. 294 pages. Delacorte. (F) **Grades 5–8**

Fifth grader Amy Lim and her parents live in a Cambodian neighborhood in Florida. She wonders why all of their friends are Cambodian, and her father explains that "life wouldn't be the same without his people, that if you didn't share the same history, then there couldn't be true understanding." Things fall apart when her mother leaves them. Amy's father begins drinking and loses his job. He and Amy move across the country to San Diego, where he becomes a mechanic. Life is different, but they settle into a routine, make friends, and find a place for themselves. When Amy sees that her mother has a new life and family, can she work through her bitterness and make California her home?
Language Arts LA1, LA9, SSII, SSIII, SSIV Cambodian Americans, East Asian Americans

Isabel's Texas Two-Step
By Annie Bryant. 2008. 235 pages. Simon and Schuster. (F) **Grades 4–7**

Part of the Beacon Street Girl series that includes an extensive interactive website, this features Isabel, one of five "BFFs" who attend Abigail Adams Junior High in Boston. Most of the titles focus on a few events in the girls' hectic lives, but a Special Adventure series involves just one character. Twelve-year-old Isabel and her family join her aunt and uncle at their ranch outside San Antonio, Texas, to celebrate her sister's quinceañera celebration. Since their mother suffers from multiple sclerosis, Aunt Inez is running the show. Adventures abound:

Isabel loses her family in the city, she and her cousin Ricardo accidentally break a glass art piece, and both spend a stormy night trapped in a cave when their horse bolts. Tensions run high as the big day approaches. The portrayal of this extended Mexican American family is warm but realistic. Spanish words throughout the text combine with Texan, Mexican, and Coahuilteca history to give a strong sense of Isabel's culture. While most characters remain undeveloped, the fast pace makes this an enjoyable title. Language Arts, Visual Arts LA1, SSII, SSIII, SSIV, SSV, VA4 **Coahuitecas, Latinos**

Kimchi and Calamari
By Rose Kent. 2007. 222 pages. HarperCollins. (F) **Grades 5–8**

Easygoing, wisecracking Joseph Calderaro isn't happy about his eighth-grade history assignment to trace his family heritage. "I don't need fifteen hundred words. Two will wrap it up nicely: I'm adopted." His Italian parents know almost nothing about his Korean birth mother—only that she left him in a police station parking lot in Pusan. Suddenly, Joseph has a desperate need to find out more about her. When his friend Nash offers to search online, Joseph agrees, but has few expectations. Too many other events fill Joseph's life at this time. He gets to know newcomer Yongsu, who grew up in Korea, fakes a Korean ancestor for his history paper and tries to figure out the best way to get a date for the spring dance. His comical, first-person narrative is packed with astute observations and hilarious commentary. As he navigates the tricky issues of race, culture, and family history, Joseph discovers more about who he really is. Language Arts LA1, SSIV **Italian Americans, Korean Americans**

Mismatch
By Lensey Namioka. 2006. 217 pages. Delacorte. (F) **Grades 7–10**

Fifteen-year-old Sue Hua finds herself combating racism on many fronts in this smoothly written tale. New to Lakeview High, her white friends match her up with Andy, a handsome Japanese American. "You're both Asian . . . And you both play in the orchestra. So you're perfect together." In fact, the two talented violinists do become involved. However, Sue's grandmother lived through the Japanese occupation of China, and Andy's father views the Chinese as "a dirty people"—and the teens have no idea how to introduce each other to their families. Namioka describes Andy and Sue's experiences with their immediate families with alternate chapters in third person singular, but the story takes a turn when the orchestra visits Japan. Andy is placed with a high-ranking Japanese family where the daughter snubs him because he isn't American enough. Sue is placed with a Korean family who is held in low social esteem because their forebears were brought to Japan as forced labor. Andy and Sue struggle to understand their place in both worlds while pursuing their own relationship. Namioka deals with a number of thorny issues without ever sounding didactic.   Language Arts HE2, HE5, LA1, LA9, SSII, SSIII, SSIV, SSV, SSIX Chinese Americans, Japanese, Japanese Americans, Korean Japanese

Seeing Emily
By Joyce Lee Wong. 2005. 268 pages. Amulet Books. (F) **Grades 7–10**

Short, sections of poetic verse trace 16-year-old Emily Wu's growing discontent with her life. Her parents annoy her (the way they eat noodles!). She doesn't like Alex Huang, the new kid her art teacher pairs her with to work on a school mural. And racist incidents she once ignored are now at the front of her mind. Emily is thrilled when the hot new boy, Nick, seeks her out, and she becomes adept at sneaking out on dates. Her best friends, Nina and Lisa, are supportive—with reservations—and at first she hesitates to react to Nick's stereotyped vision of her. When she does react, reconciling her American and Chinese heritage seems impossible. It takes a trip to visit family in Taipei for Emily to realize just who she is: "the phoenix / spreading her wings / ready to fly." Many teens will recognize their own frustrations as they follow Emily through her sophomore year.   Language Arts LA1, SSIV, VA6 Taiwanese

Stanford Wong Flunks Big-Time
By Lisa Yee. 2005. 296 pages. Arthur A. Levine. (F) **Grades 5–8**

Contrary to the stereotype, Stanford Wong is a star basketball player whose disinterest in academics causes him to miss out on basketball camp and end up in summer school. To make matters worse, his nemesis, brainy Millicent Min, becomes his tutor. Despite the fact that their grandmothers are best friends, the two have been adversaries for a long time. But Millicent's friend Emily catches Stanford's eye, and he finds that Millicent has good advice for him as he tries to attract his first crush. At the same time he has some good advice for Millicent. Stanford's voice is what makes this such a good read—his character shines through every hilarious episode.   Health HE2, HE5, LA1, PE6, SSII, SSIV, SSV **Chinese Americans**

The Tequila Worm
By Viola Canales. 2005. 199 pages. Wendy Lamb. (F) **Grades 6–9**

When Sofia is 6, her mother tells her a good *comadre* is someone who "makes people into a family. And it's what I want you and your little sister, Lucy, to grow up to be." A series of short chapters relates the experiences Sofia has growing up in a close-knit barrio in Texas and discovering what *comadre* means. Friendship, religion, holidays, family, traditions such as a quinceañera or even picking stones out of the beans with her father every week are presented in a fresh, first-person narrative revealing a bright, complex girl. She tries to figure out her own culture and her place in the wider world, particularly when she is accepted as a scholarship student at an exclusive private boarding high school. Sofia is a multifaceted character who faces situations with which many readers will relate. Peppered with Spanish words deftly explained through the text, the rich characterization, universal themes, and humor make the book an excellent choice for introducing another culture.   Language Arts LA1, LA9, SSIII, SSIV, SSV **Latinos**

3 PERFORMING ARTS

~~~~~~

DANCE, MUSIC, AND THEATER

The standards for dance, music, and theater were developed by the Consortium of National Arts Education Associations under the guidance of the National Committee for Standards in the Arts. They emphasize how these art forms relate both to other disciplines and to the study of history and culture of ethnic groups. This chapter includes biographies of performers as well as books that highlight the important and enriching role of performing arts in individuals' lives, the place of these arts forms in a wide range of cultures, and how reading about this impact clarifies our understanding of the cultures.

DANCE

Content standards for dance were implemented in 1994, although dance is not offered as a separate course in most middle schools. Standards 3, 5, 6, and 7 are most applicable to books in this section since many teachers incorporate dance in cultural studies or as part of exercise activities. Books listed here span informational books about dance to fiction books in which dance plays an integral part.

Capoeira: Game! Dance! Martial Art!
By George Ancona. 2007. Illus. 46 pages. Lee & Low. (NF) **Grades 4–7**

Ancona's photographs capture the joy of students and instructors of capoeira—a game, dance, and martial art all in one originally created by African slaves in Brazil. Double-page spreads with bright, arresting photographs of children in the U.S. and Brazil show some of the moves of capoeira, which relies on trickery as well as ability and allows men, women, boys, and girls to play together. Each student has a nickname—a leftover from the capoeiristas who had to practice in secret when Brazil declared the art illegal in the late nineteenth century. Ancona discusses musical instruments, basic techniques, and the history of capoeira. Includes a glossary, a pronunciation guide, websites, and author's sources.   Dance D5, D7, LA1, SSIII, SSV, SSVI, SSVII African Americans, Brazilian Americans, Brazilians, Chinese Americans

The Kayla Chronicles
By Sherri Winston. 2007. 188 pages. Little, Brown. (F) **Grades 6–9**

An aspiring journalist and feminist, 14-year-old Kayla sets out to expose the elite dance team in her new high school. Her Latina friend, Rosalie, is determined to prove that the "It" girls on the team won't let an ordinary—and flat-chested—girl on the team. When Kayla is accepted, Rosalie is miffed. Kayla is still dealing with her grandmother's death; she desperately misses her. She doesn't feel a part of her family, knows she has to become more assertive, and consistently embarrasses herself in front of boys. Her comic first-person narrative includes lists, e-mails, and potential headlines, making this a breezy read. Her affluent world doesn't erase the pressures of figuring out how to tame her "floppy, floofy 'fro" or combat her fashionable grandmother's attempts to make her look "perfect." Kayla's commitment to girl power and her changing view of feminism are woven throughout this engaging story.   Dance D5, D6, LA1, PE6, SSIII, SSIV, SSV African Americans, Latinos

Mao's Last Dancer: Young Readers' Edition
By Li Cunxin. 2008. 290 pages. Walker. (NF) **Grades 7–12**

Born in 1961 and chosen from millions to attend Madame Mao's Beijing Dance Academy, 11-year-old Li realizes that dance could help his family escape their oppressive poverty. In this first-person narrative, Li details the brutal conditions in which he grew up as well as the grinding schedule demanded by his teachers. He gives readers a clear view of what life was like under Mao's Cultural Revolution. When offered a scholarship, he attends the Houston Ballet Academy and falls in love with the West—and with one of his classmates. He eventually defects and becomes an international ballet star; however, he never forgets his family or his roots. Includes photographs, a short history of China, modern timeline, and a glossary of Chinese words. The first-person narrative makes it accessible to the middle school reader.   Dance D5, D7 LA1, SSIII, SSVI, SSV, SSVII Chinese

Meet the Dancers: From Ballet, Broadway, and Beyond
By Amy Nathan. 2008. Illus. 231 pages. Holt. (NF) **Grades 6–12**

In this highly readable collective biography, Nathan introduces sixteen dancers from their earliest interest in dancing to their careers in various areas of the profession. Each chapter begins with a childhood photo of the dancer and brief facts such as hometown, age when dance lessons began, favorite children's books, hobbies, and professional career. Tips for budding dancers are interspersed throughout. Includes a detailed glossary, resources (including dance companies), organizations, reference books, websites, viewing guides, acknowledgments, and an index. **Dance D3, D5, LA1, SSIV African Americans, Asian Americans, East Indian Americans, Latinos**

¡Olé! Flamenco
By George Ancona. 2010. Illus. 46 pages. Lee & Low. (NF) **Grades 4–7**

Showcasing preteen Janira Cordova as she dances with the New Mexican troupe Flamenco's Next Generation, Ancona describes the history and practice of flamenco dancing. The product of the music and dance of the Roma, also called *gypsies*, flamenco was passed down from parent to child in Spain. Today it is found around the world. Richly hued photographs of various flamenco steps and performances by modern-day dancers bring this traditional art form to life as Ancona delves into the musical instruments, actions, and dress that create the flamenco experience. From family and group gatherings to more formal stage appearances, he brings the world of these dancers to the reader. A glossary with pronunciation guide, a list of sources, and author information are provided. **Dance D3, D5, LA1, SSIII, SSVI, SSV, SSVII Cubans, Latinos, Romanies, Spanish**

Stompin' at the Savoy
By Norma Miller with Alan B. Govenar. 2006. Illus. 54 pages. Philomel. (NF) **Grades 6–9**

Norma Miller tells her story in a fast-paced, compelling narrative that captures her vibrant personality and explains what it was like to be a world-renowned dancer in the Jazz Age. A master of the lindy hop, Norma began her career in the Savoy Ballroom in Harlem—the only place in the 1930s "where blacks and whites were able to mingle and dance together." At 18 she toured Europe, and upon her return danced for Ed Sullivan; she performed in Rio de Janeiro at the onset of World War II. While her story touches upon the great events of the times, Norma remains focused on her love of dancing, making this a solid choice for aspiring dancers. The cover art is a bit young, but Martin French's rich illustrations add interest; once opened, the book is hard to put down.   **Dance D5, D7, LA1, SSII, SSIII African Americans**

To Dance: A Memoir
By Siena Cherson Siegel. 2006. Illus. 56 pages. Atheneum. (NF) **Grades 4–12**

Siegel has always danced: on the beach in Puerto Rico, where she spent her early childhood; in parking lots; and, when her family moved to Boston, in Mrs. Alcalde's basement dance studio. At 9, she saw the Bolshoi ballet; her dream to become a ballerina took center stage. Colorful, multipanel, glossy pages reveal her friendships, her hard work, and the mounting tensions between her parents as we follow her career in dance that led her family to move to New York City for her to attend the School of American Ballet. Mark Siegel's artwork for this graphic novel grabs attention: ballet shoe ribbons swirl through the panels, often with chapter headings within them. This detailed memoir, which ends when Siegel begins college, will inspire young dancers of all ages.   **Dance D5, D6, LA1, SSIV, SSV Latinos, Puerto Ricans**

A Young Dancer: The Life of an Ailey Student
By Valerie Gladstone and José Ivey. 2009.
Illus. No page numbers. Holt. (NF) **Grades 4–7**

Iman Bright is a seventh grade student at Riverdale Country School in the Bronx. Three afternoons a week she takes the bus to the Alvin Ailey American Dance Theater School where she studies dance. The rigorous program at Ailey provides the opportunity for a diverse student body to study and perform several forms of dance. Gladstone, along with photographer José Ivey, shows the energetic young dancer as a normal teen, but one who enjoys her experiences at the Ailey School—plus her violin lessons and her swimming lessons! The photo essay format gives lessons in the various dance forms students learn at Ailey, and the author's note gives the history of the Ailey School.   **Dance D3, D5, D6, LA1, SSIV, SSV African Americans**

MUSIC AND THEATER

50 Cent (Hip-Hop series)
By Hal Marcovitz. 2008. Illus. 64 pages. Mason Crest. (NF) **Grades 7–12**

To date, Marcovitz has written twenty-four books in his Hip-Hop series. Here he introduces the rapper 50 Cent (born Curtis James Jackson III). Marcovitz doesn't sugarcoat Jackson's life. He sold drugs, spent some time in prison, but says the birth of his son changed his life. He neither condones nor criticizes 50 Cent's previous activities. Using borders, text boxes, photographs, and a creative layout, the format of the books hits the mark for teens. Each book in the series includes a chronology of the singer's life, accomplishments and awards (and the date awarded), further reading and Internet sites, a glossary, an index, and picture credits. Other series titles that we recommend include *Dr. Dre, Eminem, Hip-Hop: A Short History, Queen Latifah,* and *Tupac.*   Music LA1, MU8, MU9, SSIII, SSIV African Americans

Black Cat Bone
By J. Patrick Lewis. 2006. Illus. No page numbers.
Creative Editions. (NF) **Grades 8–12**

Spare, poetic language captures the essence of blues legend Robert Johnson. The foreword sketches out the basics: born in Mississippi in 1911, son of a sharecropper, and legendary player who "spread his music all over Mississippi and Arkansas." After looking at the major events of 1911, the book presents a series of poetic vignettes that move through Johnson's short life and address the many tales that have surrounded it. Gary Kelley uses multicolor monotypes to achieve a rough, moody tone for his images of Johnson and his times. Some adult themes (e.g., a mention of the many women Johnson slept with) might make this better suited for older grades. Endnotes give further information; a bibliography is appended. Author and illustrator information are on the jacket ends.   Music, Visual Arts LA1, LA9, MU8, MU9, SSIII, SSIV, SSVII, VA4, VA6 African Americans

The Cat with the Yellow Star: Coming of Age in Terezin
By Susan Goldman Rubin with Ela Weissberger. 2006. Illus.
40 pages. Holiday House. (NF) **Grades 5–10**

After *Kristallnacht*, Ela Stein, her mother, and sister are forced to flee their home in Czechoslovakia. Three years later, they are sent to Terezin, where conditions in the converted army camp are brutal—all around is sickness, hunger, and death. Ela's life improves when she is moved to room 28, which she shares with twenty-seven other girls. Her story of daily life in Terezin centers on the children's opera *Brundibár*, in which she plays the cat. The girls of Ela's room locate one another after the war and keep their friendship alive; *Brundibár* continues to help others understand the horrors of the Holocaust. Glossy pages are filled with photographs and illustrations. An epilogue recites the grim statistics of Terezin, including the fact that only fifteen girls who were funneled through room 28 survived. Includes source notes, resources, interviews, websites, picture credits, and an index. Author notes are on the book flap. Pair this with the author's *Fireflies in the Dark: The Story of Friedl Dicker-Brandeis and the Children of Terezin* (2000). Music, Social Studies, Theater LA1, MU8, MU9, SSIII, SSIV, SSV, SSVI, SSVII, TH8 Jewish Czechoslovakians

Freedom Song:
Young Voices and the Struggle for Civil Rights
By Mary Turck. 2009. Illus. 146 pages. Chicago Review Press. (NF) **Grades 7–12**

In the mid-1950s, as the civil rights movement was just beginning, so was a fledgling choir that would become the Chicago Children's Choir (CCC). Turck intertwines the history of the CCC, the history of slavery in America, the story of the civil rights movement, and other current rights movements and shows the integral role that freedom songs have played in each. Using text, primary-source photographs, quotes from CCC members past and present, quotes from others, and a CD of freedom songs sung by the CCC, this book is an excellent compilation of music and history. Includes organizational websites, a list of historical collections of the Civil Rights Movement music, videos and DVDs, song appendix, an index, and a message from the CCC about the music on the accompanying CD. Music, Social Studies LA1, MU8, MU9, SSII, SSIII, SSIV, SSV, SSIX African Americans, AOD

The Harlem Renaissance (We the People series)
By Dana Meachen Rau. 2006. Illus. 48 pages. Compass Point. (NF) **Grades 5–8**

In this basic introduction to a few leading authors, artists, and musicians of Harlem in the 1920s and 1930s, the author sets forth factors leading to the development of Harlem as that era's "Black Capital of the World." The role of W. E.

B. Du Bois, Marcus Garvey, and Alain Locke in breaking down stereotypes and redefining African Americans prefaces the book. Short chapters introduce some of the major literary and artistic figures of that time. Although quite brief, the information is clearly presented. (For details on this series' format and style, see *The Dred Scott Decision*, page 154.) Language Arts, Music, Social Studies, Theater, Visual Arts LA1, MU8, MU9, SSII, SSIII, SSV, SSVII, TH4, TH6, VA4 African Americans

Harlem Summer
By Walter Dean Myers. 2007. 165 pages. Scholastic. (F) **Grades 7–12**

In the summer of 1925, Mark Purvis gets a job at a journal called *The Crisis*, so he doesn't have to work in his uncle's funeral parlor. Although Mark gets to meet many of the important Harlem Renaissance writers, he'd much rather play his music than work inside a hot office. However, he needs money if he and his friends want to cut a record and break into the big time. Mark gets his friends involved in some shady deals to get rich, and of course, the deals get the boys into trouble. Although the book has both humor and action, it doesn't have very many page-turning points. Myers attempts to introduce too many people who lived in Harlem during the 1920s, making it hard to keep them straight. Still, the book has merit for those interested in this period of history. Music, Social Studies LA1, MU8, MU9, SSIII, SSVII African Americans

Jazz A-B-Z
By Wynton Marsalis and Phil Schaap. 2005. Illus.
No page numbers. Candlewick. (NF) **Grades 7–12**

Noted musician Marsalis and graphic artist Paul Rogers have teamed to pay homage to twenty-four jazz greats "in a style that gives a sense of his or her sound and also reflects a particular period in time." The resulting work is nothing less than stunning. Marsalis captures the essence of each artist with various poetic forms and, often, a swirl of words, beginning with the letter for that page: "Mingus makes mad, majestic, mind-boggling music." Rogers' acrylic-and-ink illustrations are riveting. Some knowledge of jazz is necessary to fully comprehend much of the book; fortunately, even those readers without that knowledge can appreciate what's here, and perhaps even be spurred to do a bit of research. Many students will want to have a dictionary on hand as well. Language Arts, Music, Visual Arts LA1, MU8, MU9, SSII, SSIII, VA1, VA4, VA6 African Americans

Lang Lang: Playing with Flying Keys
By Lang Lang and Michael French. 2008. 215 pages. Delacorte. (NF) **Grades 7–12**

At age 3, Lang Lang was playing the piano; by age 28—in the year 2010—
he was a world-renowned concert pianist. Born into an impoverished family
in China, Lang Lang's parents sacrificed their lives to see that he had access
to the best piano teachers. However, Lang Lang had few opportunities to be
a normal child; he rarely watched television, but the stories and music from
shows such as *Tom and Jerry* helped him endure long hours practicing the piano.
While his mother remained in Shenyang to work, Lang Lang and his father
spent many months away. The relationship between Lang Lang and his father
often was stormy. A strict disciplinarian, his father drove and pushed Lang
Lang to become No. 1, sometimes making him practice ten to twelve hours per
day. French's adaptation from Lang Lang's autobiography for adults is a page-
turner and almost makes the reader feel the frenetic life that Lang Lang lived.
Music LA1, MU8, SSII, SSIII, SSIV Chinese

Lemonade Mouth
By Mark Peter Hughes. 2007. 338 pages. Delacorte. (F) **Grades 7–10**

Wen isn't sure how to deal with the massive crush he has on his father's young
girlfriend. Stella's mom is ignoring her after moving the entire family across the
country. Charlie can't get his brother Aaron's voice out of his head, even though
his twin died at birth. Olivia lives with her grandmother, visits her jailed father
as often as she can, and strives to melt away in high school. Mohini tries to be
the perfect, overachieving daughter at home, but her secret, forbidden dating is
wracking her with guilt. When afterschool detention brings this group together,
they end up forming a band that will challenge their classmates' notions of what
and who is popular. In a school where music is dropped in favor of building a
new gymnasium, where a soda vendor controls what students can or cannot
purchase, and where the jocks reign supreme, change is coming. First-person
narratives from each character adroitly spin this tale of the difficulties—and
rewards—of making new friends and taking risks while staying true to yourself.
Music LA1, MU9, SSIII, SSIV, SSV, SSVI, SSVIII East Indian Americans

The Mozart Question
By Michael Morpurgo. 2008. 66 pages. Candlewick. (F) **Grades 7–10**

In this mystery, Lesley, a young reporter, is sent to get the story of the decade from reclusive violinist Paolo Levi in Venice. Her boss warns her not to ask the Mozart question—and Lesley hasn't a clue what he means. The story turns to 9-year-old Paolo, who can't get his father to explain why he no longer plays the violin. When Benjamin, the violinist who plays at the end of the bridge, offers to give Paolo lessons, Paolo sneaks out with the violin hidden in their closet. When he finally brings Benjamin home to help him confess that he's secretly been playing the violin, Paolo learns of the tragedy that neither of his parents can forget. Michael Foreman's almost mythical illustrations turn from spirit-lifting to haunting, complementing the story's emotional tones and deftly moving readers from present to past and back again. Paolo's first-person reminiscence is filled with dialogue and moves quickly, making this a good choice for reluctant readers. Teachers should note that the story presupposes readers' knowledge of the Holocaust and gives no information about Paolo's Jewish heritage.
Music, Social Studies LA1, MU9, SSIII, SSV, SSVI, SSVII, SSIX Jewish Europeans

Ray Charles: "I Was Born with Music Inside Me"
(African-American Biography Library)
By Carin T. Ford. 2008. 128 pages. Enslow. (NF) **Grades 7–12**

Ray Charles Robinson was born into poverty, and although his mother was sickly, she expected him to do chores, even after his congenital eye disease left him blind at age 7. His mother died when he was 15, and he set out to build his life in music. He was plagued with drug and alcohol addiction and an affinity for women—inside and outside of marriage. Performing consumed him almost to his death in 2004. Ford doesn't mince descriptions of his addictions or his extramarital affairs; she presents a balanced picture of the life of the great singer. Includes a chronology of his life, a list of his Grammy Awards, a selected discography, chapter notes, further reading, websites, and an index. Other series biographies we recommend: Muhammad Ali, Maya Angelou, Halle Berry, Gwendolyn Brooks, Langston Hughes, and Will Smith. Music LA1, MU8, MU9, SSII, SSIII, SSIV African Americans

So Punk Rock (and Other Ways to Disappoint Your Mother): A Novel
By Micol Ostow. 2009. 246 pages. Flux. (F) **Grades 7–12**

In this humorous take on an old story, junior Ari Abramson starts a rock band in order to enhance his cool factor at school. His longtime friend, Jonas, will be the superstar who attracts the girls—surely some of that will rub off? The catch here is that the band consists of both the cool and the geeky from a wealthy Jewish high school in suburban New Jersey. Super-religious, chubby Yossi is included because he's the only one with a drum set—and a racquetball court in his basement where they can practice. He's allowed in the band only because his parents want his sister, Reena, to socialize more. And oh, yeah—there's always the issue of Ari's parents, who absolutely cannot know the band exists. When the group has a surprise hit with their rocked-out version of "Hava nagilah," Ari is sure he'll get the girl of his dreams—Sari Horowitz. But will he? Filled with references to Jewish traditions and peppered with texts, notebook doodles, and segments of cartoon strips drawn by Ari, this madcap, fast-paced story gives a hilarious look at one of high school's most pressing predicaments: how to deal with those around you and find your own true self in the process. **Music LA1, MU9, SSIII, SSIV, VA6 Jewish Americans**

Sophisticated Ladies: The Great Women of Jazz
By Leslie Gourse. 2007. Illus. 64 pages. Dutton. (NF) **Grades 5–9**

Presents basic career information for fourteen jazz singers, including Bessie Smith, Ethel Waters, Betty Carter, Rosemary Clooney, and Cassandra Wilson. While the author does not gloss over the difficulties faced by many of these jazz greats—the rigors of traveling on the road, discrimination, alcoholism, and difficult personal relationships—she focuses on the musical style and contributions of each. The information on each woman is limited to nine or ten paragraphs, but taken as a whole, the book can augment units on jazz and perhaps spark interest in a particular singer. Martin French's arresting, poster-style mixed-media illustrations introduce each singer, with a text block set on a vividly colored page opposite. Includes a bibliography and list of further reading, a discography, and author and illustrator information. **Music, Visual Arts LA1, MU8, MU9, SSIII, SSVI, SSVII, VA4, VA6 African Americans**

Stringz
By Michael Wenberg. 2010. 216 pages. Westside. (F) **Grades 7–10**

Jace Adams can't remember being in one place long enough to have friends. Not human ones, anyway—Ruby, his battered cello, is his dearest friend. Now, here he is, at 14, a biracial boy in a new city, living with a gruff aunt he's never met, starting high school three weeks late; and to top things off, he gets in a fight his first day at school. His decision to take Ruby and play outside Seattle's symphony hall leads him to people and events he would have never dreamed possible. Homeless Sir Lionel becomes his protector on the street; Elvis and Marcy, two teens from the school orchestra, become his friends; Aunt Bernice stands by him when his mother leaves; and Professor Majykowski gives him cello lessons in exchange for small chores on his houseboat. Jace is encouraged to enter the Volt music competition and he throws himself into practicing for the contest, but he still dreams of heading back to California.   Health, Music H2, H5, LA1, MU8, MU9, SSIV, SSV African Americans, Mixed-Race Americans

Sweethearts of Rhythm: The Story of the
Greatest All-Girl Swing Band in the World
By Marilyn Nelson. 2009. Illus. 80 pages. Dial. (NF) **Grades 7–12**

The International Sweethearts of Rhythm was an all-girl jazz band that had its heyday during World War II. Here, their story is told in a unique manner. In a New Orleans pawnshop on the eve of Hurricane Katrina, the forgotten instruments of this women's band begin sharing their experiences. Each instrument tells the story of the woman who played it, as well as the story of the events of the time. The racially mixed women's band included mostly African American women but also had white, Chinese, Mexican, Native American, and Hawai'ian members. They traveled across the U.S., playing wherever they could, but to mostly black audiences. The group disbanded in 1949. Nelson's poems, told through the voices of the instruments, are in triple meter, popular in the nineteenth century; Jerry Pinkney's artwork illustrations that incorporate graphite, color pencil, watercolor, and collage add depth and interest to the stories.
Music, Social Studies, Visual Arts LA1, LA9, MU8, MU9, SSII, SSIII, SSIV, SSV, VA1, VA4, VA6 African Americans

Take-Off! American All-Girl Bands during WWII
By Tonya Bolden. 2007. Illus. 76 pages. Knopf. (NF) **Grades 7–12**

Bolden both explains and uses language of the 1930s and 1940s to describe three popular all-girl orchestras that took off during World War II. Ada Leonard's All-American Girl Orchestra devised frilly, flouncy gowns to emphasize their femininity and counteract the prevailing attitude that girls shouldn't play jazz. The Prairie View State College Co-eds, an African American group, battled discrimination on the road but managed to sneak out to play with music greats. The International Sweethearts of Rhythm, a multicultural group, traveled in their own bus, revamped by fellow students of the Piney Woods Country Life School. Bolden recounts personal histories of individual players and touches on other popular girl bands. Black-and-white photographs and a clean layout make this easy to read; text boxes contain further information. Includes a glossary, source notes, lists of further resources, picture credits, detailed index and—best of all—a CD with samples of the bands' songs. Music, Social Studies LA1, MU8, MU9, SSII, SSIII, SSV, SSVI, SSVII, VA4, VA6 African Americans, Latinos, Mixed-Race Americans

The Tallest Tree
By Sandra Belton. 2008. 154 pages. Amistad. (F) **Grades 4–7**

Odell Davis's neighborhood has declined. The closed Regal Theater, the boarded stores, and the lone tree are stark reminders. Every day, Douglass Walker—"Little Catfish"—rushes to sit in front of the Regal with Mr. Odell, who tells him about Paul Robeson, always reminding him that Robeson was "the tallest tree" in the neighborhood. Little Catfish and Mr. Odell plan ways to improve their surroundings, and Mr. Odell creates a display highlighting the famous African Americans who once lived here. When Lamar, a teen with a chip on his shoulder, defaces the memorabilia, newspaper publicity brings offers for help in restoring the theater and the neighborhood—and Lamar finds himself part of Mr. Odell's project. Along with the interwoven biography of Paul Robeson, the story introduces other famous African Americans. Back pages list books and films about Paul Robeson and websites for information on the others.
Music, Theater LA1, MU8, MU9, SSII, SSIII, SSIV, SSV, TH8 African Americans

Tupac Shakur: Multi-Platinum Rapper (Lives Cut Short series)
By Ashley Rae Harris. 2010. Illus. 112 pages. Abdo. (NF) **Grades 5–10**

Tupac Shakur's short but eventful life is chronicled here from his childhood to his murder at age 25. Readers learn of his mother's leadership role in the Black Panthers, his time in the Baltimore School for the Arts, and his big break at the Marin City Festival. The author explores, with a fairly even approach, the mix of social activism and "thuggery" that appear both in his lyrics and his life. The book's design is inviting, with numerous photographs and sidebars, a wide black band with swirling red and gray lines at the top and bottom of each page, and well-spaced text. Organized chronologically, the book includes a table of contents; a timeline; lists of quick facts; career highlights; additional resources, including a select bibliography, websites, and organizations; glossary; chapter source notes; an index; author information; and photo credits.   Music LA1, MU8, MU9, SSIII, SSIV, SSV

Up Close: Ella Fitzgerald
By Tanya Lee Stone. 2008. Illus. 203 pages. Viking. (NF) **Grades 7–10**

November 21, 1934: at Amateur Night for the Apollo Theater in Harlem, 16-year-old Ella Fitzgerald mesmerizes the audience with her songs and wins the competition, but because she is dirty and dressed in street clothes and men's boots, she is not given the prize of a weeklong gig. She rose to become a legendary jazz singer known for her poise, grace, and generosity. It wasn't easy. Tracing her career from the segregated Jim Crow days of the 1930s until her death in 1996, this offers an inside look at the world of jazz. Includes chapter source notes, a bibliography, an index, photo credits, and brief author information. Music LA1, MU8, MU9, SSIII, SSIV, SSVII African Americans

We Shall Overcome: A Song That Changed the World
By Stuart Stotts. 2010. Illus. 72 pages. Clarion. (NF) **Grades 5–12**

Giving historical context to the antecedents of the well-known freedom song "We Shall Overcome," this traces the song from the early spiritual "I'll Be All Right" back to a hymn written by pastor Charles Tindley in the mid-1800s.

The authors examine how the song was used: a coal miners' strike in the early 1900s, a tobacco workers' strike in 1945, and, finally, the first recording by Pete Seeger in 1950. Seeger learned the song from Zilphia Horton at the famous Highlander Folk School in Tennessee. The song played a vital role in the civil rights movement and eventually took root around the world in a wide range of freedom movements, from South Africa to China to Kashmir. Numerous photographs and striking black, red, and white illustrations make this a page-turner. A CD and a print copy of the song; chapter source notes; an extensive bibliography of books, articles, recordings, films, videos, DVDs, and websites; acknowledgments; an index; author and illustrator information; and photo credits are included.   Music LA1, MU8, MU9, SSIII, SSV, SSVI, SSVII, SSIX African Americans

World of Music: Western Asia
By Kamini Khanduri. 2008. Illus. 48 pages. Heinemann. (NF) **Grades 6–12**

Khanduri introduces classical, folk, and pop traditions across Western Asia. The book opens with a map that divides the area into the Middle East, Central Asia, and India. The text covers the types of instruments, ways of sharing music, connections between music and religion, and effects of the globalization of music. Each double-page spread contains photographs, clear text boxes with concise captions, and small insets that introduce readers to well-known modern musicians and groups or provide interesting details. The whole combines to make an easy-to-follow, pleasing introduction to the vast world of Western Asian music. A glossary, a bibliography, a "webliography," and list of museums serve as resources for further research. One chart divides the world into six regions, and gives basic information on string, brass, wind, and percussion instruments, vocal styles, and dance styles. Index appended.   Music, Social Studies D5, LA1, MU8, MU9, SSI, SSII, TH8 Central Asians, East Asians, Middle Easterners, Southeast Asians

4 PHYSICAL EDUCATION

Although the focus of the standards for physical education is on physical activity and exercise, the books in this chapter support the standards in an ancillary way by introducing adolescents to a variety of sports and athletes. Novels in which a sport plays a significant role connect physical education to daily life and persuade enthusiastic sports fans to read for pleasure.

BASEBALL

Baseball Crazy: Ten Short Stories That Cover All the Bases
By Nancy E. Mercado. 2008. 191 pages. Dial. (F) **Grades 5–8**

From Little League to the majors, the authors of these stories bring special aspects of the game alive. The variety of stories, including one play, are entertaining and engaging. The book can be read in its entirety or story by story. Both boys and girls will find themselves in the book and will cheer for the protagonists. Authors include: Paul Acampora, Joseph Bruchac, Sue Corbett, Ron Koertge, Frank Portman, David Rice, John Ritter, Charles R. Smith Jr., Jerry Spinelli, and Maria Testa. **Language Arts, Physical Education LA1, PE1, PE5, PE6, SSIV AOD**

Free Baseball
By Sue Corbett. 2006. 152 pages. Dutton. (F) **Grades 5–8**

Eleven-year-old Felix Piloto can't understand why his workaholic mother doesn't like baseball. After all, isn't his dad a baseball superstar in their native Cuba? When he gets free tickets to a local farm team game, Felix ditches his babysitter and sneaks into the locker room, where he's mistaken for the opposing team's batboy. Through a fast-paced series of events, Felix finds himself in a neighboring town with a new job—and, he thinks, an opportunity to learn more about his mysterious father. Is he ready to accept the truth about his family? With its solid characterization, large doses of humor, excellent descriptions, and Spanish words and expressions that help readers relate to the world of the Cuban refugee, this book may appeal to mystery lovers as well as baseball fans.   **Physical Education LA1, LA9, PE5, PE6, SSII, SSIV Latinos**

Heat

By Mike Lupica. 2006. 220 pages. Philomel. (F) **Grades 6–9**

Orphans Michael Arroyo and his brother Carlos, immigrants from Cuba, are living alone, trying to stay together until Carlos reaches his 18th birthday. Their father was an integral part of their lives until his death three months ago. Seventeen-year-old Carlos works two jobs, and 12-year-old Michael plays baseball. Baseball is predominant in this story—Michael eats, breathes, and sleeps it. His greatest hope is that his team will play in the Little League World Series in Williamsport, Pennsylvania. Unexpected obstacles get in the way for each boy. Carlos loses one of his jobs and takes on a scalping gig. Michael's age is challenged and he is taken out of play. Worse still, the boys can't prove Michael's age because they have no birth certificate from Cuba. This will keep baseball lovers on the edge of their seats.   **Physical Education LA1, LA9, PE5, PE6, SSIII, SSIV, SSV, SSVI, SSIX Latinos**

Jackie Robinson: Champion for Equality (Sterling Biographies series)

By Michael Teitelbaum. 2010. Illus. 124 pages. Sterling. (NF) **Grades 5–9**

Baseball player Jackie Robinson hated to lose, but he cared more for others than for himself. This was true both in his personal life and professional life. His parents were sharecroppers, and life was hard. His father abandoned the family when Jackie was 1, so his mother took her four children from Georgia to California to make a better life for them. In college, Jackie set records in four sports, but his best-known accomplishment was breaking the color barrier in Major League Baseball. His first three years with the New York Dodgers were difficult: he had made a pact with Branch Rickey to remain calm and never react to slurs and prejudice; he kept his part of the bargain. Honors were heaped upon Robinson eventually, but perhaps the greatest was being inducted into the Baseball Hall of Fame. As is common with all Sterling Biographies, the book begins with a timeline of Robinson's life. Using documented photographs, engaging writing, and text boxes that give additional information about the time period, the author makes Robinson's life vibrant and engaging. Includes a glossary, a bibliography, websites, source notes, image credits, an index, and a note on the author. **Physical Education, Social Studies LA1, PE5, PE6, SSII, SSIII, SSIV African Americans**

Let Them Play
By Margot Theis Raven. 2005. Illus. 30 pages. Sleeping Bear Press. (NF) **Grades 3–6**

In the summer of 1955, the Cannon Street Little League All-Star team was looking forward to playing in the city tournament. They had high hopes of advancing to the state competition and, perhaps, the regional tournament. But the state's Little League director determined no white team would play the all-black Cannon Street team. He started his own baseball program, recruiting all the white teams and leaving the Cannon Street team with no one to play. As a result, the Little League determined they were ineligible to compete in the regional tournament. However, they invited them to Williamsport to watch the Little League World Series. When the boys arrived at the field, they were introduced as "the boycotted Negro team from South Carolina"—and the crowd cheered in welcome. When the team took the field for the traditional warm-up, five thousand people demanded, "Let them play! Let them play!" Chris Ellison's richly colored acrylic paintings capture the emotions of the boys, their coaches, and their community in this re-creation of the actual event. An epilogue discusses the team's return to the Little League World Series in 2002, and gives the names and positions of the fourteen All-Stars. **Physical Education LA1, PE5, PE6 SSII, SSIII, SSIV, SSV, SSVI African Americans**

A Negro League Scrapbook
By Carole Boston Weatherford. 2005. Illus. 48 pages. Boyds Mill. (NF) **Grades 3–8**

Weatherford uses lively poetry with an inviting scrapbook format full of archival photographs, memorabilia, and lists to describe the social climate with which the Negro Baseball League players had to contend. She gives statistics on the great players: some who broke the racial barrier, and others who didn't. The detailed index is helpful in locating information on individual players and teams. **Physical Education, Social Studies LA1, PE5, PE6, SSIII, SSIV, SSV, SSVI, SSVII African Americans**

Safe at Home

By Sharon Robinson. 2006. 151 pages. Scholastic. (F) **Grades 4–6**

Due to his father's untimely death, Jumper and his mother move from their suburban Connecticut home to his grandmother's big brownstone in Harlem. It's hard to make new friends, and Jumper hopes the neighborhood baseball camp will help. But the coach assigns him to a team led by Marcus, the one boy Jumper has already clashed with at the local arcade. Although Jumper is a great basketball player, his baseball skills are not the best. Will he ever fit in to this new world? Filled with details of baseball practice and games, this may appeal to young fans. The low reading level and dialogue-rich text make it a good choice for high-low readers, along with its sequel, *Slam Dunk* (2009). **Physical Education LA1, PE5, PE6, SSIII, SSIV, SSV African Americans**

Satchel Paige

By James Sturm. 2007. Illus. 89 pages. Jump at the Sun/Hyperion. (F) **Grades 6–12**

In 1929, 18-year-old Emmett Wilson leaves his wife and young child to play in the Negro National League. While he hits a ball off legendary pitcher Satchel Paige, Emmett destroys his knee as he slides into home base. He returns home, works as a sharecropper for the mean-spirited Jennings family, and tries to keep his young son in school and out of the fields. Through the first-person narrative of this fictional character we see the bleak reality of a sharecropper and the impact written and unwritten Jim Crow laws have on his life. Interspersed with Emmett's personal story is the story of Satchel Paige, whose inspiring feats give hope to the black community and, in this tale, serve as a small bit of justice to the Jennings brothers. Rich Tommaso's focused, clean lines in each panel of this graphic art novel lend an austere power to this thought-provoking story. "Panel Discussions" text boxes give further information about the times. **Physical Education, Social Studies LA1, PE5, PE6, SSII, SSIII, SSIV, SSV, SSVI, SSVII African Americans**

We Are the Ship: The Story of Negro League Baseball

By Kadir Nelson. 2008. Illus. 88 pages. Jump at the Sun/Hyperion. (NF) **Grades 5–12**

In the mid-1800s, African American baseball players played on teams with whites, but toward the end that century, they disappeared from those teams.

The men who loved the game formed their own Negro Baseball League. Players endured numerous forms of discrimination, often sleeping in buses or in their cars and eating alongside the road because they wouldn't be served in restaurants. Some of the greatest stars in baseball were born, although most never broke into the white major leagues. The Negro Baseball League persevered through two world wars and the Great Depression until finally, in 1947, Jackie Robinson broke the color barrier and joined the Brooklyn Dodgers. Nelson's well-researched book includes end notes, a bibliography, a detailed index, and beautiful oil paintings of individual players, teams, and games.   Physical Education, Social Studies LA1, PE5, PE6, SSII, SSIII, SSIV, SSV African Americans

BASKETBALL

A Basketball All-Star (Making of a Champion series)
By Scott Ingram. 2005. Illus. 48 pages. Heinemann. (NF) **Grades 5–8**

After an overview of basketball—its history, evolving rules, and basic play—this moves into concrete suggestions for basketball players. The author discusses coaching, nutrition, training exercises, skill-building techniques, and game strategy. The book is packed with photographs, illustrations, and text box insets with facts about players and more in-depth information on the current topic. Subheadings in bold print move the narrative briskly. With its cast of multiethnic players male and female, this is a catchy book for the middle grade athlete. A brief listing of championship records, a glossary, addresses for basketball organizations, further readings, an index, and photo credits are provided.
Physical Education LA1, PE5, PE6, SSV

Long Shot: A Comeback Kids Novel
By Mike Lupica. 2008. 182 pages. Philomel. (F) **Grades 5–8**

When he decides to run for class president, basketball player Pedro Morales realizes his challenger is Ned Hancock, the most popular athlete in Vernon Middle School. Not at all sure he can win, Pedro pursues his goal in great part due to his dad's belief that in America his son can become anything he wants. Soon Ned starts a successful campaign to thwart Pedro on the basketball court and pull him off the starting lineup. How Pedro meets this challenge with the support of his friends both on and off the court makes this a page-turner. Extensive play-by-play descriptions of the games and Pedro's warm relationship with his Mexican-born father make this a strong choice for sports fans. **Physical Education LA1, LA9, PE5, PE6, SSIII, SSIV Latinos, Mixed-Race Americans**

Game
By Walter Dean Myers. 2008. 218 pages. HarperTeen. (F) **Grades 7–12**

Senior Drew Lawson knows he's the best, but when Coach House moves Tomas, the new kid from Prague, into his position, he is livid. He knows basketball is his ticket to college, and now it looks like House is going to showcase Tomas rather than him. Everywhere Drew looks in Harlem he sees young men who have thrown away their chances and given up; he wants to avoid this at all costs. But can he keep his cool, be a team player? With a supportive mom, a hilarious and smart little sister, and a best friend whose brother—also a basketball star—is in jail, this is all about the choices one makes. Juxtaposed are classroom discussions of Othello, making this a potential partner for early Shakespeare studies. Myers' description of ball games is detailed and sure. **Health, Physical Education LA1, H2, H5, H6, PE5, PE6, SSIV, SSV, SSVI, TH8 African Americans, Czechoslovakian Americans**

Dunk under Pressure (Winning Season series)
By Rich Wallace. 2006. 119 pages. Viking. (F) **Grades 4–7**

Twelve-year-old Dunk is a free-throw specialist, which has gotten him onto Hudson City's All-Star YMCA team. Now, with middle school superstars Jared, Jason, and Spencer, he's headed for the New Jersey Shore for the summer tournament. The boys are excited—but Dunk is a little bit scared. He knows he's great at free throws, but he's just an average player in other aspects of basketball. An entire summer of practice has helped, but will he be able to keep up his end of the game? The third-person narrative is filled with dialogue, and the focus on Dunk's changing emotions brings his character to life. Lots of play-by-play action, Dunk's warm and realistic relationship with his aunt Krystal, and the joshing yet supportive interplay of Hudson City's culturally diverse team members make this a solid addition to the Winning Season series. **Physical Education LA1, PE5, PE6 African Americans**

BOARD SPORTS

Girl Overboard
By Justina Chen Headley. 2008. 339 pages. Little, Brown. (F) **Grades 7–11**

As the daughter of billionaire Ethan Cheng, 15-year-old Syrah seems to have the perfect life. Few know that she has no friends at her tony prep school, that her parents are rarely home, or that her stepbrother and stepsister hate her. Snowboarding and her one true friend, Age, have gotten her through. When her lifelong nanny, Bao-mu, retires and Age pulls away from her, Syrah must find her own way through the minefields of her life. Syrah's family history reaches back to the Cultural Revolution in China. As she uncovers family secrets, Syrah begins to understand her own place in the world. Her wry, first-person narrative is thoughtful and consuming, making this much more than a fluffy beach read.   Health, Physical Education H2, H8, LA1, LA9, PE5, PE6, SSIII, SSIV, SSVII, SSVIII, SSIX, SSX **Chinese Americans**

Ramp Rats: A Graphic Guide Adventure
By Liam O'Donnell. 2008. Illus. 64 pages. Orca. (F) **Grades 4–7**

Bounce and his best friend, Pema, are frustrated that neighborhood bully Crunch has taken over the local skate park. Bounce hopes that Marcus, his newly arrived stepbrother, can give them tips on some new moves, and maybe get Crunch to lighten up. Then Bounce and Pema discover that a motorcycle gang is vandalizing local stores, and Bounce's dad's store is targeted. Can they stop the bully *and* the gang? Mike Deas uses dark colors to create a gritty feel for this graphic novel, which teaches readers a number of skateboarding moves. Bounce's occasional first-person narrative helps keep the pace moving in this action-packed story. While cultural issues are not explored here, the protagonists reflect a multiethnic neighborhood. A third-grade reading level coupled with middle school and tween characters make this a good choice for resistant readers.   Health, Physical Education H2, H5, LA1, PE5, PE6, SSIV **African Canadians**

BOXING

Black Jack: The Ballad of Jack Johnson
By Charles R. Smith Jr. 2010. Illus. 40 pages. Roaring Brook. (NF) **Grades 4–6**

Jack Johnson, a black boxer at the turn of the twentieth century, was influential in the life of Muhammad Ali. At a time when "whites only fought whites," Johnson was shut out of many rings. Breaking the color barrier proved daunting. At last, he fought and defeated Jim Jeffries; then, in 1910 in Australia, he won over Tom Burris to become heavyweight champion of the world. Combining a pulsating rhythm in the text with bold, powerful paintings, Smith and artist Shane Evans capture the complex life of Johnson. Includes a brief "And then what happened?" along with further readings.   **Physical Education LA1, LA9, PE6, SSIII, SSIV African Americans**

Twelve Rounds to Glory: The Story of Muhammad Ali
By Charles R. Smith Jr. 2007. Illus. 40 pages. Candlewick. (NF) **Grades 4–8**

Using the twelve boxing rounds as a framework, Smith and illustrator Bryan Collier have created a vibrant biography of Ali, from his birth in 1942 to 2005. The format of the book grabs the reader quickly. Sometimes Collier's watercolor-and-collage illustrations dominate the page; other times, Smith's free-verse text takes center stage. Throughout, quotes from the text are pulled out and written in varying fonts and styles, bringing passion and tension to the book. Although no sources or bibliography appear, the book is a solid introduction and tribute to Ali and his well-known characteristics—from generosity and kindness to his tenacity in the ring.   **Health, Physical Education, Visual Arts HE2, HE5, HE8, LA1, PE5, PE6, SSIII, SSIV, SSVI, VA4, VA6 African Americans**

MARTIAL ARTS

Chinese Cinderella and the Secret Dragon Society
By Adeline Yen Mah. 2005. 242 pages. HarperCollins. (F) **Grades 5–8**

Drawing from her own childhood experiences and writings, Mah creates an exciting tale of intrigue and suspense in this fictionalized tale of a true historical incident from 1942. In this account, Chinese Cinderella, or CC, escapes from her cruel stepmother and finds refuge with Grandma Wu, where she trains with three orphaned boys to become a member of the kung fu Dragon Society of Wandering Knights and takes part in the Chinese Resistance movement. The boys, David, Sam, and Marat, are all *za zhong*—people of mixed blood—and are outcasts from their societies. In the world of the Dragons, however, their ability to perform kung fu, work as a team, and maintain secrecy make them valuable colleagues who are held in high esteem. CC's first-person narrative is fast paced, yet eloquently describes a girl searching for her place in the world. As she and her friends work to rescue American soldiers who crashed in Japanese-controlled Nan Tan, she finds her own inner strengths.   Physical Education, Social Studies LA1, PE5, SSII, SSIII, SSIV, SSV, SSVI, SSVII, SSIX Chinese, Mixed Race

Little Eagle
By Jiang Hong Chen. Trans. by Claudia Zoe Bedrick. 2007.
Illus. 32 pages. Enchanted Lion. (F) **Grades 3–6**

Taken in by kindly Master Yang after his parents are killed by the evil General Zhao, Little Eagle discovers his guardian secretly practices Eagle boxing. Every night Little Eagle watches and learns, and when Master Yang discovers him, he takes the boy on as his apprentice. Striking illustrations in lush colors bring the reader into fifteenth-century China, using a graphic novel format to show the arduous steps Little Eagle takes in order to master his art. When General Zhao attacks Master Yang, Little Eagle faces his greatest challenge. Spare, poetic language gives the story a mythic quality, leading the reader to focus on the illustrations, which are done in watercolor on paper with traditional Chinese paints and brushes and are inspired by Japanese manga. Readers should take care to read both the introduction and afterword on the end papers.   Physical Education, Visual Arts LA1, PE5, SSIII, SSIV, SSVI, SSVII, VA1, VA4 Chinese

RUNNING

Fast Company (Winning Season series)
By Rich Wallace. 2005. 119 pages. Viking. (F) **Grades 4–7**

When Coach Alvaro recruits him for the new running program, sixth grader Manny Ramos is psyched. He and Anthony, Hudson City's football lineman, set up the perfect training routine to prepare for their first meet in New York City's impressive Armory. As he becomes immersed in the world of running, Manny has less time for his friend Donald, and finds he's actually becoming friends with a girl on his new team. When overweight Anthony starts getting nasty notes at school, Manny secretly wonders if Donald is sending them. While the story focuses on the challenges of competitive racing, it also touches on the changing allegiances experienced by middle school students, body image, and the importance of friendship. As with the other books in the series, the multicultural cast of characters in this New Jersey setting is refreshing, although culture is largely unexplored.   Physical Education LA1, PE5, PE6, SSIII, SSIV African Americans, Latinos

Jesse Owens: The Fastest Man Alive
By Carole Boston Weatherford. 2006. Illus. No page numbers.
Walker. (NF) Grades 3–6

In a simple yet powerful poem, Weatherford and illustrator Eric Velasquez present Owens's path toward participation, success, and triumph in the 1936 Olympic Games. Despite growing up poor and sickly, James C. Owens, later nicknamed Jesse, ran. His junior high school track coach saw Jesse's potential to become an outstanding runner. They practiced in the mornings because Jesse had to work after school. Jesse set junior high school world records in both the long jump and the high jump. In the 1936 Games held in Berlin, Jesse's greatest opponent was Adolph Hitler, who held a hatred of all non-Aryans and wanted his German athletes to sweep the games. Jesse, an African American, won four gold medals, destroying Hitler's hopes in the Games along with his dogma of Aryan superiority. The picture-book size and format might lead only younger children toward it, but the subject and text make it appropriate for younger middle school students.   Physical Education LA1, PE5, PE6, SSII, SSIV, SSVI, SSIX African Americans

OTHER SPORTS

And Nobody Got Hurt 2! The World's Weirdest, Wackiest and Most Amazing True Sports Stories
By Len Berman. 2007. Illus. 133 pages. Little, Brown. (NF) Grades 5–8

Longtime sportscaster Len Berman recounts zany stories about baseball, basketball, football, soccer, golf, tennis, the Olympics, and more in this compilation. A "bad hair day" for tennis star Venus Williams caused her a penalty when a strand of her hair beads broke and scattered on the court. In the 1976 Olympics, Shun Fujimoto continued his gymnastics routines without revealing his newly broken kneecap, helping his Japanese team win the gold medal. Berman recounts these tales with verve, and Kent Gamble's cartoonlike caricatures of multiethnic sports men and women add further interest to this humorous collection. Physical Education LA1, PE2 AOD

They Played What?! The Weird History of Sports and Recreation
By Richard Platt. 2007. Illus. 48 pages. Two-Can. (NF) Grades 4–8

Double-page spreads with bold strips of color present various sports and recreation activities around the globe from ancient times to the present. Ballgames range from Roman handball and volleyball to Mayan *pok-a-tok*, similar to basketball. Animal races shift from camels to horses to ostriches. Bungee jumping "isn't nearly as dangerous as the Pacific Island pastime from which it grew." Small round insets give odd details for each sport, while eye-catching photographs and illustrations grab the reader's interest. While no detailed information is given here, this serves as a fun introduction to sports and recreation around the world. Physical Education LA1, PE6, SSII, SSIII, SSV AOD

Surfer of the Century: The Life of Duke Kahanamoku
By Ellie Crowe and Richard Waldrep. 2007. Illus. 48 pages.
Lee & Low. (NF) Grades 4–7

The first Hawai'ian to swim in the Olympics, Duke Kahanamoku competed at a time when racism was rampant in the U.S. His Olympic gold medal in 1912 catapulted him to stardom; sports fans worldwide clamored to see him swim. Duke was born in 1890 in Honolulu. His family, warm and loving, encouraged him to swim and surf. Even after winning numerous medals in three sets of Olympic Games and despite the racism he encountered, he was known for his modesty and kind ways. Richard Waldrep has created large, deeply colored gouache paintings detailed with colored pencil that fill one page of each double-page spread; opposite is the story's text. Includes a timeline, source notes, a source list, and author and illustrator information. Physical Education LA1, PE5, PE6, SSIV, SSIX, SSX Hawai'ian Americans, Hawai'ians

Tiger of the Snows: Tenzing Norgay: The Boy Whose Dream Was Everest
By Robert Burleigh. 2006. Illus. 42 pages. Atheneum. (NF) **Grades 4–8**

On May 29, 1953, Tenzing Norgay and Edmund Hillary made the final ascent up Chomolungma, what Westerners call Mount Everest. This short biography of Norgay begins when he is "the boy on a steep hillside,/Tending the belled yaks,/Spring in his blood,/ Wandering through patches of rhododendrons,/And as ever,/ Looking up." The free-verse exposition of Norgay's story gives the book an almost dreamlike feel, while Ed Young's lush pastel illustrations capture the grandeur of the Himalayas and the ice and snow and cold faced by the climbers. An afterword gives basic information on the expedition. **Physical Education, LA1, PE6, SSIII Nepalese**

Wild Card
By Tiki Barber and Ronde Barber with Paul Mantell. 2009.
160 pages. Simon & Schuster. (F) **Grades 4–8**

This book is football all the way. Twins Tiki and Ronde Barber, running back and cornerback for the Eagles, live for the game. When Adam Costa, the team's star kicker, is sidelined due to bad grades, the twins spring into action and offer to tutor their friend so he can pass his math and science exams. In the meantime, Tiki ends up as the Eagles' kicker—and doesn't do well. The third-person omniscient narrative lets the reader see both Tiki and Ronde's thoughts as each one struggles to figure out the best way to help the team. The supportive team atmosphere, exciting play-by-play action, and believable dialogue make this fast-paced read a strong addition to middle school collections. The Barbers have collaborated on other titles: *By My Brother's Side* (2004), *Game Day* (2005), *Teammates* (2006), and *Go Long!* (2008). **Physical Education LA1, PE5, PE6, SSIV, SSV African Americans**

5 SCIENCE & MATHEMATICS

Science and mathematics standards do not specifically address multiethnic understanding; however, it is important for all students to see scientists and mathematicians from their own ethnic or cultural group who have excelled in these areas. From the familiar to the less familiar faces, we found books to engage students in various types of scientific and mathematical inquiry. The informational books included here feature multiethnic researchers and assistants, present their topics in an inclusive or global manner, or include positive multiethnic photographs. Finding quality multiethnic science and mathematics titles was difficult; we hope publishers take note.

ASTRONOMY AND EARTH SYSTEMS

Catastrophe in Southern Asia: The Tsunami of 2004
By Gail B. Stewart. 2005. Illus. 112 pages. Lucent. (NF) **Grades 5–9**

Heavily documented with both primary and secondary sources, this presents a detailed look at the tsunami that struck parts of Indonesia, Sri Lanka, India, Bangladesh, Myanmar, Thailand, Malaysia, Maldives, Somalia, Kenya, and Tanzania on December 26, 2004. Many areas were completely devastated. The clear, compelling narrative reviews the science behind a tsunami, the traumatic effects on human life, and local and international relief efforts engendered by this horrific event. Black-and-white photographs and maps, extensive use of subheadings within the chapters, and a direct tone make this an easy-to-read, useful source for reports. Photographs of dead bodies might be disturbing for some students. Includes chapter notes, lists of further resources, source notes, an index, and picture credits.   Science, Social Studies LA1, SCIII, SCIV, SCVI, SSIII, SSVI, SSVII, SSVIII, SSIX AOD, Global

The Day the World Exploded: The Earthshaking Catastrophe at Krakatoa
By Simon Winchester. Adapted by Dwight Jon Zimmerman.
2007. Illus. 96 pages. Collins. (NF) **Grades 5–12**

Based on his dense adult book, *Krakatoa* (HarperCollins, 2003), Winchester uses detailed diagrams and photographs to give a brief introduction to volcanoes around the world. He gives the historical background of Southeast Asia, including its importance in the world's early spice trade. In the nineteenth century, technological inventions such as the telegraph and the transcontinental underwater cables made global communication faster; when Krakatoa erupted on August 27, 1883, not only was the news transmitted immediately around the world, but the explosion was so intense, its effects were felt worldwide. Winchester also includes news briefs, maps, drawings, famous paintings (with credits), a glossary, suggested volcano websites, suggested readings, and a detailed index. His informal writing style makes this book readable and interesting for even the less-scientifically inclined reader.   Science, Social Studies LA1, SCI, SCII, SCIII, SCIV, SCV, SCVIII, SSII, SSIII, SSVIII, SSIX Southeast Asians

Drought and Heat Wave Alert! (Disaster Alert! series)
By Paul C. Challen. 2005. Illus. 32 pages. Crabtree. (NF) **Grades 4–8**

Science classes looking at the water cycle, weather, agricultural practices, or the human body can connect these topics to the lives of people around the world with this catchy book. Short and to the point, it defines and describes droughts and heatwaves and their effects on people in various parts of the world. It also looks at the role of plants and trees, water conservation, urban cool-off areas, and international responses to famine caused by drought. Colorful insets provide additional information, such as the Aboriginal myth that a giant frog once created a drought by sucking up all the water, or a description of the "urban heat island effect." The book is brightly colored, with numerous photographs and well-spaced text. The global coverage shows an awareness of diversity.   Science LA1, SCII, SCIII, SCIV, SCVII AOD

Not a Drop to Drink: Water for a Thirsty World
(National Geographic Investigates series)
By Michael Burgan. 2008. Illus. 64 pages. National Geographic. (NF) **Grades 5–8**

Concern over the shortage of potable water around the world is growing as the human population grows and the climate changes. Glaciers are shrinking, oceans are warming; freshwater lakes are going dry; areas that once were inhabitable may soon become desert. Scientists from various countries are working, sometimes collaboratively, to determine the current situation and to make future predictions of water availability. Easy-to-read text and numerous documented color photographs and diagrams invite readers to explore alongside scientists. For details on this series' format and style, see *Ancient Inca: Archaeology Unlocks the Secrets of the Inca's Past*, page 99.   Science LA1, SCIII, SCIV, SCV, SCVIII, SSIII, SSVIII AOD

Ryan and Jimmy and the Well in Africa That Brought Them Together
By Herb Shoveller. 2006. Illus. 55 pages. Kids Can. (NF) **Grades 3–8**

In 1998, first grader Ryan Hreljac learned about the shortage of clean water in many African countries. His teacher said $70 would build a well (it didn't). Ryan earned the initial $70, and then earned more. At age 9, Ryan traveled to Uganda to meet Jimmy, in whose village the first well was built. The boys developed a strong bond that led to Jimmy's miraculous escape from Ugandan rebels and his coming to Canada to live with the Hreljac family. Ryan's story spread (and keeps spreading), and by 2010, Ryan's Well Foundation (www.ryanswell .ca) had built over seven hundred wells and also supports sanitation, health, and hygiene services in multiple countries. The two young men now travel around the world to tell the story of the foundation.   Science, Social Studies LA1, SCIV, SCV, SCVII, SSIII, SSIV, SSVII, SSVIII, SSIX Africans, Canadians, Ugandans

Space Rocks: The Story of Planetary Geologist Adriana Ocampo
(Women's Adventures in Science series)
By Lorraine Jean Hopping. 2005. Illus. 118 pages. Franklin Watts. (NF) **Grades 5–9**

As a child in Buenos Aires, Argentina, Adriana Ocampo loved to pretend she was an astronaut. Her family moved to the U.S., and in high school she joined a Boy Scout troop based at the Jet Propulsion Laboratory (JPL) just outside her home in Pasadena. Adriana began a permanent job at JPL, and, fascinated with the images of Mars, she turned to geology, slowly working on her university degrees and continuing to work on JPL projects. Her interest in craters led her to discover, along with other scientists, the Chicxulub crater, now known as the cause of the disappearance of dinosaurs sixty-five million years ago. For details on this series' format and style, see review of *Strong Force: The Story of Physicist*

Shirley Ann Jackson on page 91.   Science LA1, SCI, SCII, SCIII, SCVI, SSIII, SSIV, SSV
Latinos

LIFE SCIENCES AND CHEMISTRY

Animal Poems of the Iguazú: Poems
By Francisco X. Alarcón. 2008. Illus. 32 pages. Children's Book Press. (NF) **Grades 3–8**

Alarcón and illustrator Maya Gonzalez feature the animals, birds, and insects of the South American rain forest in their collection of bilingual poems and art. The book might appear as one for young children, but that is not the case. Science classes studying the ecology of the rain forest would find this especially useful. Gonzalez's brightly colored illustrations, created using paper collage and acrylic paint on archival paper, would be excellent examples for middle school art; the poems also could be used in a language arts unit.   Language Arts, Science, Visual Arts LA1, LA9, SCIV, SCVII, VA1, VA6 Latinos

Bodies from the Ice: Melting Glaciers and the Recovery of the Past
By James M. Deem. 2008. Illus. 58 pages. Houghton Mifflin. (NF) **Grades 5–12**

Across the world, as glaciers melt, climbers are discovering bodies long buried in the ice. Deem discusses some of these discoveries and what they mean to scientists trying to learn more about earlier peoples. From the Alps to the Himalayas to the Andes to the Canadian Rockies to Mount Kilimanjaro in Africa, bodies are unlocking long-kept secrets of life and human existence. Surprisingly, many have been preserved in excellent condition. Scientists and discoverers vary in their ethnicity. Includes a list of glaciers to visit, suggested websites, acknowledgments, a bibliography, illustration credits, and an index.   Science, Social Studies SCIV, SSI, SSII, SSIII, SSIV, SSV, SSIX AOD

Buffalo Song
By Joseph Bruchac. 2008. Illus. No page numbers. Lee & Low. (NF) **Grades 2–6**

In 1873, white men kill Little Thunder Hoof's mother and all the other buffalo in her herd. She is rescued by Walking Coyote's family, who nurse a small group of buffalo calves, eventually bringing them over arduous terrain to the Black Robe Fathers at the St. Ignatius Mission. The monks won't take them, leaving Walking Coyote and the Salish people of the Flathood River valley to care for the fledgling herd during the next few years. Through their efforts, and those of wealthy ranchers Michel Pablo and Charles Allard, the buffalo thrive. Bill Farnsworth's large, lush oil paintings bring both people and bison to life. In his acknowledgments, Bruchac describes his first childhood encounter with bison, as well as his sources; the afterword updates readers on the current state of bison in the U.S. Science, LA1, SCIV, SSII, SSIII, SSV, SSVI, SSVII, VA6 American Indians, Kalispels, Nez Perce, Salish

Cycle of Rice, Cycle of Life: A Story of Sustainable Farming
By Jan Reynolds. 2009. Illus. 48 pages. Lee & Low. (NF) **Grades 4–7**

On the small Indonesian island of Bali, a rhythm of rice and life was quite successful. For over one thousand years, an intricate water system brought water from the mountains to every farm on the island. This balance was nearly destroyed when the Indonesian government required farmers to raise more rice and use hybrid rice and commercial fertilizers. The result was less rice and the development of a cycle that demanded more and more fertilizer. Two American scientists studying the rice cycle finally convinced the government to allow the people to return to their proven growing methods, although it will take years for the effects of the green revolution to disappear. Breathtaking photographs of the lush island add to the appeal of the book. Science SCII, SCIV, SCVI, SCVII, SCVIII, SSII, SSIII, SSVI, SSVII, SSIX Balinese

The Eco Diary of Kiran Singer
By Sue Ann Alderson. 2005. Illus. 65 pages. Tradewind Books. (NF) **Grades 3–7**

At the edge of a public park in the middle of Vancouver is the Camosun bog, a remnant of the ice age in the midst of a busy urban landscape. When Kiran's grandma gives her a diary for her 12th birthday, she invites Kiran to join the "Crazy Boggers" as they care for this small pond. Kiran is quickly drawn into the task, writing short poems about the wonders she sees there. Each captures a different aspect of the bog, describing its plants and animals: "This tiny shrew can barely see. / He lives to eat. Hidden in the underbrush he sleeps / at most

an hour at a time." As time goes by we meet other volunteers and learn of their personal connections to the bog. The environment takes center stage here, but the multicultural cast of characters adds to the sense of a richly drawn urban community. Millie Balance's gentle watercolor illustrations bring the bog to life.
Language Arts, Science LA1, SCIV, SSIII, SSX AOD

Ethnobotany (Green World series)
By Kim J. Young. 2007. Illus. 112 pages. Chelsea House. (NF) **Grades 7–12**

Ethnobotany is defined here as the study of how people of particular cultures make use of the plants in their local environments. After a brief look at the field of science, the book covers plant classification, the emergence of agriculture, and medicinal uses of plants. The author then looks at the relationship between Native North Americans and plants, the tragedy of Easter Island, the role of plants in creating and sustaining cultures, the importance of rain forests, and the collaborative role of ethnobotanists in efforts to conserve biodiversity today. Notes, a glossary, a bibliography, a list of websites, and an index are provided. Photographs and insets that present further information add to the pleasing format. The respectful focus on indigenous cultures and the global coverage makes this a solid resource.   Science LA1, SCII, SCIV, SCVI, SSIII, SSVIII Global

The Frog Scientist
By Pamela S. Turner. 2009. Illus. 58 pages. Houghton Mifflin. (NF) **Grades 5–9**

We first meet Dr. Tyrone Hayes as he wakes his research team (which includes his son, Tyler) in Wyoming so they can catch juvenile leopard frogs. Hayes's study of the effects of the pesticide atrazine has led him here, and this photo essay describes not only his life and research, but also the many threats that are causing a rapid drop in amphibian populations around the world. Short chapters cover his life from his birth in a segregated hospital in 1967 and examine the scientific method used in Hayes's atrazine experiment, efforts to save frog species through special breeding programs, and the work and lives of some of the students assisting with the research. The sharp photos by Andy Comins bring the story to life. Well-written and easy to follow, full of interesting facts and photographs, and featuring students from many ethnic groups, this is an empowering book.   Science, LA1, SCIV, SSIII, SSIV, SSV, SSVI, SSVIII African Americans AOD

George Washington Carver: Scientist, Inventor, and Teacher
(Signature Lives series)
By Michael Burgan. 2007. Illus. 112 pages. Compass Point. (NF) **Grades 6–10**

Born just before slavery was outlawed, George and his brother, Jim, were reared by a southwest Missouri couple who treated them as their own children. When George was about 13, he moved in with an African American couple in Neosho, Missouri, to attend Lincoln School. He earned bachelor's and master's degrees from Iowa State Agricultural College (now Iowa State University) and went to Tuskegee Institute as the head of their agricultural department. His natural skill for raising plants led him to be known as the "plant doctor" almost everywhere he lived. The straightforward narrative traces his many moves as he gained an education, despite encounters with racism. One of his lifetime goals was to help black farmers improve their lives by raising more and better crops. His extensive work for the betterment of Southern agriculture is well documented. The book's layout is easy to follow and filled with photos and illustrations, with sidebars that include explanatory information. Includes an extensive timeline, source notes, extensive lists of further resources, a glossary, an index, and image credits.   Science LA1, SCIV, SCVI, SCVII, SCVIII, SSII, SSIII, SSV, SSVI, SSVII African Americans

George Washington Carver
By Tonya Bolden. 2008. Illus. 40 pages. Abrams. (NF) **Grades 3–7**

As a child growing up in southwest Missouri, George Washington Carver had great love and respect for nature. He had a quick mind but didn't attend school until he was a teen. In his early adulthood, he homesteaded in Kansas, teaching himself as much as he could. Finally, he was admitted to Simpson College and then transferred to Iowa State Agricultural College (now Iowa State University), where he earned his bachelor's and master's degrees. Carver is remembered for his many years in teaching and research at Tuskegee Institute in Alabama. In her rich prose, Bolden shows the person behind the name. Her beautiful words, moving phrases, and carefully documented photographs offer a most worthy yet quiet tribute to the unassuming man who made so many contributions to the lives and livelihood of poor southern African American and white farmers.
Science LA1, SCII, SCIII, SCIV, SCVI, SCVII, SCVIII, SSII, SSIII, SSIV, SSV, SSVIII African Americans

Neandertals: A Prehistoric Puzzle (Discovery! series)
By Yvette La Pierre. 2008. Illus. 112 pages.
Twenty-First Century Books. (NF) **Grades 5–9**

Well organized and clearly written, this follows 150 years of scientific debate over the relationship of the Neanderthals to modern humans. The first skeleton was discovered in 1856, and early twentieth–century scientists wondered if the Neanderthals were the missing link between apes and humans, or a different species altogether. Their conclusions often had more to do with their world views than to scientific evidence. The book discusses scientific processes that have helped researchers learn more about Neanderthals. Questions remain. Why did the Neanderthals disappear? Did Homo sapiens absorb their genes? Kill them off through violence? Was racism a factor? Includes captioned photographs and illustrations along with colorful boxed insets containing further information. A sparse glossary and notes section is accompanied by an extensive bibliography.
Science LA1, SCII, SCIV, SCVI, SSI, SSII, SSIII Global

People Person: The Story of Sociologist Marta Tienda
(Women's Adventures in Science series)
By Diane O'Connell. 2005. Illus. 108 pages. Franklin Watts. (NF) **Grades 5–9**

This highly personal biography begins with Dr. Marta Tienda's childhood: the loving family that struggles to make ends meet, her mother's death when she was 6, working in the fields with her siblings, and most of all, her fierce dedication to the education her father knew was important for his children's future. Along with Tienda's life choices, the work of a sociologist is discussed in detail: text insets explain what a standard deviation is, or samples are chosen for research. For details on this series' format and style, see *Strong Force: The Story of Physicist Shirley Ann Jackson*, page 91.   Science LA1, SCI, SCII, SCIV, SSIII, SSIV, SSV Latinos

Percy Lavon Julian: Pioneering Chemist (Signature Lives series)
By Darlene R. Stille. 2009. Illus. 112 pages. Compass Point. (NF) **Grades 6–9**

As an African American in the 1920s and 1930s, Percy Julian faced and overcame almost insurmountable odds to become one of the most recognized chemists in the world. He graduated with degrees in chemistry from DePauw University, Harvard, and the University of Austria; but only in Austria did he feel accepted as an equal. The racial wall continued to haunt him. Finally, he was hired by the Glidden Company, where he developed (sometimes on purpose, sometimes accidentally) synthetic hormones from soybeans. He then founded his own company to produce synthetic cortisone. Although the writing is sometimes choppy, the information, format, and photographs will keep readers engaged. For details on this series' format and style, see *George Washington Carver: Scientist, Inventor, and Teacher*, page 85.   Science SCII, SCVI SCVII, SSIII, SSVIII, SSX African Americans

Poachers in the Pingos
By Anita Daher. 2008. 123 pages. Orca. (F) **Grades 4–6**

Best friends Colly and Jaz are off for another adventure when they visit Colly's Uncle Norbert in the small town of Tuktoyaktuk. They are looking forward to exploring the *pingos*—bubble-shaped islands created when underground water pressure pushed the permafrost up. Their new friend, Tommy, guides them to the pingos, and when they stumble on a group of dead Gyrfalcons, Colly and Jaz learn about a poacher who threatens the existence of this protected species. Can they catch him before it's too late? Details about various native tribes are woven into the story: Colly's family is Dene, and Tommy is Inuvialuit. These details, along with extensive dialogue and a well-paced plot, make this a good multicultural addition to the mystery/adventure collection. Sequel to *Racing with Diamonds* (2007).   Science LA1, SCIII, SCIV, SSIII, SSIV, SSVII Canadian First Peoples, Dene, Inuvialuit

Quest for the Tree Kangaroo: An Expedition to the Cloud Forest of New Guinea
By Sy Montgomery. 2006. Illus. 79 pages. Houghton Mifflin. (NF) **Grades 5–8**

This photo essay shows how Lisa Dabek of Seattle's Woodland Park Zoo pulled together an international team of conservation biologists to travel to Papua New Guinea to find and study the rare Matschie's tree kangaroo. The author, herself an expedition member, recounts the trip in a warm and informative first-person narrative. The respectful tone she uses when describing the team and their helpers underscores the book's message that people need to work together to achieve conservation goals. Whereas similar (and older) titles often make little mention of their local partners, here much credit is given to Lisa's New Guinea friends from the village of Yawan, who join the team as trackers and porters and provide much moral support. Includes web resources, a glossary of Tok Pisin words and phrases, an index, and notes from the author as well as photographer Nic Bishop.

Science LA1, SCI, SCII, SCIV, SSIII, SSIV, SSV New Guineans

Saving the Baghdad Zoo: A True Story of Hope and Heroes
By Kelly Milner and Major William Sumner. 2010. Illus. 64 pages.
Greenwillow. (NF) **Grades 5–8**

Major Sumner, a trained archaeologist, was sent to Baghdad in April 2003. He thought his assignment was to help restore Iraq's cultural heritage. Was he ever wrong! He was asked to lead the rescue efforts at the Baghdad zoos. Here he tells the often painful yet hopeful story of the rescue and relocation of as many animals as possible. Short chapters focus on individual or small groups of animals. Accompanying primary photographs of the wreckage offer an almost-firsthand witness of the rescues. Text boxes in each chapter give fast facts about the animal or species. Hearing of the 4/64 Armor's task, trained volunteers from around the world came to assist. Includes an extensive detailed bibliography with source notes, an index, and brief biographical sketches of the major people involved in the efforts.

Science SCIV, SCVII, SSIII, SSVI, SSX AOD, Iraqis, AOD

Waste and Recycling (Green Team series)
By Sally Hewitt. 2009. Illus. 32 pages. Crabtree. (NF) **Grades 3–6**

In this look at recycling, each double-page spread covers one topic. Photographs, colored blocks of text, and clearly marked subheadings make this an excellent browser as well as a good resource for reports. "Challenge!" and "Action!" text boxes offer suggestions for students to try to increase their own recycling. Topics range from paper, plastic, and glass to cell phones and old appliances. The book ends with ideas for a recycling party and setting up home recycling. Some of the case studies included showcase successful recycling efforts in other countries; for example, a primary school in South Africa sponsors an earthworm composting project. A glossary, websites, and an index are provided. Other titles we recommend in the Green Team series (2009), all with a similar tone and format, include *Reduce and Reuse, Using Energy, Using Water, Waste and Recycling,* and *Your Local Environment.* Science LA1, SCVII, SSVIII AOD

MATHEMATICS

Benjamin Banneker: American Scientific Pioneer (Signature Lives series)
By Myra Weatherly. 2006. Illus. 112 pages. Compass Point. (NF) **Grades 7–10**

Benjamin Banneker was a free black man in the tumultuous years surrounding the American Revolution. His grandmother, Molly Welsh, an indentured servant from England, freed and then married one of the slaves she had purchased to help run her tobacco farm in Maryland. Benjamin was often under the care of his grandmother, who taught him how to read at an early age. This presents a solid introduction to Banneker's life and his work in astronomy and mathematics. The somewhat dry tone is alleviated by the series format and illustrations. The central focus is on Banneker's achievements, such as building a wooden clock with only a pocket watch as a guide. His letter to Thomas Jefferson, in which he rebuked the founding fathers for not extending freedom to all persons in America, is also included. For details on this series' format and style, see *George Washington Carver: Scientist, Inventor, and Teacher*, page 85.   Mathematics, Science LA1, M3, M4, SCIII, SCV, SCVI, SSIII, SSV, SSVI, SSVII, SSVIII African Americans

Ibn Al-Haytham: First Scientist (Profiles in Science series)
By Bradley Steffens. 2007. Illus. 128 pages. Morgan Reynolds. (NF) **Grades 7–12**

One of the most revolutionary scientists and mathematicians of all time, Ibn Al-Haytham, is today not well-known outside the field of math. He was born in Basra, Iraq, and spent his childhood there. He also spent time in Cairo, Egypt, where he discussed building a dam on the Nile River. Rather than accepting the teachings of scientists who had come before him, Ibn Al-Haytham studied their work and followed it with his own detailed research. Of all his works, only about one-third survive, but these have laid the foundation for many scientists who have come after him. The dense but well-researched book includes a table of contents, photographs, diagrams, fact boxes with pertinent information about other scientists or religious leaders of the period, a timeline, chapter source notes, detailed bibliography, websites, and an index.   Mathematics, Science LA1, M1, M3, M5, SCII, SSVIII, SSI, SSII, SSIII, SSIV, SSVIII Egyptians, Iraqis

Real World Data series
Illus. Approx. 32 pages. Heinemann. (NF) **Grades 4–8**

This series is designed to integrate mathematics with current world issues. In general, the books present information in a clear, concise manner. Chapters are organized nicely, with well-placed subheadings. Documented photographs depict people from many cultures and have appropriate captions. Text boxes provide interesting facts and tidbits. Although the pages are busy, they are clearly laid out and readable. Perhaps the strongest element in each book in the series is the presentation of graphs, charts, and tables. These help the reader grasp the main ideas presented as well as demonstrating a real-world use of mathematics. While the series shows an awareness of diversity in its choice of photographs, volumes that specifically address multicultural issues within the social studies curriculum include *Graphing Global Politics* (2010), *Graphing Immigration* (2008), *Graphing Population* (2009), and *Graphing War and Conflict* (2010).
Mathematics, Social Studies LA1, M4, SC1, SSII, SSVII, SSVIII, SSIX AOD

Blockhead: The Life of Fibonacci
By Joseph D'Agnese. 2010. Illus. 40 pages. Holt. (NF) **Grades 5–10**

This middle school–friendly picture book presents Leonardo Fibonacci's life and work in a manner that brings the Middle Ages to life. Daydreaming about numbers earns young Leonardo the nickname Blockhead in his hometown of Pisa—so, his embarrassed father, a successful merchant, takes him along on his next trip. As Leonardo travels he learns all he can about how others use numbers. Arab merchants in northern Africa show him numerals they borrowed from the Hindu people of India; Egyptian scholars teach him how the ancient pharaohs and their subjects used fractions; ancient Greek math books taught him geometry. Leonardo wrote a book about Hindu-Arabic numerals that brought him much attention and helped spread the numeric system. His presentation of the pattern now known as the Fibonacci sequence is explained in full, and clever renditions of this pattern and the spirals it creates are found in John O'Brien's drawings throughout the book. A synopsis of Fibonacci's life, a short list of activities, and author and illustrator information are included. Mathematics LA1, LA9, M2, SSII, SSIV, SSVII AOD

PHYSICS

Ellen Ochoa: First Female Hispanic Astronaut
(20th Century's Most Influential Hispanics series)
By John F. Wukovits. 2007. Illus. 104 pages. Lucent. (NF) **Grades 7–9**

After a chapter describing her childhood and college years, this book turns to Ochoa's work in optics, her efforts to gain entrance to the astronaut corps in NASA (she applied each year from 1985 until she was accepted in 1990), and her training and work at NASA. Filled with details about life in space—food, weightlessness, going to the bathroom, sleeping—this is sure to please students interested in space missions. Colored text boxes give fun facts and short biographical information about other astronauts. Quotes from Ochoa and other scientists are included, helping to offset the sometimes detail-heavy narrative. Well-documented, the book includes a timeline, chapter notes, further resources, an index, picture credits, and author information.   Science LA1, SCII, SCIII, SCV, SCVI, SSIII, SSIV, SSV, SSVI, SSVIII **Latinos**

Strong Force: The Story of Physicist Shirley Ann Jackson
(Women's Adventures in Science series)
By Diane O'Connell. 2005. Illus. 110 pages. Franklin Watts. (NF) **Grades 5–9**

A leader from an early age, Shirley Ann Jackson organized neighborhood go-kart races and cleanups and was a top student. Admitted to MIT, she endured ostracism as one of two African American freshmen there. In graduate school at MIT, Jackson studied theoretical physics and worked in earnest to ensure that minority students were treated fairly, organizing a black students' union and heading the Task Force on Educational Opportunity. After a distinguished career, she was asked by President Bill Clinton to head the Nuclear Regulatory Commission; the Senate vote for her approval was unanimous. The format here includes wide spacing, clear subheadings, extensive photographs, and numerous insets that describe physics concepts. A timeline, a glossary, a resource list, selected bibliography, and an index are appended. A website sponsored by the National Academy of Sciences (www.iwaswondering.org) gives further information and science activities.   Science LA1, SCI, SCII, SCIII, SCVI, SSIII, SSIV, SSV **African Americans**

SCIENTIFIC INQUIRY

African American Inventors
By Stephen Currie. 2010. Illus. 104 pages. Lucent. (NF) **Grades 7–12**

From the pre–Civil War era, African Americans have been inventors. Slaves gave ideas to their masters or actually invented things; however, most often their masters took credit for the inventions. Even into the mid-1900s, some African Americans couldn't afford the fees to patent their work. Stigmatizing black inventors continues even today. Currie divides the book loosely into time periods (pre–Civil War to mid-1900s), yet each chapter has a topical heading. Because few recent books provide a glimpse into the achievements of African American inventors, we chose to include this with the caveat that Currie's idealistic view of the change in racial climate mars the book. Includes chapter notes, other sources, an index, and picture credits.   Science LA1, LA9, SCVI, SCVIII, SSIII, SSV, SSVI, SSVIII African Americans

The Chinese Thought of It: Amazing Inventions and Innovations
(We Thought of It series)
By Ting-xing Ye. 2009. Illus. 47 pages. Annick. (NF) **Grades 5–8**

Readers might be surprised at the number of items we use every day that originated in China: wheelbarrows, kites, umbrellas, silk, and even playing cards! The author grew up in China and begins by introducing her country and its history using a map and timeline. Double-page spreads then outline inventions by theme, tying important innovations with social advances through China's history. Well-placed photographs and illustrations make this an enjoyable read. Includes maps, a timeline, extensive photo credits, further reading, information on authors, selected sources, and an index.   Science LA1, SCII, SCIV, SCVI, SCVII, SSII, SSIII, SSIV, SSV, SSVIII, SSIX Chinese

Exploratopia
By Pat Murphy, Ellen Macaulay, Jason Gorski, et al.
2006. Illus. 373 pages. Little, Brown. (NF) **Grades 5–9**

Eye-catching photographs, clear illustrations, and a pleasing, easy-to-follow format join with top-notch writing to make this an inviting compendium. The

book is divided into three sections: "Exploring Yourself," "Exploring Interesting Places," and "Exploring Interesting Stuff." After introductory information, most experiments include "Here's What You Need," "Here's What You Do," and "What's Going On?" Blue text boxes present letters to Professor E and answer questions such as "Why are bubbles round?" "Tools for Exploration" boxes suggest ways of taking a project even further. The section right after the introduction gives budding scientists excellent pointers on the scientific method. "Hints, Tips, and Answers" and an index are provided. San Francisco's Exploratorium Museum's website is referenced throughout for further information on specific topics. Written by museum staff members, this book features a multiethnic cast.
Science LA1, SCIII, SCIV, SCV, SCVI, SSVIII AOD

The Inuit Thought of It: Amazing Arctic Innovations
(We Thought of It series)
By Alootook Ipellie and David MacDonald. 2007.
Illus. 32 pages. Annick. (NF) **Grades 4–8**

An excellent companion book to *A Native American Thought of It* (see page 94). Now deceased, Ipellie knew his people, their lives, and customs well. Working with David MacDonald, he presents these for children and youth. The Inuit have been innovative people, finding ways to use everything at their disposal in harsh climates of the far north. With information on living in an igloo, food, clothing, entertainment, maps, and language, the book fills a need in the study of native peoples of North America. For details on this series' format and style, see *The Chinese Thought of It: Amazing Inventions and Innovations*, page 92.
Science LA1, SCII, SCIV, SCVI, SCVII, SSII, SSIII, SSIV, SSV, SSVIII, SSIX American Indians, Indians of North America, Inuits

The Leaping, Sliding, Sprinting, Riding Science Book:
50 Super Sports Science Activities
By Bobby Mercer. 2006. Illus. 80 pages. Lark Books. (NF) **Grades 4–7**

Students can use basic sports equipment and easy-to-find materials to test the scientific concepts behind dozens of sports in this highly accessible activity book. What do force, momentum, and Newton's third law of motion have to do with making an ollie on a skateboard? Why does spit on a baseball make a pitch tough to hit? Each activity includes a section on "What You Need" and "What

You Do." A final paragraph or two explains "What's Going On?" in easy-to-understand terms. Boldface words are explained further in a thorough glossary. A metric conversion chart and index round out the book. Cartoonlike illustrations by Tom LaBaff featuring Caucasian, Hispanic, and African American teens give this an inclusive feel. **Science, Physical Education LA1, PE 2, SCI, SCII, SCIII AOD**

A Native American Thought of It: Amazing Inventions and Innovations
(We Thought of It series)
By Rocky Landon with David MacDonald. 2008.
Illus. 48 pages. Annick. (NF) **Grades 4–8**

Landon, an Ojibwa band member from Ontario, learned his family's traditional practices and then studied the inventions and innovations of other groups. Photographs, drawings, and diagrams fill each page with information on topics such as food, transportation, clothing, medicine, and language. The book doesn't relegate the study of native peoples to history; it moves into modern life and contributions as well. This will both fascinate children and meet the research needs of teachers as they look for ideas to enhance studies of native peoples of America. For details on this series' format and style, see *The Chinese Thought of It: Amazing Inventions and Innovations*, page 92. **Science LA1, SCII, SCIV, SCVI, SCVII, SSII, SSIII, SSIV, SSV, SSVIII, SSIX American Indians, Canadian First Peoples, Ojibwa**

Pet Science: 50 Purr-Fectly Woof-Worthy Activities for You & Your Pets
By Veronika Alice Gunter and Rain Newcomb. 2006.
Illus. 80 pages. Lark. (NF) **Grades 4–8**

Catchy cartoon illustrations by Tom LaBaff feature a multiethnic trio of friends who guide readers through a surprisingly broad array of experiments designed to help understand animal behavior and physiology. Each experiment includes three sections: "What You Need," "What You Do," and "What's Going On?" The scientific explanation given in the latter refers directly to what the reader may have observed. ("Did your fish learn to associate food with the color red?") The friendly narrative is easy to understand and includes boldface words that can be found in an appended glossary. The experiments are designed to be fun for both pets and owners; for example, dogs find hidden treats or choose a favorite food. "Pet Smarts" inserts include safety tips; other text boxes give further information on a topic. Fun and informative. **Science LA1, SCII, SCIV, SCVII AOD**

Project Mulberry: A Novel

By Linda Sue Park. 2005. 225 pages. Clarion. (F) **Grades 5–7**

How will two suburban kids do a project in animal husbandry for the state fair? Julia Song and her best friend, Patrick, decide to raise silkworms. When the two discover that only fresh mulberry leaves will sustain their worms, Mr. Dixon agrees to let them pick the leaves from his trees. Julia's mother discourages her visits with Mr. Dixon, and only gradually does Julia comprehend that her mother has a racist attitude toward this kind African American man. Julia's exuberant first-person narrative includes her feelings about being the only Korean in her mostly white world. She also has conversations with the author that are inserted between chapters. Julia is often displeased with the author's plotline and consistently complains about her lack of control over what is supposed to be her story. This twist gives readers a view of the writing process while deepening the characterization of Julia. Despite the gravity of many of the issues tackled here, the book's fast pace and fresh presentation make this a fun read.   Science LA1, LA9, SCII, SCIV, SSII, SSIV African Americans, Korean Americans

6 SOCIAL STUDIES

The social studies chapter is the most comprehensive in the book—not necessarily by design, but because so many of the multiethnic books we read addressed specific events or time periods in world or United States history. We looked to middle school textbooks to help us arrange this chapter. Because ancient civilizations are often covered in an entire textbook, we gave these their own section. Since other areas of world history are often examined geographically, we opted to place titles within their geographic locales. Asia is subdivided into three broad regions. Because European history receives extensive coverage in most middle schools, we subdivided this section by major topics. United States history is roughly chronological to follow the organization of middle school textbooks. However, we have subdivided this section by topic area to make it easier to use. Since some subjects span a wide range of years, the chronology of the subsections is not exact; readers are urged to search by topic first and to utilize the index as necessary. The informational and fiction books in this chapter meet both the national social studies content standards and the Common Core State Standards for English Language Arts & Literacy in History/Social Studies.

WORLD HISTORY

EARLY CIVILIZATIONS

100 Things You Should Know about Pyramids
By John Malam. 2008. Illus. 48 pages. Mason Crest. (NF) **Grades 4–7**

From the pyramids of Ancient Egypt to the questionable claim of pyramids in Bosnia, Malam's hundred things about pyramids are accurate and presented in a fascinating way. The book's inviting format uses various type styles and font sizes plus colorful drawings and photographs. **Social Studies, Visual Arts LA1, SSI, SSII, SSIII, SSVIII, VA4, VA6 Ancient Egyptians, Mayans, Aztecs**

Ancient China (Excavating the Past series)
By Jane Shuter. 2006. Illus. 48 pages. Heinemann. (NF) **Grades 5–9**

Covering a span of over three thousand years, this combines basic information about its varied cultures with stories about how archaeologists have learned about ancient China. Double-page spreads are filled with maps, photographs, and text insets. Descriptive subheadings make it easy to follow the basic information. Shuter looks at a wide range of topics: earliest communities and political organization in China, warfare, lives of rich and poor, beliefs, travel and trade, and inventions. Throughout she includes archaeological tidbits. While broad, this is a solid introduction to ancient China and its archaeology. Includes both dynastic and archaeological timelines, glossary, three further resources, an index, and photo credits.   Social Studies LA1, SSI, SSII, SSIII, SSV, SSVI, SSVII, SSVIII Chinese

The Ancient Chinese World (The World in Ancient Times series)
By Terry F. Kleeman and Tracy Barrett. 2005. Illus. 174 pages.
Oxford University Press. (NF) **Grades 5–10**

"Imagine . . . a maidservant in the house of the family of the Marquis Yi of Zeng (a marquis is a low-level noble). In Hubei Province in 1977, archaeologists found his tomb, containing more than 10,000 treasures dating from around 422 BCE." Covering a vast swath of Chinese history, from Peking Man to the fifth century CE, the authors quote extensively from Chinese records and anthropological research. Using suppositional storytelling along with known facts, this volume transforms history into a gripping experience. Second-person narrative engages the reader ("When you think of a wheelbarrow, what comes to mind?"). As with other titles in this series, numerous quotes from primary sources, text boxes, photographs, maps, and illustrations further illuminate the narrative. Wide end columns contain source notes and short, explanatory definitions. Includes a timeline, further reading and websites, an index, a pronunciation guide, text credits, and author information.   Social Studies LA1, SCI, SCII, SSI, SSII, SSIII, SSV, SSVI, SSVII, SSVIII, SSIX Chinese

The Ancient Egyptian World (The World in Ancient Times series)
By Eric H. Cline and Jill Rubalcaba. 2005. Illus. 90 pages.
Oxford University Press. (NF) **Grades 5–10**

Using both fictional and historical characters, the authors weave the political history of Egypt with information about daily life, spanning the years 3000

BCE to Cleopatra's reign from 51–30 CE. An imaginary Egyptian magazine presents fashion trends: "Everyone wore heavy eyeliner . . . so much for the natural look." Fifteen-year-old Nakht, a peasant weaver buried in a humble wooden coffin, "suffered from black lung disease and desert lung disease" and a host of other maladies. His body helps readers understand life of the poorer classes. For details on this series' format and style, see the review above, *The Ancient Chinese World.*   Social Studies LA1, SCI II, SSI, SSII, SSIII, SSV, SSVI, SSVII, SSVIII, SSIX Egyptians

Ancient Inca: Archaeology Unlocks the Secrets of the Inca's Past
(National Geographic Investigates series)
By Beth Gruber, Johan Reinhard, and the National Geographic Society (U.S.). 2007.
Illus. 64 pages. National Geographic. (NF) **Grades 5–9**

Chronicles efforts of archaeologists to piece together stories of early civilizations of Peru. Maps, timelines, striking photographs, and illustrations combine with a clear, conversational writing style. Well-organized chapter headings are in the form of questions: "How do we know who lived in Peru before the Inca?" "How did engineering help the Inca rule their empire?" Within the chapters, boldface headings point the way to new topics. A glossary, a bibliography, and an index are included.   Social Studies LA1, SCI, SCII, SSI, SSIII, SSVI, SSVII, SSVIII, SSIX Inca, Peruvians

Ancient India: Archaeology Unlocks the Secrets of India's Past
(National Geographic Investigates series)
By Anita Dalal and the National Geographic Society (U.S.). 2007.
Illus. 64 pages. National Geographic. (NF) **Grades 4–8**

Replete with photographs, maps, illustrations, and timelines to help the reader make sense of a vast amount of information, this introduces the Indus Valley Civilization, Vedic Period, Mauryan Empire, and Gupta Empire. The focus on how archaeologists in the nineteenth, twentieth, and twenty-first centuries have uncovered the stories of these civilizations adds a sense of mystery and excitement to the history presented. The book ends with a brief description of the regional political and religious tensions currently hampering archaeologists' work. For details on this series' format and style, see the review above, *Ancient Inca: Archaeology Unlocks the Secrets of the Inca's Past.*   Social Studies LA1, SCI, SCII, SSII, SSIII, SSV, SSVI, SSVII East Indians

Ancient India (People of the Ancient World series)
By Virginia Schomp. 2005. Illus. 112 pages. Franklin Watts. (NF) **Grades 5–8**

Great photographs, interesting page blocks that add bits of information and intriguing stories, and a simple format with clear headers combine to make this a readable and enjoyable introduction to India's history. Packed with information, this book begins by looking at India's religious traditions and describes the roles they play within various Hindu castes. The author covers religion, royalty, government, farmers and merchants, servants, laborers and craftspeople, outcastes and slaves, and poets and playwrights. The book concludes with a detailed timeline, a biographical dictionary, a glossary, a resource section, and an index.
Social Studies LA1, SSI, SSII, SSIII, SSV, SSVI, SSVII, VA4 East Indians, Pakistanis

The Ancient Near Eastern World (The World in Ancient Times series)
By Amanda H. Podany and Marni McGee. 2005. Illus. 174 pages.
Oxford University Press. (NF) **Grades 5–10**

This absorbing history encompasses the period between 3500 BCE and 330 BCE in the Middle East, what the authors term the "cuneiform lands." These include Mesopotamia (modern Iraq), Anatolia (modern Turkey), Persia (modern Iran), the Levant (modern Jordan, Lebanon, Israel, and the Palestinian territories), and Syria. The primary source documents are fascinating. Letters between King Zimri-Lim of Mari and his wife, Shibtu, show their obvious affection and reveal inner workings of the royal household. King Shulgi of Ur tracks the flow of tax monies and boasts of his accomplishments. The priestess Adad-Guppi writes an autobiography in 547 BCE, illuminating life in the Anatolian city Harran. For details on this series' format and style, see *The Ancient Chinese World*, page 98.   Social Studies LA1, SCI II, SSI, SSII, SSIII, SSV, SSVI, SSVII, SSVIII, SSIX Anatolians, Mesopotamians, Levantines, Persians, Syrians

The Ancient South Asian World (The World in Ancient Times series)
By Jonathan M. Kenoyer and Kimberley Burton Heuston. 2005. Illus. 172 pages.
Oxford University Press. (NF) **Grades 5–10**

"If you were a student who never practiced your Vedas, or a farmer who let your land go to seed, or a craftsman who sold leaky pots, your parents or your wife or your customers would probably get angry with you. But that's not all." This second-person introduction to the concept of karma illustrates the strength of this series—it explains in detail various aspects of the cultures without speaking down to the intended audience. The writing sparks the imagination: chock full of stories, suppositions, and questions, it engages the reader every step of the way. This volume explores the sweeping history of South Asia from 7000 BCE to the early eighth century. For details on this series' format and style, see *The Ancient Chinese World*, page 98.   Social Studies LA1, SCI II, SSI, SSII, SSIII, SSV, SSVI, SSVII, SSVIII, SSIX South Asians

The Ancient World (A History of Fashion and Costume series)
By Jane Bingham. 2005. Illus. 64 pages. Facts on File. (NF) **Grades 4–8**

Using ancient artworks and archaeological evidence, this describes clothing and jewelry of about twenty groups of people ranging from the last Ice Age to the collapse of the Roman Empire. Chapters for each era or culture cover clothing, jewelry, footwear, hair, wigs, and even cosmetics. Each double-page spread includes clearly labeled photographs and illustrations; colored text boxes add interesting details. Large subheadings and much white space make this an excellent browser. Includes a timeline, a glossary, a resource list, and an index.
Social Studies, Visual Arts LA1, SSI, SSII, SSIII, SSV, SSVII, VA4, VA6 Global

Before Columbus: The Americas of 1491
By Charles C. Mann. 2009. Illus. 116 pages. Atheneum. (NF) **Grades 6–10**

In this visually appealing teen version of his acclaimed *1491*, Mann describes his quest to discover why his Pilgrim ancestors were able to colonize North America when the Indians living there vastly outnumbered them. He begins by exploring another question: "When Europeans first came to the Americas, they often described the land as 'lightly settled.' It was as if Indians hadn't built anything. How, I wondered, could that possibly be true?" Using the latest information from archaeologists and paleontologists, he describes Peruvian inhabitants who fished and traded before 10,000 BCE, the urban complexes of Norte Chico that date back to 2500 BCE, and the *milpa* system of agriculture in which farmers planted many different crops at the same time to form the basis of a well-balanced diet and allow for the growth of vast civilizations. The Olmec, Mayan,

Aztec, and Incan peoples and their highly developed societies are mapped out as well. As he presents current theories on the origins of Indians of Central and South America and on the genetic factors that allowed European diseases to wipe out tens of thousands in the "New World," Mann presents an entirely new picture of our history. Written in a conversational, highly accessible manner, this book is accompanied by striking illustrations, photographs, and maps in catchy double-page spreads. It includes a glossary, a list of further reading and websites, photo and illustration credits, and an index.   Social Studies LA1, SCI IV, SSI, SSII, SSIII, SSV, SSVI, SSVII, SSVIII, SSIX Aztecs, Inca, Indians of Central and South America, Maya, Olmecs

Cleopatra Rules! The Amazing Life of the Original Teen Queen
By Vicky Alvear Shecter. 2010. Illus. 128 pages. Boyds Mill. (NF) **Grades 5–10**

Western images of Cleopatra mostly come from the movies, but Shecter dispels the myths about this famous Egyptian pharaoh. She makes readable and humorous what could have been just another boring biography. Cleopatra was a strong leader whose only interest was to protect Egypt. Color photographs (with captions) of period art and architecture and full-page text boxes further describe people, events, and buildings relative to the story. From extensive research, Shecter surmises the Western image of Cleopatra came originally from Octavian's desire to discredit her, while the Eastern image of her is as a scholar and great ruler. Back matter includes detailed chapter endnotes, a timeline, a glossary, a bibliography (primary sources and secondary sources in separate lists), picture source credits for the 103 pictures, and an index.   Social Studies LA1, SSI, SSII, SSIV, SSV, SSVI Ancient Egyptians

Egypt (Insiders series)
By Joyce A. Tyldesley. 2007. Illus. 64 pages. Simon & Schuster. (NF) **Grades 5–10**

This book provides a thorough overview of the geography, history, religion, life, tombs, and temples of ancient Egypt. Pages busy with fact boxes and sidebars are colorful yet engaging. Used along with other books, whether fiction or nonfiction, this could be an excellent resource. It includes an index, a glossary, diagrams, maps, a timeline, and photographs and drawings of a multitude of items. Social Studies LA1, LA9, SSI, SSII, SSIII Egyptians

The First Americans:
The Story of Where They Came From and Who They Became
By Anthony Aveni. 2006. Illus. 125 pages. Scholastic. (NF) **Grades 5–10**

Aveni, Distinguished Professor of Astronomy, Anthropology, and Native American Studies at Colgate University, invites his readers to examine the theory (which he supports) of how early peoples migrated from Asia across the Bering Strait Land Bridge approximately twenty thousand years ago. He posits that these people were the ancestors of native peoples in the Northwest, Northeast, Southwest, and Southeast; the Mississippi Valley; and the Caribbean islands. Using a second-person conversational tone, his engaging writing combines with archival documented photos, maps, artifacts, and illustrations by S. D. Nelson to provide a rich resource for research on Native American groups. One caveat: the title could be misleading. This is strictly a historical look at native peoples and does not include their place in today's United States. Social Studies LA1, SCII, SCVII, SCVIII, SSI, SSII, SSIII American Indians

The Golden Bull
By Marjorie Cowley. 2008. 206 pages. Charlesbridge. (F) **Grades 4–7**

Jomar and Zeta's parents send their children to the towering city of Ur to save them from starving. Jomar works as an apprentice to the temple goldsmith and tries to find his little sister a safe position. They've already clashed with Malak, an evil temple overseer. Now Zeta is missing and stands accused of stealing a precious lapis bead from the shop. Jamar knows he must act and turns to the one powerful person in Ur he knows—someone who can destroy him as easily as help him. Filled with details about life in early Mesopotamia (now Iraq) and the processes of early gold work, this is a well-crafted mystery. Social Studies, Visual Arts LA1, SSII, SSIII, SSIV, SSVI, SSVII, SSVIII, VA4, VA6 Ancient Iraq, Mesopotamia

Life in Ancient Egypt series
By Kathryn Hinds. 2007. Illus. Approx. 72 pages.
Marshall Cavendish Benchmark. (NF) **Grades 6–9**

During the period known as the New Kingdom, from about 1550 BCE to about 1070 BCE, Egypt was highly respected and led by strong, capable rulers. The four books in this series about the New Kingdom—*The City, The Countryside, The Pharaoh's Court*, and *Religion*—incorporate photographs of actual sites and artifacts with engaging text and firsthand accounts from people who lived during the period. Written in a conversational tone, the chapters are subdivided and the text is augmented by color photographs, map, and illustrations on almost every page. Each title includes a table of contents, glossary, map, further readings, online sources, bibliography of sources used, sources for quotations, and an index. Although having a good timeline would be beneficial, the book stands on its other strengths.   Social Studies LA1, SSI, SSII, SSIII, SSV, SSIX Egyptians

Life in the Ancient Indus River Valley (Peoples of the Ancient World series)
By Hazel Richardson. 2005. Illus. 32 pages. Crabtree. (NF) **Grades 4–6**

Replete with catchy illustrations and photographs, this very basic introduction traces two ancient civilizations, the Harappans and the Aryans, from their beginnings in the Indus River Valley (present-day Pakistan). The author touches on the fact that no archaeological evidence shows the Aryans destroyed the Harappans and works on the premise that the two cultures eventually intermixed. The timeline at the beginning of the book guides the reader through the sometimes murky chronological progression of both civilizations. Trade, cities, farming, daily life, religions and beliefs, arts, and inventions are all introduced. A glossary and an index are provided.   Social Studies LA1, SCVI, SSI, SSII, SSIII, SSV, SSVI, SSVII, VA4 East Indians, Pakistanis, South Asians

Pharaoh's Boat
By David Weitzman. 2009. Illus. No page numbers.
Houghton Mifflin Harcourt. (NF) **Grades 4–12**

A captivating book on several levels: a history of ancient Egypt; details of construction and reconstruction of Cheops's boats; a biography of Hag Ahmed Youssef Moustafa, the man who with his crew painstakingly learned how to rebuild the boat; and the story of efforts to rebuild and preserve the second boat found in the same pit. Weitzman's drawings and illustrations of the boats, the tools used to craft them, and the men who built them are meticulously well crafted. The final four-page spread of the boat is magnificent! In his afterword and acknowledgments, Weitzman tells of his interest in ancient Egypt and the work still in progress on the boats. He offers suggested resources for those inter-ested in the work.   Social Studies, Visual Arts LA1, SSI, SSII, SSIII, SSVIII, SSIX, VA1, VA2, VA4, VA6 Egyptians

Seven Wonders of Ancient Africa (Seven Wonders series)
By Michael Woods and Mary B. Woods. 2009. Illus. 80 pages.
Twenty-First Century Books. (NF) **Grades 5–9**

While most students are probably familiar with the Great Sphinx, they are less-familiar with the history surrounding the temples of Abu Simbel, the Kush Pyramids, the civilizations of the Swahili Coast, and the cities of Aksum, Great Zimbabwe, and Timbuktu. Intended as an introduction to these ancient cultures, the authors bring history to life: "The Swahili coast was like a huge ancient shopping mall—with thousands of items for sale." They discuss some of the racial prejudices that have colored this history, citing, for example, the fact that for a long time Europeans did not believe Great Zimbabwe could have built such a large and grand city (a fallacy dispelled by archaeologists in the 1930s). Each chapter places its wonder in historical context, at times giving details about its rediscovery by European archaeologists or explorers. This series is beautifully produced with impressive, well-captioned photographs, maps, and illustrations; clear subdivisions; and text boxes with intriguing factoids that fill glossy pages. The many primary source quotations and engaging writing invite further study. Includes a timeline, an invitation to readers to "Choose an Eighth Wonder," a glossary and pronunciation guide, source notes, a selected bibliography, a list of further reading and websites, an index, author information, and photo acknowl-edgments.   Social Studies LA1, SCI, SCII, SSI, SSIII, SSVI, SSVII, SSVIII, SSIX Ancient Africans

Seven Wonders of the Ancient Middle East (Seven Wonders series)
By Michael Woods and Mary B. Woods. 2009. Illus. 80 pages.
Twenty-First Century Books. (NF) **Grades 5–9**

This inviting introduction to some of the cultures in the Ancient Middle East covers the Ziggurat at Ur, library of Nineveh, city of Persepolis, King Solomon's temple, rock city of Petra, Hagia Sophia, and Krak des Chevaliers. It is full of primary source quotations, such as the wording of the Charter of Cyrus, who conquered Babylon in 539 BCE and freed the enslaved Jewish people. Written in an engaging manner, it places the reader within the culture responsible for each wonder—we can imagine the wonderful gardens of Nineveh or feel part of a ceremony celebrating New Year's Day in Persepolis. For details on this series' format and style, see the review above, *Seven Wonders of Ancient Africa*. Social Studies LA1, SCI, SCII, SSI, SSIII, SSVI, SSVII, SSVIII, SSIX Ancient Middle Easterners

Tutankhamun
By Demi. 2009. Illus. No page numbers. Marshall Cavendish. (NF) **Grades 3–7**

Born into ancient Egyptian nobility, Tutankhaten (later renamed Tutankhamun) was the first and only son of King Akhenaten and a minor queen, Kiya. His childhood was interrupted when he was 9—his father died and Tutankhaten became king. Torn between the wishes and commands of his two advisors, he was made to change his name to Tutankhamun. Just as his adult life was truly beginning, King Tut was murdered. His favored advisor had the young king secretly buried; his tomb went undetected until 1922, when Howard Carter, a British archeologist, located it. From that time forward, the glory of King Tut grew as the treasures of his tomb became known all around the world. Demi's compact text and opulent, yet minutely detailed, uncluttered Egyptian-style art transport readers to ancient Egypt. Includes a genealogy of King Tut's ancestors and a map of Lower Egypt showing the location of his tomb. Social Studies, Visual Arts, LA1, SSI, SSII, SSIII, SSIV, SSV, SSIV, VA4, VA6 Ancient Egyptians

Who Was First: Discovering the Americas
By Russell Freedman. 2007. Illus. 88 pages. Clarion. (NF) **Grades 5–12**

Large colorful paintings, illustrations, and maps make this a page-turner. Freedman presents the exciting stories of not only Columbus, but of Admiral Zheng He, Leif Ericsson, and unnamed explorers who left their traces in sites throughout the Americas. He recounts evidence refuting the concept of the Clovis people crossing the Ice Age land bridge known as Beringia; namely, a band of hunters and gatherers lived at the site of Monte Verde in Chile about 14,500 years ago. Newer theories posit that ancient peoples probably came to the Americas by boat and slowly made their way south. Freedman provides information on archaeological techniques and theorizing as he explores various theories. Replete with primary source quotations, heavily documented with sources, credits, and a thorough index, this is a prime research tool as well as a fascinating read. Social Studies LA1, SCI, SCII, SSI, SSIII, SSVI, SSVII, SSVIII, SSIX Chinese, Greenlanders, Icelanders, Norwegians, Spanish

AFRICA

A Brief Political and Geographic History of Africa:
Where Are Belgian Congo, Rhodesia, and Kush? (Places in Time series)
By John Davenport. 2008. Illus. 111 pages. Mitchell Lane. (NF) **Grades 4–8**

The book looks at the history of Africa as a whole, but particularly at Egypt, Sudan, the Congo, and Zimbabwe. Filled with color photographs, a timeline, maps, and interesting facts, this report book becomes much more, even for adults. Includes a bibliography and index. Other books in the series focus on the Middle East, Asia, Europe, Latin America, and North America. Social Studies LA1, SSI, SSII, SSIII, SSV, SSIX Africans, Congolese, Egyptians, Sudanese, Zimbabweans

Burn My Heart
By Beverley Naidoo. 2009. 209 pages. Amistad. (F) **Grades 8–12**

Mugo and Mathew Grayson have grown up together in Kenya, but they've never been equals. This becomes more apparent as the Mau Mau uprising spreads in the early 1950s. Mugo's father cares for the *bwana*'s horses on land that his family owned for generations before the British. Mugo works in the *bwana*'s kitchen but maintains a tenuous friendship with Mathew. Trouble for Mugo and his family begins when Lance Smithers' family moves to the adjoining farm. Lance's father, a white extremist, creates illegal "gathering" places where the Kenyans are persecuted or killed, and Lance incites fear and hatred in Mathew, leading him to turn against the Kenyans he knows. Through alternating chapters from Mugo's and Matthew's viewpoints, Naidoo presents a vivid picture of an oppressed people, siding more with the Kenyans than the British and opening a window to the dark decade of the 1950s in Kenya. Social Studies LA1, LA9, SSII, SSIII, SSIV, SSV, SSVI, SSIX Africans, British, Kenyans

Child of Dandelions
By Shenaaz Nanji. 2008. 214 pages. Front Street. (F) **Grades 7–11**

When brutal dictator Idi Amin issues an edict in 1972 to evict all Indians from Uganda within ninety days, Sabine's father dismisses it. After all, he and his family are native Ugandans, and his businesses keep the economy going. But when Indian shops are looted, her uncle disappears, and her best friend, Zena, begins to talk about the need for "Dada Amin" to liberate her people from the "foreigners," Sabine begins to doubt her father's certainty. The 15-year-old struggles to keep her family safe in the midst of turmoil. The day-by-day countdown, rich dialogue, and evocative descriptions bring the reader into the heart of Sabine's dilemma in this many-layered story of friendship, betrayal, entitlement, and oppression.   Social Studies LA1, LA9, SSII, SSV, SSVI, SSVII Africans, East Indian Ugandans, Ugandans

City Boy
By Jan Michael. 2009. 188 pages. Clarion Books. (F) **Grades 5–8**

Losing first his father, then his mother to "The Disease" (AIDS), Samuel Sangala suddenly is an orphan. Accustomed to having the amenities of city life Sam now has nothing and goes to live with his aunt in the Malawian countryside. He feels alone and underappreciated by the village children. His blue shoes, the last gift from his mother, are stolen, *and* he must share his few things with his cousins. As the story progresses, Sam deals with his mother's death and understands the importance of family, not things. Michael, a native of the Netherlands, presents the reality of life in Malawi where poverty is high and nearly 15 percent of the population is infected with HIV, leading to soaring deaths from AIDS. Orphaned children often aren't as fortunate as Sam—they have no relatives and end up in orphanages with little hope.   Social Studies LA1, LA9, SSII, SSIII, SSIV, SSV, SSIX Africans, Malawians

Civil Wars in Africa (Africa: Progress & Problems series)
By William Mark Habeeb. 2007. Illus. 110 pages. Mason Crest. (NF) **Grades 7–10**

Currently, an estimated 20 to 25 percent of Africa's 885 million people have been affected by ongoing civil wars. After a series introduction that emphasizes the enormous diversity of Africa, this book looks at the human, economic, and global consequences of civil war. It turns to the causes of these wars; chief among them is the impact of colonialism, which exploited almost the entire continent and actively caused discord among cultural groups. As various country-states achieved independence in the second half of the twentieth century, authoritarian governments continued to exploit their country's resources for a select few; this, and economic mismanagement, led to conditions that readily fomented civil war. Chapters focus on the role of ethnicity, religion, and ideology in these conflicts. A final chapter looks at efforts for resolving Africa's civil wars. For details on this series' format and style, see *Religions of Africa*, page 217.   Social Studies LA1, SSI, SSIII, SSV, SSVI, SSVII, SSIX Africans

Ethiopia (Cultures of the World series)
By Steven Gish, Winnie Thay, and Zawiah Abdul Latif. 2007. Illus.
144 pages. Marshall Cavendish Benchmark. (NF) **Grades 5–10**

The authors present a balanced view of Ethiopia, giving its history, yet describing modern-day life in both rural and urban areas. Although designed more for research, the book is written to engage a middle grade student's interest in another part of the world. Includes photographs, an index, map, "fast" facts about the economy and culture, a timeline of Ethiopian history, a glossary, and further readings. The series is ongoing. Newer titles (2010) worth consideration include *Bangladesh, Ghana, Guatemala, Honduras,* and *Kuwait.*   Social Studies LA1, SSI, SSII, SSIII, SSV, SSVI, SSVII, SSVIII, SSIX Africans, Ethiopians

A Long Walk to Water
By Linda Sue Park. 2010. 121 pages. Clarion. (F) **Grades 6–9**

It is 2008. Eleven-year-old Nya spends eight hours a day walking in the baking sun to get water for her family—four hours walking to the water and four hours back with the now-heavy plastic container. When the rains stop each year, her family leaves their village and camps by the big lake that supplies water for the Neur tribe and the rival Dink tribe. Nya likes not spending her days hauling water, but this year she realizes her mother hates the camp and fears their family might be hurt or killed as the Nuer and Dinka continue their rivalry. Alternating between Nya's and Salva's stories, we go back to 1985 and see how 11-year-old

Salva struggles to stay alive in the midst of the Sudanese civil war. Told by their teacher to run from their school, Salva joins other refugees, not knowing where his family is. He finds other Dinka from his village, eventually makes his way to a refugee camp, and then, through a twist of fate, leads 1,500 other boys to safety in Kenya. The stories come together in 2009 as Salva, who has ended up in the U.S. and started a nonprofit company, comes to Nya's village to build a well—a well that, with luck, will help end the rivalry between their tribes. Short, fast-paced, and suspenseful, this not only informs about Sudanese culture, it also shows the power of determination and the impact one person can have on many. Science, Social Studies LA1, SCIV, SSIV, SSVIII, SSX Africans, Sudanese

Making of Modern Africa (Africa: Progress & Problems series)
By Tunde Obadina. 2007. Illus. 128 pages. Mason Crest. (NF) **Grades 7–10**

Beginning with a chapter on "Defining Africa," this describes both North Africa and sub-Saharan Africa but points out that "Africans from all parts of the continent commonly dispute such regional division." The brief outlines of Pan-Africanism, European imperialism and colonialism, African nationalism, and the impact of globalization set the tone for the history of the immensely diverse lands and cultures on the continent. The early history of Africa with its large kingdoms and transportation lines is followed by descriptions of the European incursion and eventual colonial rule. The author looks at what may have given Europeans advantages in their development over indigenous peoples living on the African continent. Nationalism, independence movements, and postcolonial development lead to the final chapter on "Africa Today." The emphasis on the variety of cultures and institutions found in Africa helps make sense of this broad topic. For details on this series' format and style, see *Religions of Africa*, page 217. Social Studies LA1, SSI, SSIII, SSV, SSVI, SSVII, SSIX Africans

Mzungu Boy
By Meja Mwangi. 2005. 150 pages. Groundwood. (F) **Grades 5–8**

In 1950, British colonial rule was in place in Kenya. Many Africans were slaves, although not called slaves. Twelve-year-old Kariuki dislikes the chores his mother gives him and the slaps his father gives him; he prefers sitting quietly by the river watching a family of ducks. His life changes when he meets Nigel, the grandson of the white plantation owner. The two become friends despite the trouble the friendship brings. They spend hours together chasing rabbits and an old warthog. Kariuki knows something unsettling is going on, yet he and Nigel feel free to wander miles from home. Things change when the boys are kidnapped and bound by the Mau Mau. Kariuki's brother, Hari, finds the boys and sets them free; this action has dire consequences. The first-person voice pulls the reader into the story. The publisher's note gives a brief overview of the Mau Mau rebellion that took place in Kenya in the 1950s. First published in England in 1990. Social Studies LA1, LA9, SSII, SSIII, SSIV, SSV, SSVI Africans, British, Kenyans

Over a Thousand Hills I Walk with You
By Hanna Jansen. 2006. 342 pages. Carolrhoda. (F) **Grades 6–12**

In April 1994, Jeanne d'Arc Umubyeyi's family was killed in the genocide in Rwanda. Though she witnessed and experienced horrible things, Jeanne survived without being raped or mutilated. The 8-year-old had an incredible desire to live. In 1996, she was adopted by Hanna and Reinhold Jansen, a German couple who already had twelve other children, mostly war orphans. Hanna Jansen organizes the book to give the reader pause between chapters so Jeanne's story can be taken in small chunks. Elizabeth Crawford's translation focuses on Jeanne's courage and allows a middle school student to deal with the horror of war.   Social Studies LA1, LA9, SSIII, SSIV, SSIX Africans, Rwandans

Women in the African World (Women's Issues, Global Trends series)
By Joan Esherick. 2005. Illus. 112 pages. Mason Crest. (NF) **Grades 6–12**

In this collective biography, Esherick states, "African people as a whole tend to identify most with their cultures, tribes, or heritages, rather than their nations." She asserts there is no such thing as a "typical African." The book begins with women in African history and concludes with the future for African women. Many facts and informational tidbits are presented in text boxes; these, along with striking photographs and illustrations and a running border at the bottom of each page, create an effective graphic layout. Includes a list of further reading, websites, a glossary, an index, picture credits, and author information. Although some sources are credited within the text, there is unfortunately no comprehensive source list.   Social Studies LA1, SSIII, SSIV, SSIX Africans

ASIA

Because physical or political maps of Asia differ in delineating and identifying boundaries of Asia, we have chosen to follow the divisions as identified by *Encyclopædia Britannica*. A good general map can be found at WorldAtlas (www .worldatlas.com). Thus, the books in the Asia section of the chapter are arranged in this order: Middle East, East Asia and North Central Asia, and South Asia and Southeast Asia. Books overlapping two or more of these geographical areas are found in the predominant area's section.

MIDDLE EAST

Benazir Bhutto: Pakistani Prime Minister and Activist (Signature Lives series)
By Mary Englar. 2006. Illus. 112 pages. Compass Point. (NF) **Grades 7–10**

Benazir Bhutto's upbringing was different from other Pakistani women of her era. Born in 1953, educated in Catholic schools, she then studied comparative government at Radcliffe and Oxford. She hadn't planned to go into politics—as a child, the violence that often surrounded politics in Pakistan scared her. Clear narrative with quotes from Bhutto's autobiography and interviews provide an overview of her life through 2005, including her father's political rise and fall, his murder, subsequent family arrests and murders, and her own rise to power as prime minister. Readers should conduct further research to learn more about accusations of corruption within her government, her return to Pakistan, and her assassination in 2007. For details on this series' format and style, see *George Washington Carver*, page 85.   Social Studies LA1, SSII, SSIII, SSVI, SSVII Pakistanis

Beneath My Mother's Feet
By Amjed Qamar. 2008. 198 pages. Atheneum. (F) **Grades 6–10**

An excellent student, 14-year-old Nazia's greatest dream is a college education; but when her father is injured, her mother pulls her out of school to clean houses in Karachi. As her father's shiftless ways take the family further into poverty, Nazia works to keep them afloat and is proud her sewing earns extra money. Always a dutiful daughter, Nazia wonders about her mother's path for her. Must she marry her cousin, who may be as irresponsible as her father? Why can't she finish school and change her destiny? Fast-paced and with plenty of dialogue, this thought-provoking story shows the many layers of prejudice within Pakistan. Health, Social Studies H4, H6, LA1, SSIII, SSIV, SSV Pakistanis

A Bottle in the Gaza Sea
By Valérie Zenatti. Trans. by Adriana Hunter. 2008. 149 pages.
Bloomsbury. (F) Grades 7–12

Seventeen-year-old Tal Levine learns to bury the fear that comes with living in Jerusalem in 2003. When a bomb goes off in her neighborhood, killing a young bride-to-be, her fear grows, and she decides she must do something to counteract the hatred in her world. She asks her brother, Eytan, an Israeli soldier, to throw a bottle with a message in the Gaza Sea. Tal hopes a Palestinian girl in the Gaza Strip will find it and respond. The sardonic, in-your-face reply she receives is not from a girl, but a boy who calls himself "Gazaman." Tal's sincerity and persistence move Gazaman—really named Naïm—and the two begin to share their innermost thoughts. When Tal witnesses the bombing of a city bus, she writes to Naïm for solace: "I saw bodies, dead people, things I don't want to describe . . . I heard screams, I didn't know human beings could produce noises like that." Through their correspondence, Tal and Naïm show readers how different life can be for those living a mere sixty miles apart—and how their dreams for a different world can be the same despite the Arab-Israeli conflict. Social Studies H2, LA1, SSIII, SSIV, SSIX Israelis, Palestinians, Arabs, Jews

Children of War: Voices of Iraqi Refugees
By Deborah Ellis. 2010. 128 pages. Groundwood. (NF) Grades 6–12

In the fall of 2007, Ellis traveled to Jordan to interview children who were refugees from Iraq. The children and teens range in age from 8 to 19; most live in deplorable conditions; most live in abject poverty because as refugees neither they nor their parents are allowed to work. Some of the children attend school; some do not. Each moving interview is prefaced with a brief introduction that explains how unsafe conditions were and are in Iraq. Not surprisingly, many of the children suffer from mental trauma and harbor hard feelings and anger toward the invading American troops and former president George Bush. They miss their homes in Iraq; those who lost family members mourn. These children wish for a bright future, but few think it will come to them. The interviews would provide a backdrop for discussion of the Iraq wars. Includes a glossary and organizations to contact for further information. Social Studies LA1, SSI, SSII, SSIII, SSIV, SSVI, SSIX Iraqis

Dawn and Dusk

By Alice Mead. 2007. 152 pages. Farrar, Straus and Giroux. (F) **Grades 5–8**

In her introduction, Mead explains that Kurdistan, a territory that stretches over parts of Turkey, Iraq, Iran, and Syria, is home to over twenty million Kurds. In each country, however, "Kurds have been marginalized and subjected to forceful repression." Thirteen-year-old Azad lives in Sardasht, a small Iranian town caught up in the war between Iraq and Iran. His parents divorced when he was 7, and he shuttles between his father's ill-kept home and his uncle Mohammad's house, where his mother lives. He and his friend Hiwa love to hang out, play soccer, and are looking forward to buying the new game, Pac-Man. As Azad helps prepare for Mohammad's wedding, he begins to realize just how involved his mother and uncle are in the deadly struggle for Kurdish independence—and why his mom had to divorce his father. Then the chemicals fall on Sardasht. Azad's first-person narrative strikes a fine balance between the everyday life and thoughts of a young teen and the political realities of a close-knit, activist family struggling to survive in a dangerous and unpredictable world. Social Studies LA1, SSI, SSIII, SSIV, SSV, SSVI Kurds

Good Night, Commander

By Ahmad Akbarpour. Trans. by Shadi Eskandani and Helen Mixter. 2005/2010. Illus. No page numbers. Groundwood. (F) **Grades 3–6**

In most wars, children are often innocent victims. In the eight-year-long Iran-Iraq War, the protagonist, Commander, is an unnamed young boy who lost a leg and his mother; now his father is about to remarry. Not wanting to face having a new mother, Commander spends most of his time secluded in his room lost in imagining he can avenge his own mother's death. Akbarpour's text is poignantly sparse told first-person dialog. Morteza Zahedi's moving childlike pencil drawings so resemble the way a child would draw his room—one-dimensional and flat, but from a detached, outside perspective. Both author and illustrator are Iranian, living in Iran. The book was named an International Board on Books for Young People Outstanding Book for Young People with Disabilities.

Social Studies, Visual Arts LA1, SSI, SSII, SSIII, SSIV, SSV, SSVI, VA4, VA5 Iranians

Out of Iraq: Refugees' Stories in Words, Paintings and Music
By Sybella Wilkes. 2010. Illus. 70 pages. Evans. (NF) **Grades 5–12**

Working with the United Nations Relief Agency (UNHCR) has given Wilkes opportunities to hear the heartbreaking stories of Iraqi refugees. All have suffered great losses—family members, homes, and livelihood. Yet they still hope for a better future; many hope to return to their homeland. Using a photo essay format, she features the personal story of a child, a teen, or an adult. Color photographs and paintings (some by children, some by displaced artists) depict the devastation of Iraq and living conditions in refugee camps. She gives historical background for wars in Iraq, the rise and downfall of Saddam Hussein, and information about UNHCR and its efforts to assist the refugees. She offers teachers suggestions on ways to use the books with students. Her effective way of telling these stories without detailed description of each situation makes this an appropriate book for middle grade readers and would be an excellent introduction for Deborah Ellis's *Children of War: Voices of Iraqi Refugees* (see page 113). One word of caution: some spellings are different due to the use of British English.   Social Studies LA1, MU9, SSI, SSII, SSIII, SSIV, SSVI, SSIX, VA4 Iraqis

Santa Claus in Baghdad and Other Stories about Teens in the Arab World
By Elsa Marston. 2010. 198 pages. Indiana University Press. (F) **Grades 7–12**

Decision making is at the heart of each of these short stories, highlighting what it is like for teens to grow up in the Middle East today. Although most of the stories were previously published in other collections, they are brought together here to emphasize the difficulty each teen faces, and the hope each holds for a better life for themselves and their families. Marston studied in the Middle East and sets each of her fictional characters in a historically and culturally accurate situation. She spares no brutal reality. In her author's note, she provides the geographical, historical, and cultural background for the eight stories. Although she gives no further readings, her personal experiences lend credibility to the collection.   Language Arts, Social Studies H2, H5, LA1, LA9, SSIII, SSIV, SSV Egyptians, Iraqis, Jordanians, Lebanese, Palestinians, Syrians, Tunisians

The Shepherd's Granddaughter
By Anne Laurel Carter. 2008. 222 pages. Groundwood. (F) **Grades 7–12**

Amani has fought to become the family's shepherd, just like her grandfather; but the Israelis are building new highways and settlements on lands farmed and grazed by Palestinian families for hundreds of years. In this bittersweet story, readers see the complex relationships within Amani's close-knit family as they struggle to retain traditional ways of living in the face of political realities. Her father uses his cell phone to organize resistance to the takeover of land; her cousins attend school in town; but Amani cares for her sheep. When she meets an American boy who has moved into a nearby settlement, Amani realizes that as a homeschooler, she cannot learn enough English to communicate, so she begins attending school with her cousins. Issues of family solidarity, gender roles, and, above all, tensions created by living in an occupied land abound in this complex coming-of-age tale. Westerners get a perspective of the Arab-Israeli conflict not often presented. **Social Studies LA1, SSIII, SSIV, SSV, SSVI, SSVII, SSVIII, SSIX Israelis, Palestinian Arabs, Palestinians**

Silent Music
By James Rumford. 2008. Illus. No page numbers. Roaring Brook Press. (F) **Grades 3–6**

Ali lives in Baghdad in 2003. He loves soccer, playing with his friends, and his parents' loud music, but he loves learning calligraphy more. His mother calls him Yakut, after a famous calligrapher who lived in Iraq in the 1200s. The story goes that when the Moguls attacked Baghdad in 1258, Yakut went to a tower and there wrote for days. When the bombs begin to fall on Baghdad in 2003, Ali finds solace in practicing his calligraphy all night for several nights. He finds *peace* the hardest to write; even when the bombing is stopped, he still struggles with the word. The protagonist is probably 11 or 12, but the subject matter of the book is solemn and would provide a thought-provoking backdrop for a discussion on the Iraq and Afghanistan wars. Rumford's art, calligraphy, and sparse text make for a powerful book. **Social Studies, Visual Arts LA1, SSII, SSIII, SSIV, SSV, SSVI, SSIX, VA4, VA6 Iraqis, Muslims**

Tasting the Sky: A Palestinian Childhood
By Ibtisam Barakat. 2007. 176 pages. Farrar, Straus and Giroux. (NF) **Grades 6–12**

In 1981, 18-year-old Ibtisam Barakat is detained by Israeli troops outside Ramallah. As she waits, she traces her childhood memories in this beautifully written memoir. Ibtisam was 3 when the Six-Day War began in June 1967. Her story begins there. As her family flees, she struggles with her shoe and is separated from them. Although reunited later that night, her terror at this separation colors the rest of her childhood. At the end of the Six-Day War, Israel occupied the Gaza Strip and the West Bank and took over East Jerusalem—lands that had been under Arab administration since the 1948 war and the establishment of Israel. Ibtisam's memories involve the occupation of her homeland, but also encompass everyday activities and interesting events from a child's point of view. The historical note prefacing her memoir gives background information crucial to the story. A map gives a clear sense of where events occur.   Language Arts, Social Studies LA1, SSIII, SSIV, SSV, SSVI, SSVII, SSIX Palestinians

Thunder over Kandahar
By Sharon E. McKay. 2010. 258 pages. Annick. (F) **Grades 7–10**

Fourteen-year-old Yasmine feels trapped in Afghanistan. She is Afghan but was born in England and has just come to Afghanistan for her father to teach in a university. However, his Western views make Harat unsafe for his family. After Yasmine's mother is beaten by the Taliban, the family moves to a village in Kandahar province. Here Tamanna, a peasant girl, is hired to help the family; the girls become like sisters. Things don't improve. The Taliban shoot and seriously wound Yasmine's parents as they try to get her mother to a doctor. Because they are also British, they are airlifted to Kandahar Airfield (KAF), but Yasmine is left behind to collect family documents. Risking her life to get medicine to Tamanna, Yasmine finds Tamanna beaten and won't leave her behind. The rickshaw driver hired to take the girls to KAF only takes them partway before throwing them off. The girls' lives take a sharp turn as they begin the harrowing walk toward the Pakistani border. In a page-turning story, McKay brings the war in Afghanistan up close and personal. In preparation for writing this story, McKay spent time in Afghanistan. Includes a glossary and an accurate timeline (for fictional characters).   Social Studies LA1, LA9, SSII, SSIII, SSIV, SSV, SSVI. Afghans

Travels of Benjamin of Tudela: Through Three Continents in the Twelfth Century
By Uri Shulevitz. 2005. Illus. No page numbers. Farrar, Straus and Giroux. (F) **Grades 4–7**

In 1159, just over a century before Marco Polo made his extensive travels, a little-known Jewish traveler, Benjamin, left Tudela, Spain, wanting to see places mentioned in the Bible. Fourteen years later he returns home and relates his adventures, as well as tales he heard along the way. In this picture book for older readers, each two-page spread features sparse text and lush illustrations that represent the place or event. In the author's note, Shulevitz explains that he made this a first-person fictionalized account because Benjamin's own *Book of Travels* was straightforward facts and lacked descriptions of dangers and traveling conditions. For the illustrations, Shulevitz relied on art from later medieval periods or from his own imagination to convey Benjamin's experiences. He includes a detailed bibliography of sources he used for research. **Social Studies LA1, SSI, SSIII, SSIV Jewish Italians**

Under the Persimmon Tree
By Suzanne Fisher Staples. 2005.
275 pages. Farrar, Straus and Giroux. (F) **Grades 7–12**

In alternating voices, Staples tells the stories of two people whose lives intersect in war-torn Afghanistan in the early part of the twenty-first century. Young Najmah, or Star, holds her very pregnant mother back as ruthless members of the Taliban pillage their farm and force her father and older brother to join their unit. Shortly after baby Habib is born, American bombs destroy the farm; Najmah finds her mother's and brother's bodies, and mutely acquiesces when old neighbors come to take her to a refugee camp and safety. Her first-person narrative alternates with the third-person tale of Nusrat, a young American whose conversion to Islam and subsequent marriage has brought her to Pakistan. While her husband staffs a clinic in northern Afghanistan, Nusrat sets up an informal school for refugee children in Peshawar. Staples effectively weaves detailed facts about the Taliban, the mujahideen, the many types of Muslim believers, and the daily lives of Afghans and Pakistanis during this tumultuous time. These never interfere with the story but propel it toward its moving conclusion. Strong characterization, a well-paced plot, dialogue that includes many words from the region (a glossary is appended), and solid descriptive language make the story and setting come alive. **Social Studies LA1, LA9, SSII, SSIII, SSV, SSIX, SSX Afghans, Pakistanis**

Where the Streets Had a Name
By Randa Abdel-Fattah. 2008. 313 pages. Scholastic. (F) **Grades 5–9**

Thirteen-year-old Hayaat's grandmother longs to visit her home once more, but that isn't possible: the house now belongs to an Israeli family, and Hayaat's family lives on the wrong side of the wall in the West Bank town of Bethlehem. Believing her grandmother would be happy just to get some soil from her village, Hayaat hatches a plan. She and her friend Samy skip school to make a trip. The distance isn't far, and under normal circumstances it would take less than one hour to get there. However, one never knows where mobile Israeli checkpoints will be, and the two kids don't have the proper papers to enter Jerusalem. Attempting to appear fearless, they embark on what will become a day to remember. They climb the wall (a forbidden activity) but find themselves in a situation that seems hopeless. Will they get the soil? Will they get home safely? The Israeli-Palestinian conflict is central, but Abdel-Fattah successfully weaves three story threads into the novel: the family's longing for things lost, the preparations for Hayaat's sister's wedding, and the events that led to the scars on Hayaat's face. She brings the novel to a satisfying conclusion, despite the conflict's ever-present cloud.   Social Studies LA1, SSI, SSII, SSIII, SSIV, SSV, SSVI, SSIX Israelis, Palestinians

Women in the Arab World (Women's Issues, Global Trends series)
By Joan Esherick. 2005. Illus. 112 pages. Mason Crest. (NF) **Grades 6–12**

There are about three hundred million people living in Arab nations in a wide array of cultural contexts. Esherick begins by showing the vast differences in the lifestyles of Arab women, and stresses the need to avoid stereotyping. Using stories of individual girls, she looks at opportunities provided (or not) according to various countries' forms of government, geographical heritage, and, especially, religious beliefs. The role of women's honor within the extended family is central, affecting a girl's educational opportunities and her ability to move within and outside of her community. The author strives to present cultural differences in a balanced manner. She notes that "even within Arab society, women disagree over their status. Some Arab women feel valued, loved, and cherished by men in a system that protects them; others feel oppressed and abused." The closing chapters point out challenges that some Arab women are working to overcome. For details on this series' format and style, see *Women in the African World,* page 111.   Social Studies, LA1, SSI, SSIII, SSV, SSVI, SSVII Arabs, Muslims

EAST ASIA AND NORTH CENTRAL ASIA

The Adventures of Marco Polo
By Russell Freedman. 2006. Illus. 64 pages. Arthur A. Levine. (NF) **Grades 5–9**

To his death, Marco Polo claimed he traveled to China and beyond. Skeptics scoffed at him, claiming that he had a vivid imagination. Scholars even to the present time sit on opposing sides—some believe he indeed made the long journey described his *Description of the World* (otherwise known as *The Travels of Marco Polo*); others doubt much of his writing. In the final chapter of this book, Freedman presents both sides of this argument, but makes Marco Polo come alive for readers. Whether or not everything that appears in Marco's book is true, he is the best-known medieval traveler who influences many explorers, including Columbus. Quoting heavily from Marco's own work, Freedman takes readers along on Marco's nearly twenty-four-year journey to the courts of Kublai Khan and back to Venice. Enhancing Freedman's flowing prose is Bagram Ibatoulliene's well-researched, intriguing period paintings. A note in the book explains the style the artist chose for each of the paintings. The book is also filled with well-chosen archival period artwork; these paintings reflect the European understanding and image of those different from themselves. There are detailed notes on each of the archival art pieces used in the book.   **Social Studies, Visual Arts LA1, SSI, SSII, SSIII, SSIV, SSIX, VA4, VA6 Asians, Chinese, Mongolians, Venetians**

Adventures on the Ancient Silk Road
By Priscilla Galloway and Dawn Hunter. 2009. Illus.
168 pages. Annick. (NF) **Grades 5–9**

In this eminently readable and interesting book about the Silk Road, the stories of three men who traveled it give an intriguing look at the history of the many trade routes it comprised. Stretching from China to India and Europe, encompassing cities such as Baghdad, Constantinople, Samarkand, Moscow, and Venice, the Silk Road connected many cultures. Xuanzang, a Chinese Buddhist monk, headed to India in 629 CE to collect Buddhist scriptures from India. His journey, during which he staved off bandits and was befriended by several local rulers, took sixteen years. Genghis Khan used the Silk Road beginning in 1207 CE so his invading armies could move quickly. He also set up outpost buildings along its routes. Marco Polo used the Silk Road (1271–1295 CE) for trading, and wrote a book about his travels detailing trading practices among the people he visited. While careful research is evident, the writers have chosen to tell the most dashing tales concerning the Silk Road. The colorful graphic format and well-placed photographs, illustrations, and maps add interest. Includes an afterward, further reading, acknowledgments with author information, photo credits, and an index. Social Studies LA1, SSI, SSII, SSIII, SSV, SSVI, SSVII, SSIX Asians, Chinese, Mongolians, Venetians

Boy on the Lion Throne: The Childhood of the 14th Dalai Lama
By Elizabeth Cody Kimmel and Dalai Lama XIV Bstan-'dzin-rgya-mtsho.
2009. Illus. 160 pages. Roaring Brook. (NF) **Grades 5–8**

The story of the Dalai Lama's childhood and youth reads like an adventure novel. Born in a remote mountain village in 1935, Lhamo Thondu was found, at 2½ years of age, to be the reincarnated successor of the thirteenth Dalai Lama. At age 4, he and his family were moved to Lhasa, the center of Tibetan Buddhism, where his life changed drastically. As the most revered person in Tibet, great care was taken to teach him—and to keep him alive. Lhamo himself, completely composed in his new role, was curious and quick, and especially interested in the Western world, from its cars to its movies. But China's quest to rule Tibet created continual tension. When Mao Tse Tung invited the 19-year-old leader to Beijing, many Tibetans feared for his life. Kimmel seamlessly weaves information on Tibet, its particular form of Buddhism, and the politics of the times into the story. She includes details and photographs that allow readers to envision events. The story ends with the Dalai Lama's harrowing escape from Chinese soldiers in Lhasa in 1959. A short epilogue brings readers up-to-date on his continued exile. Includes a bibliography, online resources, photo credits, an index, information on Tibet Aid, a note on place names, and a short foreword from the Dalai Lama himself. Social Studies LA1, SSI, SSIII, SSIV, SSV, SSVI, SSIX Tibetans

The Diary of Ma Yan: The Struggles and Hopes of a Chinese Schoolgirl
By Ma Yan. Ed. by Pierre Haski. Trans. by He Yanping and Lisa Appignanese.
2005. 166 pages. HarperCollins. (NF) **Grades 5–12**

Thirteen-year-old Ma Yan is in her seventh year of schooling—rare for a girl in her remote corner of China. When French journalist Pierre Haski and his team (the first foreign journalists to visit since the 1930s) visited her community in 2001, Ma Yan's mother gives her daughter's diary to Haski. The team went to Shanghai and read the diary; they were so intrigued they returned to interview her. Ma Yan recounts daily life both at school (she and her brother walk twelve and a half miles through hilly country, a four- to five-hour trek) and at home. Her focus on family members and day-to-day occurrences of her life make her diary come alive. The diary gives an unprecedented glimpse of the hardships many poor Chinese families endure to give their children an education. Short chapters interspersed throughout the book help readers understand more about Ma Yan's life: her grandparents; the poverty in her region; how the schools work; harvesting *fa cai*, a wild grass; and more. Footnotes help clarify unfamiliar terms. Black-and-white photographs and a simple page design add appeal.   **Language Arts, Social Studies H1, H2, H5, LA1, LA9, SSII, SSIV, SSV, SSVI, SSVII, SSVIII, SSIX Chinese**

Elephants and Golden Thrones: Inside China's Forbidden City
By Trish Marx. 2008. Illus. 48 pages. Abrams. (NF) **Grades 4–8**

Packed with colorful photographs, maps, and illustrations, this book presents information on the Forbidden City in northern China, from which twenty-four emperors ruled for over five hundred years. Arranged chronologically, very short stories based on historical records preface most chapters, giving readers an intriguing glimpse of the ceremonies, tasks, and private lives of six emperors, plus Dowager Princess Su and Empress Cixi. Snippets of Chinese culture are presented for each time period. While the lack of source notes, an index, and documentation for some artwork makes this an imperfect source for reports, the lush overview of the Forbidden City may spur students to further research topics in China's history. Includes a timeline of important dates and emperors, a glossary, a bibliography, an author's note, and photo credits. The preface by the executive deputy director of the Palace Museum provides an excellent introduction to the book.   **Social Studies LA1, SSII, SSV, SSVI, SSVII, VA4 Chinese**

Genghis Khan
By Demi. 2009. Illus. No page numbers. Marshall Cavendish. (NF) **Grades 3–7**

In this reprint of her 1991 book *Chingis Khan*, Demi uses stylized Asiatic illustrations with gold overlay to present the life of Temujin, who would later become Genghis Khan. From his birth in 1160, Temujin was trained and groomed to become a great leader who would succeed his father in leading the Mongol kingdom. When Temujin was 9, his father was poisoned; thus, Temujin became the head of the Yakka Mongols. Taking the remnants of the tribe to the desolate part of Mongolia, Temujin proved that his early training had prepared him to lead his people. By 1206 he had reunited all the Mongol tribes and was named Genghis. From that time till his death in 1227, his conquests led to great expansion of his kingdom. Demi's concise text and illustrations depict Genghis's power and conquests without an overemphasis on brutality. The only weakness of the book is a lack of sources. Social Studies, Visual Arts LA1, SSI, SSII, SSIII, SSIV, SSVI, VAI, VAIII, VAIV, VAVI Mongolians

Kubla Khan: The Emperor of Everything
By Kathleen Krull. 2010. Illus. No page numbers. Viking. (NF) **Grades 3–6**

Born and reared in Mongolia, Kubla became an even greater emperor than his famous grandfather, Genghis Kahn. In 1260, he became "khan of all khans." Although he conquered tribes and countries, he treated the subjugated honestly and fairly. He accomplished his major goal—conquering China—and set up his capital in what is present-day Beijing. Kubla's opulent lifestyle didn't get in the way of his doing great things for the citizens, sponsoring the arts and sciences, or expanding trade with the West. In fact, when Marco Polo came to Kubla Khan's court in 1275, he remained seventeen years! As Khan aged and grew obese, he began to lose control over parts of his realm. However, his influence continued beyond his death in 1294. Other than the information Marco Polo presents in his book, little is known about Khan. Robert Byrd's detailed paintings and drawings extend and enhance Krull's interesting and well-written text. Social Studies LA1, SSI, SSII, SSIII, SSIV, SSV, SSVI Mongolians

Marco Polo
By Demi. 2008. Illus. No page numbers. Marshall Cavendish. (NF) **Grades 3–7**

Marco Polo was fifteen when he first met his father because he was born shortly after his father left Venice on a trading expedition. Just two years later, in 1271, loaded with gifts for Kublai Khan, Marco accompanied his father and uncle on their long trip to China and back. After some twenty years in service to the great

Kublai Khan, they finally returned to Venice in 1295. Marco settled down to a merchant's life in Venice but continually told stories about his great travels. Despite the popularity of his book *Travels of Marco Polo*, people only laughed at his fantastical tales. The back endpages give a colored map of Polo's journey. Demi's author's note gives the sources she consulted. Her rich illustrations, created with Chinese ink-and-gold overlays, reflect the Eastern culture of the thirteenth century. The art style of the borders and the design of the clothing subtly change as the explorers move from country to country. **Social Studies, Visual Arts** LA1, SSI, SSII, SSIII, SIV, SSIX, VA4, VA6 **Global**

Real Samurai: Over 20 True Stories about the Knights of Old Japan!
By Stephen R. Turnbull. 2007. Illus. 48 pages. Enchanted Lion. (NF) **Grades 4–8**

From its etched endpapers to its large, deeply colored double-page spreads, this introduction to the "knights of old Japan" is a page-turner. Turnbull clearly intends to entice young readers to further study the samurai and their country. Each chapter is divided into short sections that tell a tale and give details of interest concerning various aspects of the samurai, such as their armor and weaponry. A glossary and an index are appended. **Social Studies** LA1, SSIII, SSV, SSVI, SSVIII, SSIX **Japanese**

Revolution Is Not a Dinner Party: A Novel
By Ying Chang Compestine. 2007. 248 pages. Holt. (F) **Grades 5–8**

When Comrade Li comes to live with her family, 9-year-old Ling has no idea how it will affect the next four years of her life. Her loving father, who once patiently gave her English lessons, grows more and more somber, and is assigned to be a janitor at the hospital where he once was a surgeon. The food and items her family once enjoyed have disappeared from the stores; it seems that only Comrade Li and his gang can obtain them. As China's Cultural Revolution continues, Ling's childhood innocence disappears as she learns to keep her mouth shut. She begins to understand the dangers of this new world under Communism. Not close to her mother, Ling is bereft when her father is taken for "re-education." The author draws from her childhood experiences to create a chilling story of the consequences of resistance during the revolution. **Social Studies** LA1, SSII, SSIII, SSIV, SSV, SSVI, SSVII **Chinese**

Su Dongpo: Chinese Genius
By Demi. 2006. Illus. No page numbers. Lee & Low. (NF) **Grades 4–8**

In her characteristically minimalist writing style and her intricate artistic style, Demi presents the life of one of the greatest Chinese men who ever lived. According to her introduction, Su Dongpo (1036–1101) was "a statesman, philosopher, poet, painter, engineer, architect, and humanitarian." An inspiration to the Chinese and to the world, Su Dongpo was satisfied with life regardless of whether he was in a high service position for his country or living in poverty in exile on an island. Demi adroitly incorporates several of Su Dongpo's poems into her narrative, making his life appear all the richer. Her block, mostly pastel, illustrations are surrounded by a gold border and show the strong Eastern influence on her work.   Social Studies, Visual Arts LA1, SSI, SSII, SSIII, SSIV, SSV, SSVI, SSIX, VA4, VA6 Chinese

Warriors in the Crossfire
By Nancy Bo Flood. 2010. 142 pages. Front Street. (F) **Grades 6–9**

Joseph, the son of a native chief, and his half-Japanese cousin, Kento, are about to see their families and culture torn apart. Their life on Japanese-controlled Saipan has been routine, filled with the traditions of their people. Now the native peoples of the island are caught in the vicious battle between the Japanese and Americans near the end of World War II. Over thirty thousand Japanese and Americans are killed, but there is no recorded total of islanders killed. Before Joseph's father leaves to fight, he takes Joseph to a high, secluded cave and tells him to bring the family there when the fighting begins. Thankfully, Joseph remembers the path and takes his family on the arduous journey to the cave. How will they survive as their food and water dwindle? The book includes a historical note about the battle of Saipan and the other Mariana Islands.   Social Studies, LA1, SSII, SSIV, SSV, SSIX. Chamorros

Women in the World of China (Women's Issues, Global Trends series)
By Ellyn Sanna. 2005. Illus. 112 pages. Mason Crest. (NF) **Grades 6–12**

After an introduction giving a snapshot of the status of women worldwide, this covers the historical role of Chinese women and the effects of the Cultural Revolution on women's status. Sanna examines the lasting negative effects of Confucian thought on the role of women, and then turns to the roles of daughter, wife, and mother within the family. Throughout the book, cultural differences are acknowledged, with respect given to the many differences between Western and Chinese customs. Stories of individual women help the reader understand the variety of circumstances in which Chinese women live. Statistics are depressing; for example, "domestic violence occurs in at least 30 percent of mainland China's families . . . A woman is still little more than an animal in the minds of many Chinese families." Efforts to change the underlying thoughts about women's roles are stressed, and a chapter on strong Chinese women adds a hopeful note. For details on this series' format and style, see *Women in the African World*, page 111. **Social Studies LA1, SSI, SSIII, SSV, SSVI, SSVII Chinese**

SOUTH ASIA AND SOUTHEAST ASIA

Anila's Journey
By Mary Finn. 2008. 309 pages. Candlewick Press. (F) **Grades 7–10**

When Anila's father left India to return to his home country, Ireland, he promised Anila and her mother he would come back for them; he didn't. Anila's mother has become the mistress of another white man just so they can survive. Now 14, orphaned, and under the guardianship of Miss Hickey, an accomplished artist, Anila hasn't given up on her father. Rather than leave Calcutta with Miss Hickey, she takes a job drawing birds for kindly Mr. Walker. As they head up the Ganges with a small expedition, Anila learns they will pass her grandfather's village. Should she visit her mother's family? Then Mr. Walker's nefarious aide, Carlen, says he knows what happened to her father, but he will not tell her without "payment." Told in alternating chapters, the story moves tautly from Anila's childhood to the present day, where it seems Mr. Walker has more in mind than just birds. What are those pits he keeps exploring? Filled with details of nineteenth-century British India, this layered tale looks at racism and the damaging effects of colonialism through the somewhat naïve eyes of one young artist. The Dublin author wisely had her details checked by a Calcutta historian. **Social Studies LA1, SSII, SSIII, SSVI, SSVII, VA4 Indians, Mixed-Race Indians, Mixed-Race Irish**

Bamboo People: A Novel
By Mitali Perkins. 2010. 272 pages. Charlesbridge. (F) **Grades 5–8**

Father has been arrested for his medical treatment of an enemy of the state, and 15-year-old Chiko hopes to take an exam that will allow him to become a teacher and bring home a much-needed salary. Instead, he is gang-pressed into the Burmese military. With the help of a street orphan, Tai, he survives boot camp and its physical rigors. When their hate-filled captain assigns Tai to a "special" jungle mission, Chiko volunteers to take his place—and tragedy results. The second part of the book describes the struggles of Tu Reh, a 16-year-old Karenni boy who lives with his family in a Thai refugee camp. On his first mission with his father, he hopes to earn the respect of his parents and his best friend. Instead, he rescues the enemy—Chiko—and must justify his action when he moves him to the camp. Tu Reh is torn between his desire for revenge on the Burmese soldiers who burned his home and his knowledge that Chiko is just as unhappy with the Burmese government as he is. Both boys are believable, as are secondary characters that hold important places in their hearts. Each recounts his story in first-person narrative that moves at a fast pace and is filled with dialogue. Further background is available in the author's short section about modern Burma, an author's note, information on the usage of *Burma* rather than *Myanmar*, and acknowledgments. **Social Studies LA1, SSIII, SSIV, SSVI Burmese, Karennis**

Bangladesh (Enchantment of the World series)
By Tamra Orr. 2007. Illus. 144 pages. Children's Press. (NF) **Grades 5–9**

Beginning with a fictional diary of a "Save the Tiger Foundation" employee, this introduction to Bangladesh covers the usual range of topics. The country's complex history includes rule by Great Britain and Pakistan before gaining independence in 1971. While high poverty and low education rates are not glossed over, the author attempts to focus on the positive, particularly in her chapters on the family, religion, and culture. Vivid color photographs show modern urban and rural Bangladeshis, both well-to-do and poor. Despite the tendency to lump all Bangladeshis together, this is a solid introduction to a fascinating country. **Social Studies LA1, SSI, SSIII, SSV, SSVI, SSVII, VA4 Bangladeshis**

Climbing the Stairs
By Padma Venkatraman. 2008. 247 pages. Putnam. (F) **Grades 7–11**

Caught in a street protest, 15-year-old Vidya watches in horror as her father tries to protect a fallen woman, only to be beaten by a British soldier. Vidya blames herself; if she had not run into the street, her father, Appa, would not be brain-damaged. Her family must move to Madras to live with her uncle's family, where they clearly are not welcome. The household is very conservative: the women serve the men and sleep on different floors of the house. Vidya's aunt and uncle restrict her every action, and she misses her friends and the rich life she had enjoyed in school and with her lively, liberal family. To make things worse, her brother, Kitta, is considering joining the hated British army to fight the Nazis. Rich characterization, the broad sweep of history as India struggles for independence while supporting the Allies, and a fast moving plot with elements of romance make this coming-of-age novel an engrossing read. **Social Studies LA1, LA9, SSII, SSIV, SSV, SSVI, SSIX East Indians**

Gandhi (DK Biography series)
By Amy Pastan. 2006. Illus. 128 pages. DK. (NF) **Grades 6–10**

This straightforward, well-written biography weaves the history of Mohandas Gandhi's era with his life, placing him in the context of the turbulent times in which he lived. Numerous photographs, illustrations, and sidebars accompany the text, making this a visual exploration of Gandhi's world and adding depth to the text. The use of primary sources, an excellent timeline, and good resources for further study make this a solid choice. **Social Studies LA1, SSII, SSIII, SSV, SSVI, SSVII East Indians**

Gandhi: The Young Protester Who Founded a Nation
By Philip Wilkinson. 2005. Illus. 64 pages.
National Geographic Society. (NF) **Grades 4–8**

Born on October 2, 1869, Mohandas Karamchand Gandhi grew up to lead a nation in its struggle for independence. While many biographies focus on his adult life, this shows more of his childhood and student days before looking at his accomplishments. The inclusion of many family photographs personalize his story, making him more accessible to student readers. Replete with photographs, maps, illustrations, insets, and a timeline that runs on the bottom of each page, this format helps the author weave in a good deal of background on India as well as providing solid information on Gandhi's life and relationships. **Social Studies LA1, SSII, SSIII, SSV, SSVI, SSVII East Indians**

Going to School in India

By Lisa Heydlauff. 2005. Illus. 97 pages. Charlesbridge. (NF) **Grades 4–9**

Colorful photographs by Nitin Upadyhe accented with bright graphics show various ways children throughout India go to school. They travel by bicycle, boat, cable swing, rickshaw, *chackara*, and even bullock cart. Schools might be a tent in a desert, a schoolbus that reaches homeless children in Mumbai, an old building on an island in Kashmir, or a night school for girls who must work during the day in Rajasthan. Often, the children themselves run their schools through a special children's parliament. The book is packed with information covering a wide range of topics and includes many comments from the children. One of the best presentations of contemporary life in India. **Social Studies LA1, SSIII, SSV, SSVI, SSVII East Indians**

Keeping Corner

By Kashmira Sheth. 2007. 288 pages. Hyperion. (F) **Grades 5–8**

Married at 9, 12-year-old Leela is excited to move in with her husband's loving family when she turns 13. However, when her husband dies of a snakebite, Leela is utterly unprepared for "keeping corner," the Hindu practice in which a widow remains in the husband's house for one year. She must break her glass bangles, put away her jewelry, shave her head, and wear the dull brown sari of the widow. While her older brother is outraged, Leela's parents know that breaking from tradition will ensure total ostracism in their small village. When the principal of her school arranges to come teach her each week, Leela hesitates. As she begins reading the paper and taking notice of the world around her, she learns that Gandhi's reasons for peaceful resistance extend beyond opposing the British colonists and the caste system that limits her own life choices. Tumultuous and engaging, this brings to life rural Gujarat in the early 1900s with a deftly told, wholly engaging story. **Health, Social Studies H5, LA1, LA9, SSIII, SSIV, SSV East Indians**

Mumbai (Global Cities series)
By Jen Green. 2007. Illus. 60 pages. Chelsea House. (NF) **Grades 5–8**

Mumbai lies in central India. With a population of over eighteen million, it is one of India's main ports and a thriving center for industry and commerce—yet home of one of the world's largest slums. This looks at Mumbai's history, religious and ethnic groups, housing, education, and health care. It also covers sectors of the economy, including the informal economy, city management, transportation, culture and tourism, and environmental and energy challenges. Packed with modern photographs that capture a cross-section of life in Mumbai, maps, charts, and case studies that highlight individuals and their work, this is a competent introduction to a complex city. Includes a glossary, a bibliography, and an index.   **Social Studies LA1, SSIII, SSV, SSVI, SSVII, SSVIII East Indians**

Rickshaw Girl
By Mitali Perkins. 2007. 91 pages. Charlesbridge. (F) **Grades 4–6**

Naima is quite the artist; she wins awards for the traditional alpana patterns she paints on the sides of her family's home. Her family is poor, and Naima wants to help bring in money. She also faces age restrictions; now that she is 10, she and Saleem are too old to play together, and soon she must begin wearing a saree rather than her *salwar kameez*. One day while her exhausted father is napping, Naima decides to drive the rickshaw; she wrecks it and then must tell father, who wearily wonders how they will fix it. Taking matters into her hands, Naima goes to the neighboring village to seek work at the rickshaw repair shop. To her surprise, the female owner of the shop gives Naima the chance to prove herself. The author and her husband lived in Bangladesh three years and began to see sex-role shifts that allow women the chance to own and run their own small businesses, giving hope to their poverty-stricken families. Jamie Hogan's occasional black-and-white illustrations bring Naima to life. The story is geared for younger middle schoolers and offers an inside look into a lesser-known culture.   **Social Studies, Visual Arts LA1, SSII, SSIII, SSIV, VA1, VA4 Bangladeshis**

Teens in India (Global Connections series)
By Lori Shores. 2007. Illus. 96 pages. Compass. (NF) **Grades 4–12**

This well-designed, catchy book focuses on how teens in various parts of India live. The authors discuss school (or, for some, work), then move to religion, meals, family activities, holidays, ceremonies such as marriage and birth, working, sports, and leisure activities. While it focuses on Hinduism and overgeneralizes in some areas, it attempts to treat the diversity of lifestyles teens experience: a poor rural boy might work full time in agriculture, while his urban counterpart may work in a *walla*, or roadside shop. Other teens may attend school until they obtain graduate degrees. Bright, modern photographs and explanatory insets help the western reader better understand Indian traditions and teenagers' lives. Includes a historical timeline, a glossary, additional resources, source notes, a bibliography, an index, image credits, and information about the author and the content advisor. Among the other thirty-four titles in the series are: *Teens in . . . China, Cuba, Egypt, Ghana, India, Iran, Japan, Kenya,* and *Pakistan.*   Social Studies LA1, SSII, SSIII, SSV, SSVI, SSVII, SSVIII East Indians

Teens in Thailand (Global Connections series)
By Sandra Donovan. 2009. Illus. 96 pages. Compass Point. (NF) **Grades 5–12**

Packed with photographs featuring modern-day urban teenagers, here is a glimpse of life in Thailand today. The author carefully includes some information on the differing lifestyles of rural teens and poor teens, but the emphasis is on middle-class teens in the city—where over one-third of Thailand's sixty-five million residents live. The book follows the Global Connections series format to present the structure of the school system and a typical school day, home life, religious celebrations, and the world of work. It ends with "Hanging Out and Having Fun"—from listening to pop music from around the world on MP3s; going to dance clubs; or participating in family events. Quick facts are presented in "At a Glance." For details on this series' format and style, see the review above, *Teens in India.*   Social Studies LA1, SSII, SSIII, SSV, SSVI, SSVII, SSVIII Thai

Town Boy
By Lat. 2007. Illus. 191 pages. First Second. (NF) **Grades 7–12**

"I became a town boy at the age of ten . . ." So begins Lat's childhood memoir, which details his family's move to Ipoh, a city north of Kuala Lumpur in Malaysia. Richly detailed pen-and-ink drawings present humorously drawn cartoon characters, adding depth to his story of life in the 1960s. Lat's best friend is Frankie, who introduces him to Elvis, Bobby Darin, and the Beatles, inviting him to his home to listen to records. Ipoh's multicultural citizenry, streets filled with activity, and busy classrooms form the backdrop for a number of adventures, from taking part in the high school's annual cross-country race to hanging out at the cinema with hopes of spotting the school beauty, Normah. A celebrated cartoonist who produced his first book at age 13, Lat's childhood memories were first published in 1979 as *Kampung Boy*; this reissued version was originally published in 1980 but remains relevant today.   Social Studies, Visual Arts, LA1, SSIV, SSV, SSIX, VA4, VA6 Malaysians

Tsunami: Helping Each Other
By Ann Morris and Heidi Larson. 2005. Illus. 32 pages. Millbrook. (NF) **Grades 4–8**

Focusing on two brothers, 12-year-old Chaipreak and 8-year-old Chaiya, the authors tell how the tsunami of 2004 devastated Khao Lak, a popular tourist destination. Glossy pages feature photographs from before and after the event, and highlight the great variety of people and organizations from around the world and throughout Thailand that came to help the residents and the tourists. Buddhist monks minister to relatives of the deceased and missing; UNICEF and Red Cross personnel help with relief and rebuilding; and volunteers assist members of the Thai army in rebuilding the boys' school. The brothers find their mother but not their father. A website set up by the International School of Bangkok describes their Tsunami Relief Network, organized "to make a significant difference in the lives of the poorest children who were tsunami victims in Thailand." Although the format of this nonfiction work follows that of a picture book, the small print and packed pages make it most suitable for middle grade students.   Social Studies LA1, SSII, SSIII, SSV, SSVI, SSVII Thai

EUROPE

WORLD WAR I

Home Is Beyond the Mountains
By Celia Barker Lottridge. 2010. 224 pages. Groundwood. (F) **Grades 5–9**

World War I in Europe is in its final year (1918); battles over territories are still taking place. Turkey, who had sided with the Germans, controls the southern part of Persia (modern-day Iraq), but now is invading the northern part of Persia (modern-day Iran). The worst Turkish invasion into Persia occurs in the summer of 1918. The Assyrians and Armenians who live in the villages have no warning and flee for their lives—men and boys going one direction, women and

children left to make a harrowing three-hundred-mile trip on their own. It is into this fray that Samira begins the arduous journey over the mountains with her mother and younger sister. After both her mother and sister die along the route, Samira wanders alone into a British refugee camp at Baqubah. Miraculously, her older brother, Benyamin, also finds his way to the same camp. Over the next six years, Samira, Benyamin, and approximately three hundred orphans walk from orphanage to orphanage. Their last walk, on which they retrace many of the same miles of their first journey, is filled with fear and hope. What will they find? Who will be left? Lottridge bases the book on things her mother told about growing up in Persia. Susan Shedd, the director of the orphanage, is her mother's sister, who played a vital role in the welfare and safety of the children.
Social Studies LA1, SSII, SSIII, SSIV, SSV, SSVI Armenians, Assyrians

Murder on the Ridge
By Ted Stenhouse. 2006. 240 pages. Kids Can Press. (F) **Grades 5–8**

In small Grayson, Canada, in 1952, racial tensions and unanswered questions abound. Thirteen-year-old Will and Arthur have been friends since age 6. Will is white and Arthur is Blackfoot, and now they find themselves entwined in the racial tensions. As they help their biracial friend, Catface, and his grandmother reroof the shack in which she lives, they begin to question how her Blackfoot husband died on France's Vimy Ridge in World War I. Through Arthur's Blackfoot grandfather and their experiences in the sweat lodge, the boys are transported back to Vimy Ridge to experience the battle. They return with an answer—but who will believe their story? What will they tell their families and townspeople? This is the third book about Will and Arthur, but the author gives enough background to allow the book to stand alone. Fast-paced, action-packed, and with plenty of dialogue in short chapters, this time-travel mystery engages readers from the start. Language Arts, Social Studies LA1, SSII, SSIII, SSIV, SSVI American Indians, Blackfoot, Mixed Race

The Night of the Burning: Devorah's Story
By Linda Press Wulf. 2006. 210 pages. Farrar, Straus and Giroux. (F) **Grades 5–9**

Once, Devorah and her little sister, Nechama, lived with their loving parents in the small village of Domachevo in Poland. Then came the Great War, hunger, and disease, and the dreadful Night of the Burning. Now the girls face a new challenge: they have been chosen to leave their orphanage in Pinsk to move to South Africa. Devorah tells their story in alternating chapters that move from flashbacks of their happy and then harrowing experiences in Domachevo to their current journey and eventual adjustment to their new homes in 1920s South Africa. Throughout, readers see Devorah's fear and sorrow as she struggles to keep her family together and make sense of her new world. Background information is found in an author's note, an epigraph, an afterword, and a historical note that touches on the precursors of apartheid. Includes a glossary of Hebrew and Yiddish words. Social Studies LA1, SSIII, SSIV, SSV, SSVI Jewish Poles, Jewish South Africans

The War to End All Wars: World War I
By Russell Freedman. 2010. Illus. 176 pages. Clarion. (NF) **Grades 6–10**

When historians look back at the beginning of World War I, they note that some in Europe were looking for a reason to go to war. They also acknowledge, however, that if communications among the leaders and their followers had been better, the "war to end all wars" might have been averted or lessened. Freedman gives readers the political and relational background of the leaders of Europe, detailing their kinship to one another. Relationships between Austria-Hungary and the small nation Serbia were at odds. The Serbs had won their freedom from Turkey in 1878 and were trying to gain respect with power and threat rather than diplomacy. After a young Serbian assassinated Franz Ferdinand of Austria in Sarajevo, Austria knew she would have to fight the Serbs. Germany, a rising young nation competing for broader influence in trade and colonies, was a strong ally of Austria and saw this war as a potential way to capture Paris. The war that all thought would last only a few months dragged on from August 1914 until November 11, 1918. Europe was decimated; whole towns in Belgium and France were laid to waste; and untold millions of soldiers and civilians were slaughtered. Freedman's own father fought in the war in 1918, and the author paints a true picture of World War I: the text is exceptionally approachable for middle grade students, and the plentiful archival photos of the war's devastation add faces to the war. Includes detailed chapter source notes, a selected bibliography, picture credits, and index. Social Studies LA1, SSI, SSII, SSIII, SSV, SSVI, SSIX AOD, Eastern Europeans

Unraveling Freedom:
The Battle for Democracy on the Home Front during World War I
By Ann Bausum. 2010. Illus. 88 pages. National Geographic. (NF) **Grades 6–12**

From the chilling cartoon strips at the beginning of the book to the timeline in the back that tracks major U.S. events and decisions limiting or granting freedoms from 1917 to 1993, Bausum presents a little-studied aspect of American history. Including the book in our bibliography stretches our definition of *multiethnic*, but it examines serious discrimination of immigrants to America. The sinking of the British passenger liner *The Lusitania* in 1915 opened the door for governmental curtailment of individual freedoms. It also gave President Woodrow Wilson a reason to ask Congress to declare war against Germany in 1917 and send American troops to participate in World War I. Frenzied anti–German American sentiment arose across the country: German Americans were harassed—some jailed, some killed; German language study in schools was curtailed; German breweries were put out of business. Many governmental acts that were instituted restricted freedoms for all Americans, not just those of German descent. Includes an afterword, a guide to wartime presidents (from 1797 through present) and ways freedoms were unraveled, a timeline to track major events in U.S. history that pertained to World War I and Woodrow Wilson, notes and acknowledgments, a bibliography, a resource guide, citations for quotes, an index, and illustration credits. Social Studies, LA1, SSI, SSII, SSIII, SSIV, SSV, SSVI, SSIX. African Americans, AOD, German Americans

WORLD WAR II AND THE HOLOCAUST

Anne Frank and the Children of the Holocaust
By Carol Ann Lee. 2006. 242 pages. Viking. (NF) **Grades 5–12**

Readers think they know Anne Frank from reading her diary, but coupling it with Lee's biography, the picture is more complete. The heading for each chapter is a quote from *The Diary of Anne Frank*. Lee has written four other books about Frank; here she intertwines the Frank family's story with events and historical facts about World War II and the plight of East European Jews. Statistics are chilling: of the nearly 216,000 Jewish children who were sent to Auschwitz, only 451 under age 16 were liberated. Lee intersperses primary source photographs, and includes a map, charts (by country) of Jewish populations before and after World War II, detailed chapter source notes, a bibliography and further readings, and text permissions. Social Studies LA1, SSII, SSIII, SSIV, SSV, SSVI, SSIX Jews

The Boy in the Striped Pajamas: A Fable
By John Boyne. 2006. 215 pages. David Fickling. (F) **Grades 7–10**

Germany 1942: 9-year-old Bruno comes home from school to find the maid packing his things. No one explains why his family is moving to "Out-With," other than to say it's for his father's job. At "Out-With," from his bedroom window, Bruno sees people behind a fence; and, one day, out of curiosity, he goes to the fence. He meets Shmuel and begins secretly meeting him at the fence. He has many questions but gets no answers. Readers read between the lines to figure out Bruno's father is the commandant of Auschwitz where Shmuel is a Jewish prisoner. Bruno's last visit with Shmuel changes everything when Bruno slips under the fence to look for Shmuel's father. In a quiet, moving, yet disturbing way, Boyne presents the story of Holocaust through the eyes of an innocent boy. Social Studies LA1, SSIII, SSIV, SSV, SSVI, SSIX Jewish Germans

Escape—Teens on the Run: Primary Sources from the Holocaust (True Stories of Teens in the Holocaust series)
By Linda Jacobs Altman. 2010. Illus. 128 pages. Enslow. (NF) **Grades 6–10**

Oral history interviews, diaries, memoirs, and survivor testimonies provide chilling, fascinating, and inspiring views of the many ways that teenagers escaped Nazi persecution during WWII. Some escaped without their parents in rescue operations such as the Kindertransport program or the ocean liner *St. Louis*. Others escaped from labor camps after seeing their parents shot. Still others made it out with one or more members of their family and the help of underground rescue organizations. The text here provides the background necessary to understand what was happening in these teens' worlds, effectively linking the narratives and forming a well-organized, easy-to-follow book. Differing typefaces, clear subheadings, and numerous photographs contribute to the page-turning effect. Includes a timeline from 1938–1945, chapter notes with websites for many of the sources, as well as a list of additional related websites; a glossary, a list of further reading, an index, and illustration credits. Social Studies LA1, SSIII, SSIV, SSV, SSVI, SSIX Jewish Europeans

The Grand Mosque of Paris:
A Story of How Muslims Saved Jews during the Holocaust
By Karen Gray Ruelle and Deborah Durland DeSaix. 2008.
Illus. 40 pages. Holiday House. (NF) **Grades 4–8**

In 1940, after the Nazis capture France, anti-Jewish laws were created and enforced. Jews who had escaped to Paris in previous years now were in grave danger. One little-known and rather unlikely place for protection was the Grand Mosque in Paris. With its connections to the subterranean tunnels of Paris, it offered safe passage to other countries. Combining the story shrouded in mystery, with hauntingly beautiful paintings, this presents a picture of Muslim leaders who risked their lives to protect these Jewish people. When French filmmaker and novelist Derri Berkani began to research the North African resistance in 1974, he interviewed Muslims who had led the World War II movement. He viewed the register of people in the mosque from the war years; but when he returned a few years later, no such register existed. This meticulously researched book contains a detailed afterword, a glossary, acknowledgments, references, a bibliography, films, interviews, recommended books and films, and a detailed index. Social Studies LA1, SSII, SSIII, SSIV, SSV, SSVI, SSIX, SSX French, Jewish Europeans, Muslims

Hidden Child
By Isaac Millman. 2005. Illus. 73 pages. Farrar, Straus and Giroux. (NF) **Grades 4–7**

Isaac Sztrymfman (Millman) was a happy child with parents who loved him; but life changed one afternoon in 1941 when his father was ordered to register the family as Jews. Soon Isaac's father was taken to the Pithiviers internment camp. Isaac and his mother visited only once. As persecution of Jews in Paris grew worse, Isaac's mother used the last of her money to transport the two of them to safety, but the small group they were traveling with was captured and imprisoned. In prison, Isaac saw his mother give a guard her jewelry for his safekeeping. His mother was eventually deported, and after the war Isaac lived with various people until Widow Devolder took him. In 1948, an American Jewish couple adopted him. Millman, who had drawn throughout his life, tells his story in text, photographs, and watercolor montage paintings that look like photographs. The text is divided into sections with one to three family photographs and double-page colored paintings illustrating the preceding pages. In an author's note, he explains that of his family, only one cousin, one uncle, and he survived the Holocaust. Language Arts, Social Studies, Visual Arts LA1, SSII, SSIII, SSIV, SSV, SSVI, SSIX, VA1, VA4, VA6 Jewish Americans, Jews

The Journey That Saved Curious George:
The True Wartime Escape of Margret and H. A. Rey
By Louise Borden. 2005. Illus. 72 pages. Houghton Mifflin. (NF) **Grades 4–9**

Known worldwide for their Curious George books, Hans and Margret Reyersbach both grew up in Hamburg, Germany. They met early in their careers in Rio de Janeiro, Brazil, where they formed a working partnership (Margret was a photographer) and married. They were living and working at the Hotel Terrass in Paris in 1940 when the Nazis invaded. On June 12, along with more than five million other people, they fled south to escape the German invaders. With their most precious possessions in their bike baskets—including the original manuscript and drawings for *Curious George*—they pedaled to the south of France, where they caught a train for Bayonne and eventually reached Brazil. Told in free verse that is surrounded on each page by illustrations in the style of the 1940s, the layout is inviting, with photographs, reprints of Hans's artwork and diary, and other primary source documents adding interest to a fascinating tale. The book ends with a short synopsis of the Reys' life and a partial bibliography of their works. Language Arts, Social Studies, Visual Arts LA1, SSIII, SSV, SSIX, VA4, VA6 Jewish Americans, Jewish Germans

Lonek's Journey: The True Story of a Boy's Escape to Freedom
By Dorit Bader Whiteman. 2005. 141 pages. Star Bright. (NF) **Grades 5–8**

"On a sunny day in August 1939, eleven-year-old Lonek was cheerfully walking home." When he arrives home, his father says he is leaving to join the Polish army. As Polish Jews, the family is targeted by the Germans; Lonek is captured and taken to a Siberian labor camp. Escaping from the camp, he slowly makes his way to Palestine. This moving story takes place over a two-year period during which Lonek traveled thousands of miles. The author states that it represents a little-known part of the Jewish escape to Palestine, one that resulted in the freedom of nearly one thousand children. Whiteman, an escapee from Nazi-occupied Vienna in 1938, paints a serious picture of the horrors of World War II. The book includes maps, black-and-white photos, a glossary, and an explanation of what happened to Lonek's family after being separated during the Holocaust. Social Studies LA1, SSII, SSIII, SSIV, SSV, SSVI, SSIX Jewish Poles

Someone Named Eva
By Joan M. Wolf. 2007. 200 pages. Clarion. (F) **Grades 5–7**

When Milada awakens to loud noises, her grandmother quickly hands her a garnet pin, saying, "Remember who you are. Remember where you are from. Always." Nazi soldiers take her family. Blonde, blue-eyed Milada is taken to a Lebensborn center in Poland, where she and other girls are stripped of their identities, immersed in German language and culture, and indoctrinated with Nazi beliefs. Milada is now Eva. She successfully hides her grandmother's pin; it helps her remember her true identity after being adopted by a high-ranking German family. As the war turns against the Germans, things get bad for her new family. Eventually, a knock at the door brings Milada a choice that will change the direction of her life. Wolf bases this story on a little-known aspect of World War II: the destruction of the people and town of Lidice, Czechoslovakia. Of the 105 Lidice children, only seventeen survived the war; nine of those had been adopted by German families.   Social Studies LA1, SSII, SSIII, SSIV, SSV, SSVI, SSIX Czechoslovakians

The Year of Goodbyes: A Story of Friendship and Farewells
By Debbie Levy. 2010. Illus. 136 pages. Disney-Hyperion. (NF) **Grades 5–8**

Jutta understands difficult things are happening around her, but she and her friends at the Jewish School for Girls in Hamburg, Germany, still have fun. During 1938, Hitler and the Nazis impose more restrictions on German Jews, and Jutta's father spends more time trying to acquire visas and travel documents for his family. Levy uses entries from her mother's 1938 *poesiealbum* (poetry album) as the introduction to the poems in the book. Each poem expresses her mother's 11-year-old thoughts as, unknowingly, the classmates say goodbye to one another. In her afterword, Levy includes a brief history of her family, particularly her mother; information about Hitler's rise to power, and the persecution and extinction of the Jews; information on each of the girls who wrote in Jutta's album; family photos; a timeline from Jutta's birth to 1939; source notes; and a selected bibliography.   Social Studies LA1, LA9, SSIII, SSIV, SSVI Jewish Germans

Yellow Star

By Jennifer Rozines Roy. 2006. 227 pages. Marshall Cavendish. (F) **Grades 4–8**

Of the 270,000 Jews forced into the Lodz ghetto by the Nazis, only eight hundred survived. Twelve were children. The author's aunt, Syvia Perlmutter, was one of them. Through extensive interviews, Roy has recast Syvia's story into a first-person, free-verse poetic narrative that effortlessly weaves day-to-day incidents with a broader view of life in Poland during the Holocaust: "Yellow / is the color of / the felt six-pointed star/that is sewn onto my coat. / . . . I wish I could / rip the star off / (carefully, stitch by stitch, so as not to ruin / my lovely coat), / because yellow is meant to be / a happy color, / not the color of / hate." Each small incident is given a boldface heading that moves Syvia's compelling story along. The story is separated into five chronological parts, each prefaced by a short explanatory chapter describing what was happening in the war during that time. The author's introduction and final note give further information on Syvia's family; a timeline gives a broad view of major events of World War II.   Social Studies LA1, SSIII, SSIV, SSV, SSVI, SSIX Jewish Poles

ETHNIC CONFLICTS

Broken Song

By Kathryn Lasky. 2005. 154 pages. Viking. (F) **Grades 5–9**

In this companion book to *The Night Journey* (1981), on a terrible night in 1897, Cossack troops invade Reuven Bloom's town and home, changing his life forever. Dressed as an old peasant woman and carrying his 2-year-old sister, Rachel, in a basket on his back, Reuven escapes to Poland, where he sends Rachel safely to America. He then becomes the best demolition man for the Bund, the underground Jewish Workers' Federation. Reassigned, he saves the family of his future wife, Sashie (the protagonist of *The Night Journey*), and ultimately decides to leave his violent life and join Rachel and her adoptive family in America. While the adventurous plot is compelling, it is Lasky's skillful characterization of Reuven and his oh-so-feisty sister that bring the story into focus. Contains plenty of dialogue, unobtrusive explanations of the historical context of the story, and a happy (if improbable) ending.   Social Studies LA1, SSII, SSIII, SSV, SSIX Jews-Russian

The Day of the Pelican
By Katherine Paterson. 2009. 145 pages. Clarion. (F) **Grades 5–8**

In the spring of 1998, 12-year-old Meli Lleshi and her family, Albanian Muslims, must flee their comfortable home in Kosovo after her older brother, Mehmet, is beaten and left for dead by Serbian militants. They find refuge first in the mountains with the Kosovo Liberation Army, then, as the months pass, with their relatives at the family farm. When Serbian intruders burn down the house, the Lleshis are forced to make a harrowing journey to a Macedonian refugee camp. There Baba decides his family will escape the hatred and desire for revenge by moving to America. Meli wonders, will it work? Can Mehmet ever forget? Can she? When they finally settle into a small Vermont town, Meli is hopeful—until she and Mehmet are targeted in the aftermath of 9/11. A short afterword gives background on the tangled history of Kosovo and on Slobodan Miloševi's horrific ethnic cleansing that destroyed the lives of so many Albanian citizens. Social Studies LA1, SSI, SSIII, SSIV, SSV, SSVI Albanian Americans, Albanians

The Lace Dowry
By Andrea Cheng. 2005. 113 pages. Front Street. (F) **Grades 6–8**

Mama insists 12-year-old Juli have a dowry, but Juli says, "Mama, it is 1933 and I don't need a dowry. Nobody in Budapest has a dowry anymore." However, Mama contends Juli's dowry must include a handmade tablecloth. She plans their first train trip to the lace maker in Halas. There Juli meets Roza, the lace maker's daughter. The girls are the same age but from different socioeconomic situations. As Juli and her mother make their bimonthly trips to Halas, Juli and Roza become true friends. But in these troubled times, can their friendship endure? In her author's note, Cheng, whose parents were Hungarian Jewish immigrants, explains the history of the Halas lace and uses the story of her aunt's dowry lace tablecloth as the basis for this book. Social Studies LA1, LA9, SSIII, SSIV, SSIX, VA4, VA6 Jewish Hungarians

Memories of Babi: Stories
By Aranka Siegal. 2008. 116 pages. Farrar, Straus and Giroux. (F) **Grades 4–7**

Aranka Siegal spent many special times with her Jewish Babi in Little Komjaty, Ukraine, in the 1930s. She uses those times as the basis of her stories of Piri, a Hungarian city girl. Both Christians and Jews live in Little Komjaty; they are poor, hard-working farmers who mostly respect one another's religion, but experience some ethnic conflict as well. Piri has some superstitions, particularly about death and the cemetery, but her grandmother dispels them and teaches her many life lessons. Each of Siegal's nine stories stands alone; as a whole, they offer a satisfying look at simple Ukrainian country life and customs. Siegal gives several recipes for foods she mentions in the book. In the last story, she talks about how death has touched her life so many times, but her memories sustain her, even as she considers her grandmother's last experiences when taken from her home by the Nazis.   Language Arts, Social Studies LA1, LA9, SSII, SSIII, SSIV Jewish Eastern Europeans, Jewish Hungarians, Jewish Ukrainians

Mixing It
By Rosemary Hayes. 2007. 185 pages. Frances Lincoln. (F) **Grades 7–12**

Caught in a sudden bomb explosion on her way to school, Fatimah keeps a boy in the rubble from bleeding to death. When their photograph hits the front page of the newspaper with the misleading headline "Muslim Girl Saves Schoolboy Friend," Fatimah and Steve become targets for a terrorist's rage. Told in alternating chapters, the teens struggle to understand each other as the local vicar and imam work to persuade the two families to set an example for their British city by becoming friends. To make matters worse, Fatimah and Steve begin to realize they are attracted to each other—something their cultures will never accept. And then the threatening notes begin. Author Hayes visited with Al-Noor Girls' Group and had them vet the book, giving readers a modern look at one aspect of young British Muslim society. The result is somewhat didactic, but this can serve as an introduction to some of the thorny issues faced by immigrant teens today.   Social Studies LA1, SSIII, SSIV, SSV Muslim British

My Childhood under Fire: A Sarajevo Diary
By Nadja Halilbegovich. 2006. 120 pages. Kids Can. (NF) **Grades 6–10**

"Nadja, you're not going to school today." With this greeting from her parents on April 6, 1992, life changes drastically for 12-year-old Nadja. The war in Bosnia and Herzegovina had begun; Sarajevo, the city which held the Winter Olympics in 1984 was now under siege. To keep herself occupied, Nadja begins keeping a diary on May 31, 1992. Her last entry is August 6, 1995. In the diary, she writes about what is happening all around her—with her family, in their apartment building, in Sarajevo, and in the country. War, destruction, and death are everywhere. Throughout the war, she and her family try to keep some semblance of normalcy, although at times they fear for their lives. Often her feelings are raw; her pain and her confusion about the atrocities are evident in her poignant entries. She wonders particularly about the senseless killing of children who will never know the joy of life. In this published version, her present-day thoughts and comments are interspersed with the entries. As she looks back at her experiences, she fills in important information to give readers a better sense of life under siege. Includes photographs of Nadja, her family, and destruction in Sarajevo. **Social Studies LA1, SSI, SSIII, SSIV, SSVI Bosnians, East Europeans, Serbs**

Under a Red Sky: A Memoir of a Childhood in Communist Romania
By Haya Leah Molnar. 2010. 302 pages. Farrar, Straus and Giroux. (NF) **Grades 6–9**

In the late 1950s in Bucharest, Romania, young Eva slowly learns about the history of her eccentric and talented family, who survived mass murders incited by fascist Romanian groups in World War II. Her father, a concentration camp survivor, now makes films for Romania's government-owned film studio; her mother teaches ballet. Protected by her parents, grandparents, aunts, and uncles, Eva does not know she is Jewish until she is 8 years old. Her family applies for passports to emigrate to Israel and lose their jobs as a result. During the years of waiting to emigrate, Eva becomes a Young Pioneer in school (she is relieved she can't be singled out now) and studies Hebrew in secret. Her lively, dialogue-filled accounts bring to life the joy of spending time with her friend, Andrei, and her doting family in the midst of the fear that comes from living under an anti-Semitic, repressive regime. **Language Arts, Social Studies LA1, LA9, SSI, SSIII, SSIV, SSVI Jewish Romanians**

SOUTH AND CENTRAL AMERICA, MEXICO, AND THE CARIBBEAN

Fidel Castro, Leader of Communist Cuba (Signature Lives series)
By Fran Rees. 2006. Illus. 111 pages. Compass Point. (NF) **Grades 6–9**

As with other titles in the series, this begins with a pivotal moment in Fidel Castro's life: his speech in Havana on January 8, 1959, that signaled the beginning of his leadership in Cuba. After briefly covering his childhood, Rees discusses Castro's life as a student, his leadership in the Cuban revolution, the defeat of the U.S.-sponsored Cuban exile army at the Bay of Pigs, his role in the Cuban missile crisis of 1962, and his life up to the 1990s. Unfortunately, while the overall description of events is accurate, the author fails to provide sufficient historical background to give a balanced view of the reasons behind Cubans and other South Americans support of Castro or of his disdain for the U.S. government. Yet, in the hands of a teacher well versed in Latin American history, this could be a useful resource. For details on this series' format and style, see *George Washington Carver*, page 85. Social Studies LA1, SSII, SSIV, SSV, SSVI, SSVII, SSIX

Cubans, Latinos

Firefly Letters: A Suffragette's Journey to Cuba
By Margarita Engle. 2010. 151 pages. Henry Holt. (NF) **Grades 5–7**

In 1851, Fredrika Bremer, a Swedish novelist and suffragette, spent three months in Cuba. She went looking for paradise but instead found the dichotomy of slavery and elite society. At the end of the three months, she left behind two changed young women: a slave girl, Cecilia, and her rich mistress, Elena. Because Cecilia spoke English and Spanish, she became Fredrika's translator. The two traversed the countryside, where Fredrika interviewed and sketched slaves and freed slaves. Elena, on the other hand, could only sit by her window watching the two rescuing fireflies in the marketplace. Escaping the watchful eyes of her mother, Elena joined the others in the small cottage and soon hatched a plan to make enough money to purchase the freedom of Cecilia's unborn child. As the three women narrate their stories in free-verse poems, readers learn their inner thoughts and see their transformation. The book includes a historical note about Bremer and a list of references. Language Arts, Social Studies LA1, LA9, SSII, SSIII, SSIV, SSV, SSVI

Africans, Cubans, Swedes

Journey of Dreams
By Marge Pellegrino. 2009. 250 pages. Frances Lincoln. (F) **Grades 6–10**

A skilled artist, 13-year-old Tomasa sees pictures everywhere. She and her family live peacefully in a Mayan village in the Guatemala Highlands, where her father raises corn and her mother sells colorful woven clothing. Tomasa weaves too and is proud her work is beginning to sell. Then the soldiers and helicopters come, capturing boys for the army and destroying homes. When the family begins receiving threatening notes, Mama and 14-year-old Carlos flee north. Not long after, as their village is torched, Tomasa, her father, little brother, and baby Maria flee. Throughout their long, harrowing journey to safety in the U.S., Papa's storytelling comforts and teaches them. Hardest to bear is missing Mama and Carlos—will they ever be reunited? Tomasa's first-person narrative is matter-of-fact and poignant. While steadfastly containing her fear each day, her dreams, sprinkled throughout the story, effectively reveal her confusion and dread. Pellegrino bases Tomasa on the many young asylum seekers with whom she has had contact in her work in the Sanctuary Movement. Details about the Guatemalan government's campaign that destroyed 440 villages, and of the Sanctuary Movement, which helped refugees from war-torn Central America in the 1980s, are given in an afterword. Social Studies LA1, SSII, SSIII, SSIV, SSVI, SSVII, SSIX, VA4 Guatemalans, Maya, Mexicans

Jungle Crossing
By Sydney Salter. 2009. 215 pages. Harcourt. (F) **Grades 5–8**

On a family vacation to Cancún, Mexico, Kat, just out of seventh grade, goes with her younger sister on guided day trips to historical Mayan sites. They sit in the front of the bus behind their Mayan guide, Nando, and listen as he tells the story of Muluc, a girl who lived in the time of the Mayan empire. Kat pretends she isn't interested in the story, yet she sketches elements of each day's story. One day Nando sees her sketches and realizes she isn't the typical uncaring, thoughtless American teen tourist. After Kat and Barb attend his sister's quinceañera and spend the night in his village, Nando and Kat apologize to each other for their incorrect assumptions and acknowledge their friendship. The author bases the book on her own experiences in Mexico. While the story of Muluc is from her own imagination, it is also based on much research and study. She includes websites on the Mayan culture and archeological treasures for further exploration. Social Studies LA1, LA9, SSII, SSIII, SSIV, SSIX Maya, Mexicans

The Poet King of Tezcoco: A Great Leader of Ancient Mexico
By Francisco Serrano. Trans. by Trudy Balch and Jo Anne Engelbert. 2007. Illus. 34 pages. Groundwood. (NF) **Grades 4–7**

On April 28, 1402, Prince Acolmiztli Nezahualcóyotl was born in Tezcoco, located in a valley to the east of Lake Tezcoco—now covered by Mexico City.

As prince, and later as king, Nezahualcóyotl became known for his poetry and his will to rule his people with kindness rather than terror. In this beautifully illustrated book, readers meet this king, learn of his battles, share his inner struggles and his reverence of nature, and appreciate his poetry. The book includes a chronology of the king's life, a glossary, an introduction, and further readings. Although no pronunciation guide is provided, it offers a thorough look at the advanced kingdom-states that existed before the Europeans destroyed them. Language Arts, Social Studies, LA1, SSI, SSII, SSIII, SSIV, SSV, SSVI, VA1, VA4, VA6 Acolhuas, Mexicans

The Poet Slave of Cuba: A Biography of Juan Francisco Manzano
By Margarita Engle. 2006. 183 pages. Holt. (NF) **Grades 7–12**

Juan Francisco Manzano was born into slavery in 1797. Doña Beatriz de Jústiz, La Marquesa, sets his mother free and allows her to marry Juan's father; Juan, however, must remain her slave. He becomes her poodle, her pet, and learns to bark and sit on command; he memorizes poetry and play lyrics for La Marquesa so he can perform for her friends. When she dies, Juan is transferred to La Marquesa de Prado Ameno, who treats him cruelly. Juan finally escapes. The author's historical account gives more about Manzano's life. He spends several years in hiding in Havana. While there, he marries Delia and eventually purchases his freedom. In 1842, in Cuba's *Año del Cuero* ("year of the lash"), Juan is jailed for supposedly inciting a riot. His work is the only known autobiographic account of Latin American slavery. Margarita Engle has chosen to write these poems in Manzano's poetic style. Using alternating voices for the poems makes the book more dramatic. Language Arts, Social Studies LA1, LA9, SSII, SSIII, SSIV, SSV, SSVI, SSIX Cubans

The Red Umbrella
By Christina Diaz Gonzalez. 2010. 284 pages. Knopf. (F) **Grades 6–10**

As Fidel Castro takes power in Cuba in 1961, 14-year-old Lucía Alvarez and her 7-year-old brother, Frankie, witness the soldiers' brutality towards people who oppose the revolution. The Alvarez family is being watched; as May moves into June, trouble increases. Papá and Mamá quickly find a way to send the children to the U.S. Scared and sad, the children arrive in Miami and promptly are sent to the Kendall facility for Cuban children. By chance, the young man who supervises the boys' dorm recognizes their last name and remembers how their father once helped him. He places the children with Mr. and Mrs. Baxter in Grand Island, Nebraska. The Baxters and the children come to love each other deeply; but the infrequent phone calls with their parents make Lucía realize the increasing dangers their parents face. The significance of the red umbrella isn't apparent until the end of the book. In her author's note, Gonzalez explains her "research began at home" because the story is based on her family's history. Includes a pronunciation glossary of Spanish words.   Social Studies LA1, SSII, SSIV, SSV, SSVI Cuban Americans, Cubans

Tropical Secrets: Holocaust Refugees in Cuba
By Margarita Engle. 2009. 199 pages. Holt. (F) **Grades 5–9**

Daniel, a Jewish boy, escaped Nazi Germany, but not before seeing his grandfather killed on *Kristallnacht*, "The Night of Broken Glass." After making a pact with his parents to meet in New York, Daniel boards a ship headed for the United States. The ship is turned away in New York and sails for Cuba. Once there, Daniel is lucky; he is allowed into the country. Homeless, penniless, and distraught, he is befriended by two people: David, an older Jewish man married to a Christian, and Paloma, the daughter of a wealthy Cuban merchant. Each of the three has personal secrets, but they come to trust and depend upon one another. Spanning the years 1939 through 1942, Engle uses the three fictional characters to tell the little-known history of Jews who were fortunate enough to find refuge in western countries. (Many ships carrying Jews were made to return to Europe, where most people were exterminated in death camps.) In alternating free verse, the three characters share their journeys toward acceptance, love, and freedom. A historical note and author's note are appended.   Social Studies LA1, SSII, SSIII, SSIV, SSVI, SSIX Cubans, Jewish Cubans, Jewish Germans

The Walls of Cartagena
By Julia Durango. 2008. 152 pages. Simon & Schuster. (F) **Grades 5–9**

Beginning with a letter dated 1639 CE, the story of Amadeo de Angola skips backward and forward. Amadeo has no memory of his mother, who died in childbirth on a slave ship. Bought, raised, and educated in the household of Doña Isabel until his 13th birthday, he earns the nickname Calepino because of his quick wit and ability to learn and speak eleven languages. Calepino dreads mornings he serves as Father Pedro's interpreter to those on the slave ships. He retches at the stench of suffering and death, yet marvels at the kindness the priest shows the terrified slaves. His life changes when only he speaks the language of a mother and son, Mara and Tomi, on a slave ship. When Mara delivers a stillborn child the following day and is herself near death, Calepino is called to the slave holding pen to interpret for Dr. López, a Jewish doctor who works in the leper colony. Soon Calepino is serving with the doctor, learning valuable lessons about friendship and loyalty, and helping Mara and Tomi. Then Dr. López is imprisoned as a Jew. Can Calepino help his friends when they need him the most? **Social Studies LA1, SSII, SSIII, SSIV, SSV, SSVI, SSIX Africans, Colombians**

U.S. HISTORY

To align with the many history textbooks used by middle schools, we have arranged this chapter by major topic. While we have tried to place titles chronologically, at times a topic spans a wide number of years. Therefore, readers should look for titles by topic; the index contains more specific topics than those found in the following subheadings. Because we could not find quality multiethnic titles written between 2005 and 2010 about some of the significant events in U.S. history, readers will note some gaps in the following bibliography.

COLONIZATION

Blood on the River: James Town 1607
By Elisa Lynn Carbone. 2006. 237 pages. Viking. (F) **Grades 5–8**

Twelve-year-old-orphaned Samuel Collier comes to the New World as page to Captain John Smith. After their first encounter with native peoples, Samuel wonders what he is "in for." A natural loner, he learns this won't work. Through the first harsh year, if not for Smith's native friends, the English would have perished. As he sees how the British encroach on the native lands and loot and kill, Samuel understands why the native people dislike the British. In 1610 as wounded Captain Smith heads back to England, Samuel and others head to Point Comfort to begin a new fort. Soon, the natives burn James Town in retaliation for the British actions. Carbone gives a fresh look at the English in the New World. She includes an afterword describing events in the years following the story, an author's note, and primary source notes with websites for each chapter. Social Studies LA1, SSII, SSIII, SSIV, SSV, SSVI American Indians, Powhatans

Fort Mose and the Story of the Man Who
Built the First Free Black Settlement in Colonial America
By Glennette Tilley Turner. 2010. Illus. 42 pages. Abrams. (NF) **Grades 5–9**

Sometime before 1700, a Mandingo boy was born. He was captured by the English and brought as a slave to fledgling Charles Town. Little is known about his early years; but in 1724, he and nine other African men (mostly from West Africa) escaped and arrived in St. Augustine, Florida. The Spanish purchased them as slaves but gave them roles of responsibility. Here the Mandingo man took the name by which he is known: Francisco Menendez. Freed at last, Menendez and approximately one hundred former slaves were the first freedmen to live in the newly formed Spanish Fort Mose (moh-say), the early southern destination of the Underground Railroad. By 1738, thirty-eight families lived there. With the Spanish and English trading ownership of the fort, the people's fate was at jeopardy, and Fort Mose was abandoned in 1763. After being captured and enslaved by the British once again, Menendez ended up in Cuba where he died at age 70. The site of the fort and most of its history were lost until late in the twentieth century, when archeologists used thermal photography to identify its original site just off Florida's coast. The historical significance of Menendez and Fort Mose is still unfolding. An author's note, acknowledgments, a glossary, notes, sources, an index, and illustration credits are included.
Social Studies LA1, SSII, SSIII, SSIV, SSV African Americans

Hispanic America series
By Roger E. Hernández. 2009. Illus. Approx. 80 pages.
Marshall Cavendish Benchmark. (NF) **Grades 5–12**

This comprehensive series gives students a new look at Hispanic and Latino American participation in every phase of U.S. history. It spans five centuries, from early Spanish explorations of the New World to present-day involvement. Each volume includes interesting drawings, maps, and photographs. Crisp graphics and fonts with a lot of white space keep the text from overpowering the reader. Well-placed subheadings help organize an immense amount of information. Each title includes a timeline, a glossary, a list of further readings including books and websites, an index, author notes, and photo credits. While a bibliography is given, the authors unfortunately quote from the books without citing the specific source; nor do they give citations for the multitude of statistics presented. Still, we recommend this series because of its significant contribution to students' understanding of the key roles of various Hispanic and Latino individuals and groups. Titles include *Early Explorations: The 1500s; New Spain, 1600–1760s; The Civil War, 1840s–1890s; The Spanish-American War, 1898 to World War II; 1950s–1960s; 1970s–1980s; 1990s–2010.* Authors include Roger E. Hernández, Steven Otfinoski, and Richard Worth. Social Studies LA1, SSII, SSIII, SSV, SSVI, SSVII, SSVIII, SSIX, SSX Latinos

Pocahontas: A Life in Two Worlds (Sterling Biographies series)
By Victoria Garrett Jones. 2010. Illus. 124 pages. Sterling. (NF) **Grades 5–9**

"Larger than life" succinctly describes the image Americans have created of Pocahontas. Jones gives a more accurate portrayal of her life—from her birth (probably in 1595) to her death in 1617. She was Powhatan's favored daughter, but her escalating interactions with the British finally led to her father's rejection. In 1607 when the first British arrived, the men of the Powhatan nation watched with curiosity, alarm, and hostility at the invasion of their lands. The friendship between Pocahontas and John Smith proved crucial to a tenuous peace between the Native Americans and the English. She became the intermediator for the English. Although she was tricked and captured by the British in 1613, she continued to work for peace until her death in England in 1617. For information on format, style, and back matter see *Jackie Robinson: Champion for Equality*, page 68. Social Studies LA1, SSII, SSIII, SSIV, SSV American Indians, Powhatans

REVOLUTIONARY WAR

The Escape of Oney Judge
By Emily Arnold McCully. 2007. Illus. No page numbers.
Farrar, Straus and Giroux. (F) **Grades 3–6**

Taught to work with her mother in the mansion for Martha Washington, young Oney Judge knows her life is easier than being a field slave. It chafes her, though, that while she can play with Mrs. Washington's granddaughter, she cannot learn to read. Despite her good standing in the Washington household, Oney knows she could be sold at a moment's notice. This simple yet powerful picture book details Oney's life with the Washingtons and tells of her eventual escape to a free life in Portsmouth, New Hampshire. An author's note gives sources and further information about Ona Maria Judge. The fluid watercolor illustrations help place the reader in the late 1700s and highlight Oney's emotions as she struggles as a slave in a newly "free" country.   Social Studies LA1, SSIII, SSIV, SSV, SSVI, SSVII

African Americans

Everybody's Revolution:
A New Look at the People Who Won America's Freedom
By Thomas J. Fleming. 2006. Illus. 96 pages. Scholastic. (NF) **Grades 5–9**

Fleming introduces people from varied cultural and ethnic backgrounds who participated in the American Revolution. His introduction, "What Does the American Revolution Have to Do with Me?" makes the book personal and draws the reader to ask the same question. In an almost conversational style, he makes the people come alive. Although the documented primary source photographs show only white male faces, Fleming explains the cultural or ethnic background of these men. They had all come to America to escape the tyranny of leaders in their homelands. They believed in the ideals of the Declaration of Independence and were willing to fight for this fledgling new country. From events leading to war and throughout the long battle, others joined in the fight: Bernardo de Galvez, a Spaniard in charge of New Orleans, became a secret aid to the Americans; African American men, some freedmen and some slaves, were instrumental in battle; Jewish men fought and raised money for the war effort; Polish generals "won enduring fame" for their valiant leadership; Swiss and Dutch men provided food and military assistance; the Oneida Indians were loyal to the Americans and fought courageously, even facing other Indians who were loyal to the British; women, including Abigail Adams, were outspoken about the war and found ways to engage themselves in the effort—some were spies, some were soldiers; some children served as buglers, while others were spies and runners. Fleming is recognized as a scholar on the American Revolution. Although he does not include source notes, he includes a list of newer books (1998–2004 copyright dates) for further reading, respected websites, a glossary, and a detailed index. The primary source photographs from respected collections are credited on the verso of the title page. Social Studies LA1, SSII, SSIII, SSIV, SSV, SSVI, SSX American Indians, AOD, Dutch, English, French, Germans, Irish, Jews, Oneida, Scottish, Spanish, Swiss

Forge
By Laurie Halse Anderson. 2010. 297 pages. Atheneum. (F) Grades 5–9

In the brief prelude, Anderson provides enough background for those who haven't read *Chains* (2008) to understand that 15-year-old Curzon and Isabel have successfully escaped slavery. The story picks up nine months later, in October 1777. The two have been separated, and Curzon finds his way into the continental army during the winter at Valley Forge. He must let no one know he is an escaped slave. By February 1778, Curzon's owner, Bellingham, identifies him. This changes Curzon's role, and the future looks grim. After spotting Isabel serving Bellingham, he wonders if they can ever escape Bellingham. Will they ever be free? Chapters of the book are headed by days with a quotation from a diary or historical document. Anderson seamlessly weaves her fictional characters into a historically accurate account of conditions during the winter at Valley Forge. End matter—including questions for discussion, Anderson's detailed explanations of her research, and an extensive glossary—adds to the value of this impressive book. Social Studies LA1, LA9, SSII, SSIII, SSIV, SSV African Americans

Liberty or Death: The Surprising Story of Runaway Slaves Who Sided with the British during the American Revolution
By Margaret Whitman Blair. 2010. Illus. 64 pages.
National Geographic. (NF) Grades 5–9

In 1775, Lord Dunmore, British Royal Governor, promised freedom and land to runaway slaves who would side with and fight for the British in the Revolutionary War. Thousands (estimated between fifteen thousand to a hundred thousand) fled to cities occupied by the British. The promises made to them were not as forthcoming as hoped, and by 1783, the question was, "Where could the black loyalists go?" Loyalists, both black and white, went first to Nova Scotia—there, the whites received land before the blacks; the same happened in Sierra Leone, but, there the black loyalists flourished despite injustices imposed upon them. Their descendents live in Freetown. Includes a timeline, resource guide, an index, sources, and photo credits. Social Studies LA1, SSII, SSIII, SSIV, SSV African Americans

SLAVERY

Africa: A Look Back (Drama of African-American History series)
By James Haskins and Kathleen Benson. 2007. Illus. 68 pages.
Marshall Cavendish Benchmark. (NF) **Grades 6–9**

With arresting maps, illustrations, and ample use of primary source material, this opening volume of the series will leave readers wanting more. Using the slave narratives of Olaudah Equiano, Ayuba ben Suleiman Diallo, Mahomma Gardo Baquaqua, and Venture Smith, the authors explore the background cultures of the men and look at each individual's life in some detail. The introductory chapter gives a brief history of Africa; the men's stories show the complexity of their home societies. Day-to-day details allow students to compare their own lives with the lives of Americans and Europeans during those historical periods. Future titles in this series trace the journey of millions of African Americans through the history of the United States. This spotlight on African culture puts a human face on the stories to come. No source notes are given; however, the book includes a glossary, a resource list, a bibliography, an index, picture credits, and author information. Social Studies LA1, SSII, SSIII, SSIV, SSV, SSVI, SSVII, SSIX African Americans, Africans

Day of Tears: A Novel in Dialogue
By Julius Lester. 2005. 177 pages. Hyperion. (F) **Grades 7–12**

In his author's note, Lester writes, "On March 2 and 3, 1859, the largest auction of slaves in American history took place in Savannah, Georgia. Some accounts put the number of slaves sold at 429, while others . . . at 436." Pierce Butler must sell his slaves to pay a gambling debt. Through dialogue and interludes, flashbacks, and flash-forwards, Lester presents the heartwrenching stories of people whose lives were affected forever. Using first person, each character draws the reader into that life. Emma, the 12-year-old slave girl, and Sarah, the owner's younger daughter, play significant roles. Each reminisces about the time and mourns the loss of their friendship. The stories are made even more powerful and poetic by the heavy rain that fell during the two days of the sale, which became known as "the Weeping Time." Social Studies LA1, LA9, SSII, SSIII, SSIV, SSVI African Americans

The Dred Scott Decision (We the People series)
By Jason Skog. 2007. Illus. 48 pages. Compass Point. (NF) **Grades 7–10**

Dred Scott's long legal battle for freedom led to a Supreme Court decision many say helped push the United States toward the Civil War. The author's conversational tone belies his work as a reporter. The introductory chapter describes the scene at the 1857 ruling and gives information on previous legal precedents. The book then covers Scott's early life as a slave, his marriage to Harriet Robinson, and his many moves with owners both in and out of slave territory. The stops and starts of the case in the Missouri Supreme Court, the lawyers involved, and the arguments for Scott's freedom are all here, along with the public's reaction to the final decision that Scott remain a slave. Clear, concise writing and organization make the book easy to read. Well-placed colorful borders, interesting photographs and illustrations, and an extensive bibliography, index, glossary, and timeline enhance the text. Social Studies LA1, SSII, SSIII, SSV, SSVI African Americans

Elijah of Buxton
By Christopher Paul Curtis. 2007. 341 pages. Scholastic. (F) **Grades 4–8**

Eleven-year-old Elijah is immersed in the community of Buxton, a Canadian settlement of runaway slaves not far from Detroit, Michigan. After school he helps Mr. Leroy clear fields for Mrs. Holton, who is saving to buy her husband's freedom. He does numerous chores for folks, such as fetching the mail or catching and delivering fish. He's just figuring out the world of adults but is often tricked by the shifty Preacher, a man who seems nice on the surface but who often gets the better of the naive boy. Curtis places the reader in Buxton with surety, showing both the hopes and fears of its residents. The story takes a darker turn when Preacher steals the money Mr. Leroy hopes to use to free his family, sending Elijah into the dangers of Detroit—and the possibility of capture despite his freeborn status. Elijah's endearing, first-person, colloquial narrative perfectly presents an 11-year-old's view of life. An author's note presents the historical facts underpinning the story. Social Studies LA1, SSII, SSIII, SSIV, SSV, SSVI, SSVII African Americans, African Canadians

Fleeing to Freedom on the Underground Railroad:
The Courageous Slaves, Agents, and Conductors (People's History series)
By Elaine Landau. 2006. Illus. 88 pages.
Twenty-First Century Books. (NF) **Grades 5–12**

Using primary source documents, photographs, diaries, books, and preserved interviews, Landau presents a thoroughly researched and documented history of the Underground Railroad. She weaves unthinkable living and working conditions of slaves with the hopeful accounts of those who escaped to the North. Chapter subdivisions and generous placement of black-and-white or sepia-toned photographs break the text into manageable chunks. The writing is clear and engaging. Full of interesting, reliable information. The book includes sections of the Fugitive Slave Act of 1850, part of the Emancipation Proclamation, source notes, selected bibliography, further reading and websites, places to visit, a detailed index, and acknowledgments for photo and map credits. Few other books in the series have a multiethnic focus.   Social Studies LA1, SSII, SSIII, SSIV, SSV, SSVI African Americans

I, Dred Scott
By Shelia P. Moses. 2005. Illus. 96 pages. Margaret K. McElderry. (F) **Grades 6–10**

No one knows precisely what combination of factors led to Dred Scott's famous decision to sue for freedom under the Missouri Compromise. Here, Sheila Moses has created the fictional voice of Dred Scott to tell his story. In the dialect of the time, he describes his early life as the slave of Peter Blow. "I ain't got no memory of ever belonging to nobody other than he and his wife Miss Elizabeth Blow. It's safe to reckon they bought me when I was nothing but a youngster." As this sparely told tale unfolds, the reader learns of Scott's marriage, his travels with his new master, and of the years he spent on "free soil" in Illinois and Wisconsin—years that should have earned his wife's and his freedom. This is a beautifully designed book, with well-spaced text and wood engraved illustrations. The dedication, foreword, and detailed author's note with quotes from primary sources are important reading. Includes a helpful timeline, bibliography, and author information. Pair this with Jason Skog's *The Dred Scott Decision* (page 154) for readers who want a thorough understanding of the Supreme Court decision that is often cited as a primary cause of the Civil War.   Social Studies LA1, LA9, SSII, SSIII, SSIV, SSVI, SSVI, SSVII African Americans

John Brown: His Fight for Freedom
By John Hendrix. 2009. Illus. 39 pages. Abrams. (NF) **Grades 4–6**

Combining his almost larger-than-life (tall tale–like) illustrations of John Brown with accessible text, Hendrix shows the intense personality of Brown, his hatred of slavery, and his passionate desire to abolish it. Particularly haunting is Brown sitting inside the engine house at Harper's Ferry. Hendrix draws from his own research of John Brown's life to develop this picture biography of a select period in Brown's life. He makes Brown's struggles, beliefs, and fears real. In his author's note, he explains his interest in Brown; the controversy that has shrouded Brown's life for nearly 150 years; and, how, although he lost his own life, Brown stood for the downtrodden and oppressed. Includes maps, an index, and selected readings. **Social Studies LA1, SSIII, SSIV, SSVI African Americans**

The Letter Writer: A Novel
By Ann Rinaldi. 2008. 217 pages. Harcourt. (F) **Grades 7–9**

In 1831, Nat Turner led the bloodiest slave rebellion in American history in Virginia, killing 57 people—white and black. In this fictionalized account of the Southampton Insurrection, Rinaldi presents 11-year-old Harriet, an illegitimate daughter, whose half-brother, Richard, asks her to write letters for her blind stepmother. When the charismatic preacher Nat Turner is brought to her plantation to make furniture, Harriet finds an outlet for her sympathy toward the slaves Richard treats harshly. When Nat asks her for a map of the region she complies, little dreaming of the consequences. Harriet is a feisty, believable character whose observations highlight the difficulties of life in antebellum Virginia. **Language Arts, Social Studies LA1, SSIII, SSIV, SSV, SSVI, SSVII African Americans**

Letters from a Slave Boy: The Story of Joseph Jacobs
By Mary E. Lyons. 2007. 208 pages. Atheneum. (F) **Grades 5–8**

Following her biography of Harriet Jacobs in *Letters from a Slave Girl* (Scribner, 1992), Lyons presents a biographical fiction account of Harriet's son, Joseph. She bases his story on fragments from Harriet's letters and intertwines it with factual information about Harriet and the years 1839–1860. In exchange for teaching Josiah, a white boy, how to fish, Josiah teaches Joseph to read and write.

Their white father claims neither Joseph nor his younger sister, Lulu. After Harriet escapes to New York, first Lulu and then Joseph join her, but they are always evading slave hunters. Joseph spends much of his life on his own—on a whaling ship, as a printer's apprentice, and searching for gold. He always hopes to earn enough to buy his mother's and sister's freedom, but gambling and cards get in his way. Through all his travels, he writes letters to his mother and others. These letters allow readers to learn about Joseph and his family. **Social Studies LA1, LA9, SSII, SSIII, SSIV, SSV, SSVI African Americans**

Maritcha: A Nineteenth-Century American Girl
By Tonya Bolden. 2005. Illus. 47 pages. Harry N. Abrams. (NF) **Grades 4–8**

Maritcha Lyons, a young, gifted black woman, is determined to become a teacher. Born in 1848, she grows up in lower Manhattan until the 1863 New York City draft riots force her family to move to Providence, Rhode Island. As committed abolitionists, her parents harbor escaped slaves in their boardinghouse. Maritcha remembers meeting many luminaries of the black community throughout her childhood. She also remembers speaking, at age 16, to the Rhode Island legislature to convince them to allow her to attend the then-segregated Providence High School. Using Maritcha's memoir, Bolden's descriptions include meticulously researched details of daily life of the era. Every double-page spread includes photographs and illustrations. The result is a well-documented, fascinating glimpse into one girl's life. **Social Studies LA1, LA7, SSII, SSIII, SSV, SSVII African Americans**

My Name Is Sally Little Song
By Brenda Woods. 2006. 182 pages. Putnam. (F) **Grades 5–8**

Sally May, born in Georgia in 1790, is 12 when she and her brother are to be given to their master's brother. Her father decides the family will run away— south to the swamps rather than north to Canada. They make their way to Seminole territory in Florida. They run for several harrowing days, eating what they find and getting sick from swamp water. The slave hunters are not far behind them, and before long, the whole Seminole village is in grave danger. This intense, fast-paced story sheds light on a little known piece of American history. The Seminole allowed escaped slaves to enter their village, live with them, and

be productive members of their community.   Social Studies LA1, SSIII, SSIV, SSV
African Americans, Seminoles

The Slave Trade and the Middle Passage
(Drama of African-American History series)
By S. Pearl Sharp, and Virginia Schomp. 2007.
Illus. 70 pages. Marshall Cavendish Benchmark. (NF) **Grades 5–8**

This well-researched book examines the "spiraling cycle of supply and demand" that spurred the transatlantic slave trade. After a brief look at slavery within Africa, which was often a form of indentured servitude and not hereditary, the authors explore Portugal and Spain's entry into what became a huge market. Using the story of Ottobah Cugoano, kidnapped from Ghana in 1767, and other individuals' stories, this looks at the political and economic forces that propelled the slave trade forward in Europe and the New World. The final chapter focuses on the abolition of the slave trade and the eventual rescinding of slavery laws, and offers a brief look at slavery's impact. The authors point out the irony of the "free" society of the United States built through the enslavement of millions of Africans. For details on this series' format and style, see *Africa: A Look Back*, page 153.   Social Studies LA1, SSII, SSIII, SSV, SSVI, SSVII, SSX African Americans, Africans

The Time of Slavery (American Voices series)
By Elizabeth Sirimarco. 2007. Illus. 114 pages.
Marshall Cavendish Benchmark. (NF) **Grades 6–9**

Sirimarco uses primary sources to present the history of slavery in the United States. The preface gives students various approaches to using these sources, encouraging them to ask questions and conduct further investigation. Almost every double-page spread includes an illustration or photograph from the era or event discussed or depicting that era or event. Clearly written and well organized, the author gives just enough background information for the sources presented to make sense, closing each section with a "Think About This" series of thought-provoking questions. The book begins with Olaudah

Equiano's narrative of how his sister and he were kidnapped from their home in Nigeria and Mahommah G. Baquaqua's description of the horrors of the Middle Passage. The author presents the laws and codes of early America that supported slavery, and includes narratives of slaves describing their lives. A chapter on "Escape and Revolt" includes information on the Turner rebellion in 1831. The book ends with the passage of the Thirteenth Amendment to the Constitution in 1855. An excellent introduction to the use of primary sources, this includes a timeline, glossary, extensive bibliography, a list of websites with a cautionary note on credibility, and an index.   Social Studies LA1, LA9, SSII, SSIII, SSIV, SSV, SSVI, SSVII, SSX African Americans, Africans

Up Before Daybreak: Cotton and People in America
By Deborah Hopkinson. 2006. Illus. 120 pages. Scholastic. (NF) Grades 5–9

Hopkinson grew up in Lowell, Massachusetts, a city whose lifeblood had been cotton mills. When the cotton industry closed plants in the United States and moved them to other countries, cities like Lowell became shadow cities. The book's accounts are based on interviews with former slaves conducted as part of the Federal Writers' Project during the Great Depression. Acknowledging that the interviews are perhaps biased by the fact that the interviewers were white, Hopkinson believes the stories show the important intertwining of cotton with the lives of millions of people and thus reflect a history that must be told. The interviews, both text and audio, are recorded in the Library of Congress American Memory archives. Hopkinson has edited the language for greater ease of reading. The stories cover the period before the Civil War and progress through the Great Migration and the Great Depression; freely interspersed in each are archival photographs. Includes further readings for young people; a selected bibliography of books; another of articles, oral histories, narratives, bulletins, pamphlets, and websites; detailed chapter notes; text permissions; photo credits (most from museums and the Library of Congress); and a detailed index.   Social Studies LA1, SSIII, SSV, SSVI, SSVII, SSVIII African Americans

WESTWARD EXPANSION

Bad News for Outlaws:
The Remarkable Life of Bass Reeves, Deputy U.S. Marshal
By Vaunda Micheaux Nelson. 2009. Illus. 42 pages. Carolrhoda. (NF) **Grades 3–6**

Born into slavery in 1838, as an adult, Bass Reeves was the epitome of a great man on the western frontier. Because of his temperament as a child, his mother feared he would become an outlaw. Instead, his owner taught him how to use a gun and entered him in shooting contests which he nearly always won. Colonel Reeves even took Bass along when he joined the Civil War. However, an argument between the two led Bass to strike his master, and he ran from Texas to Indian Territory. A group of native people hid him till the war ended. Now free, he bought a piece of land in Arkansas, married Jennie, settled down, fathered eleven children, and became one of two hundred deputy marshals who covered the 74,000 square miles of the territory. R. Gregory Christie's illustrations are riveting. In the end pages, the author gives a bit of background on Judge Parker; more on the Indian Territory; a glossary of Western words; a timeline; further readings about her research, including a detailed bibliography of sources she used; and how she was first introduced to Bass Reeves.   Social Studies LA1, SSII, SSIII, SSIV, SSVI African Americans

Bear Dancer: The Story of a Ute Girl
By Thelma Hatch Wyss. 2005. 181 pages. Margaret K. McElderry. (F) **Grades 5–8**

Set in the Rocky Mountains and the Great Plains, this story is divided into three sections: 1860–1861, 1861–1863, and 1863. There is unrest and fighting between the Utes, the Arapahos, and the Cheyenne, much of it caused by white soldiers and settlers trading with the Arapahos. The Utes live in the mountains; the Arapahos in the plains, but the Arapahos are invading Ute territory, taking their horses, and their women. Life is rich for 12-year-old Elk Girl until her brother asks her to go north to live with the old White River Ute chief and his wife. Shortly after arriving, two Cheyenne men capture her. She spends a year as a slave of the Cheyenne and is "rescued" by white settlers with whom she spends a year. Through the kindness of Uriah Curtis, who is taking a treaty to her brother, Elk Girl goes home but finds things different. We realize she was rescued by whites, but with the author's notes that explain how she worked with the great-great-great-granddaughter of Elk Tooth Dress to re-create her life, we support this book. It is a quick read designed for a younger audience or for older readers who need simpler books.   Social Studies LA1, LA9, SSII, SSIII, SSV, SSVI American Indians, Indians of North America, Tabeguache Ute, Ute

Black Storm Comin'
By Diane Lee Wilson. 2005. 295 pages. Margaret K. McElderry. (F) **Grades 4–8**

Twelve-year-old Colton Wescott and his family head west in a covered wagon, but as a racially mixed family they face many obstacles. Grudgingly, they are allowed to tag along at the end of a wagon train. An accident at the beginning of the journey doesn't bode well for the family. They drop further behind the wagon train, run out of supplies, and Colton realizes it is up to him to save his family. Wilson's fast-paced, action-filled story keeps readers on edge. They experience the racial tensions Colton faces; they run the brutally cold, exhilarating race against time and weather along with him; they fear for his and his family's safety—all the while sharing African American experiences during the westward expansion in 1860 and learning about the Pony Express.   Social Studies LA1, SSII, SSIII, SSIV, SSVI African Americans

Crooked River
By Shelley Pearsall. 2007. 249 pages. Yearling. (F) **Grades 6–9**

In 1812, tensions mount between the Ojibwa and the white settlers as the white encroach upon Ojibwa territory in Ohio. Whites live on one side of Crooked River; the Ojibwa on the other. Thirteen-year-old Rebecca Carver and her 17-year-old sister, Laura, their brothers, and father have a small farm near Crooked River. Their pa was mean before their mother died—and now he is meaner. The children know he is up to no good. Pa brings Amik, an Ojibwa, to their cabin, ties him up, and forces him into the loft. Pa tells the girls to guard Amik, but Rebecca is angry to see him treated so harshly. She risks her life to befriend Amik because she doesn't believe he murdered a shifty trapper. The story is told in alternating voices—Rebecca's in first-person narrative, Amik's in poetry. Pearsall includes a selected bibliography of related informational books for young adults, plus two museum resources.   Social Studies LA1, LA9, SSII, SSIII, SSIV, SSV, SSVI American Indians, Ojibwa

Dancing at the Odinochka
By Kirkpatrick Hill. 2005. 257 pages. Margaret K. McElderry. (F) **Grades 5–8**

When Russia owned Alaska, Russians, Indians, and Eskimos (Yupik and Inupiat) lived there. This book, set at the Nulato *odinochka* ("trading post") on the banks of the Yukon River, is based on the brief five-page memoir of Erinia Pavaloff Callahan, whose father managed the Russian American Company trading post. Twice a year when the Kaiyuh people came to the post to trade, Erinia was excited to visit with her good friend, Nilaat. Things changed when the telegraph men came. The United States purchased Alaska, the trading company became part of the U.S. government, gold was discovered in Alaska, steamships made travel up and down the Yukon easier, and new settlements sprang up all along the Yukon. The old ways disappeared; the new ways came to stay. **Social Studies LA1, LA9, SSII, SSIII, SSV, SSVI American Indians, Kaiyuh, Russians**

The Indian Removal Act: Forced Relocation (Snapshots in History series)
By Mark Stewart. 2007. Illus. 96 pages. Compass Point. (NF) **Grades 6–12**

Stewart uses his first chapter to describe the events on the Trail of Tears march. With this beginning sentence of chapter 2: "The Indian Removal Act was the result of a process that took place over a period of more than 200 years," Stewart connects the numerous painful events that led to Andrew Jackson forcing the approval of the Indian Removal Act in 1830. It took nearly eight years for the final group of Cherokees to march toward Oklahoma. Some descriptions from soldiers who marched with the Cherokee are moving. In his concluding statement, Stewart says, "The only positive thing to come out of the Indian Removal Act . . . is it serves a lesson of the terrible things one race can do to another when its members consider themselves superior." Includes a detailed timeline from 1540 to 1924, a vetted source of websites, historic sites, a glossary, chapter source notes, a select bibliography, further readings, information about the author, picture credits, and content and reading advisors. **Social Studies LA1, SSI, SSII, SSIII, SSIV, SSV, SSVI American Indians, Cherokees, Chickasaw, Choctaw, Creeks, Seminoles**

Nat Love (Legends of the Wild West series)
By Barbara Lee Bloom. 2010. Illus. 103 pages. Chelsea House. (NF) **Grades 6–9**

Nat (pronounced Nate) Love was born in slavery, but escaped and ended up as a cowpuncher in the Wild West. He was restless and always looking for his next adventure. The numerous illustrations include photographs of Love and his family, photographs of the period, drawings (one almost a caricature), and two clearly recent color photographs (not labeled as such). Bloom inserts too much historical background about the times, making it difficult to piece together a coherent biography of Love; but despite its shortcomings, Nat's escapades and adventures will hold middle schoolers' attention. Includes a chronology of Love's life, a historical timeline, a glossary, a bibliography, further resources (including several websites), an index, picture credits, and a brief biography of the author. Social Studies LA1, SSII, SSIII, SSIV, SSV African Americans

Pappy's Handkerchief (Tales of Young Americans series)
By Devin Scillian. 2007. Illus. No page numbers. Sleeping Bear. (F) **Grades 3–7**

Rich, sweeping acrylic illustrations bring to life the story of Moses and his family as they leave their faltering fish stall in Baltimore to take part in the land run for the territory of Oklahoma. Excited by the prospect of owning land—something his father and grandparents dreamed of when they were enslaved—the family sold everything they owned, bought horses and a wagon, and set out west. Overcoming a number of obstacles (an ice storm, white riders who said, "Negroes weren't allowed in the land run," and fever), they made it to the starting line just in time. When the race begins their wagon crashes into a creek bed, and it's up to Moses to ride out to stake their claim using Pappy's handkerchief. Moses's first-person narrative is direct and engrossing, moving the story along quickly, yet containing enough detail to intrigue readers to find out more about this historical event. The author's note explains that between 1889 and 1895, five land runs were actually held. Word spread among African American communities, and despite African Americans' fears that their color would preclude them from settling, at one time "Oklahoma had more all black towns than any other state." The author does note that the Native Americans in Oklahoma "endured unspeakable hardships" due to the opening of the new territory. Social Studies LA1, SSII, SSIII, SSVII, VA6 African Americans

The Trail of Tears (Cornerstones of Freedom series)
By Deborah Kent. 2005. Illus. 48 pages. Scholastic. (NF) **Grades 4–6**

Kent provides a short history of the encounters among the five native groups in the southeastern United States and the encroachments of white settlers. Her cogent discussion of the multiple failed treaties between the U.S. government and the native groups, particularly the Cherokee, is especially good for younger audiences. She doesn't shy away from describing the harsh treatment of native peoples as they were forced off their land following the signing of the Indian Removal Act of 1830. Includes a glossary, timeline of the Trail of Tears from 1791–1993, a bibliography, and an index. Picture credits are given on the verso of the title page. The lack of documented sources weakens the book, but its overview is worth considering.

Social Studies LA1, SSI, SSII, SSIII, SSIV American Indians, Cherokees, Chickasaw, Choctaw, Creeks, Seminoles

The Trail of Tears: The Relocation of the Cherokee Nation
By Lydia Bjornlund. 2010. Illus. 104 pages. Lucent. (NF) **Grades 6–12**

Beginning with a timeline of important dates and an introduction defining the Trail of Tears, Bjornlund proceeds to provide information about the Cherokee nation, how and where they lived before the invasion of Europeans. She continues with descriptions of the failed treaties the U.S. government initiated with the Cherokee, and of various state governments' treatment of the Cherokee people. She doesn't spare the harshness of the journey from the east to what was the Oklahoma territory, but concludes with how the Cherokee began to start over. Although more of a report book, the engaging text will lead some to read the entire book. Includes archival photos (with photo credits), detailed chapter notes, further resources (including recent books and websites), and an index.

Social Studies LA1, SSI, SSII, SSIII, SSIV, SSV, SSVI American Indians, Cherokees

CIVIL WAR AND RECONSTRUCTION

African Americans during the Civil War (Slavery in the Americas series)
By Deborah H. DeFord. 2006. Illus. 112 pages. Chelsea House. (NF) **Grades 4–8**

African Americans played an integral part in the Civil War. Early-on they weren't allowed to fight for the Union, but from the outset of the war, free blacks and slaves served as laborers in the Confederate army. Abolitionists and career Union officers brought the repeal of a 1792 law that forbade black men to serve in the army. Even with racism in the forces, African Americans played a significant role in important battles of the war. This includes well-captioned photographs and illustrations, a timeline, a glossary, further readings, websites, and an index. Sources are provided for the photographs but not the illustrations; author and editor information is given, but no source notes exist. Despite these omissions, the book is solid. Social Studies LA1, SSII, SSIII, SSV, SSVI, SSVII African Americans

The Brothers' War: Civil War Voices in Verse

By J. Patrick Lewis. 2007. Illus. 31 pages. National Geographic. (NF) **Grades 6–12**

The superb wordplay of J. Patrick Lewis breathes new life into the speeches of Lincoln, the letters of Grant and Lee, and the moving human drama of the Civil War. The author draws on primary sources to inspire each poem, bringing the ordinary and extraordinary voices of the Civil War to light. The book includes a note from the photo editor on the authentic period images.
Language Arts, Social Studies LA1, SSIII, SSIV, SSV African Americans

Cruisers

By Walter Dean Myers. 2010. 126 pages. Scholastic. (F) **Grades 5–8**

What if the Civil War had been settled before it began? Rather than being expelled from their gifted academy in Harlem, Zander, Kambui, LaShonda, and Bobbi are assigned to accomplish just this. To contest the expressed views of the Sons of the Confederacy, they create a newspaper, *The Cruiser*. Editorials in *The Cruiser* and the school paper *The Palette* cause tensions to run high during this "experimental" Civil War unit. Toward the end of the unit when Zander and his friends design and wear signs with the slogan "We Are Degraded," students come to realize discussions of the Civil War must include slavery and race. The editorials and student essays are set apart in bold font and add a different dimension to this first book in the Cruisers series. Social Studies LA1, SSIII, SSIV, SSVI African Americans

Harriet Tubman, Secret Agent: How Daring
Slaves and Free Blacks Spied for the Union during the Civil War

By Thomas B. Allen. 2006. Illus. 191 pages. National Geographic. (NF) **Grades 5–9**

Physical size, font style, photographs, illustrations, and broadsides make this book resemble one from the 1800s. Although these features are appealing, it is the story that truly engages the reader. It is more than a biography of Harriet Tubman. The title insinuates the book covers only the Civil War period, but it goes further back. Following Harriet from before she escapes till her death, the reader comes to claim her as a friend. Intertwined with her story are the lives of other brave African Americans who risked their lives to gain freedom and then fight for equality. Over and over again, Harriet entered dangerous Southern territory to bring others to freedom and to spy for the Union Army. Sadly, many papers and documents that could have shed more light on her life were destroyed or simply thrown away following the war. Allen has used only primary source documents for the book, and includes primary source photographs, maps, a bibliography, a timeline, source notes, and further readings.

Social Studies LA1, LA9, SSII, SSIII, SSIV, SSV, SSVI African Americans

March toward the Thunder
By Joseph Bruchac. 2008. 298 pages. Dial. (F) **Grades 6–12**

To help his mother financially, 15-year-old Louis Nolette, an Abenaki Indian from Canada, joins the Irish Brigade to fight the Confederates in 1864. He sees no sense in slavery: "How can one man own another?" He never expected war. For four grueling months he suffers indignities: fleas, poor food, churning battles, and bloodied comrades. Although he experiences prejudice, the focus is on the bonds created by war. The third-person narrative is detailed and evocative; Louis' thoughts, set in italics, make the story personal and accessible. Bruchac bases the book on the experiences of his great-grandfather and uses extensive research to give a compelling view of an average soldier's experiences in the Civil War.   Social Studies LA1, SSIII, SSIV, SSV, SSVII Abenakis, African Americans, American Indians, Indians of North America, Mohawks

Racing to Freedom Trilogy series
By Alison Hart. 2007. Approx. 160 pages. Peachtree. (F) **Grades 5–8**

In the first book, *Gabriel's Horses* (2007), 13-year-old Gabriel is left to care for Mr. Giles's horses after his father, a free African American, goes to fight for the Yankees. Mr. Giles entrusts the horses to Gabriel, sees his abilities, and gives him his freedom. In the second book, *Gabriel's Triumph* (2007), the reader follows newly freed Gabriel to Saratoga, New York, to ride in the Saratoga Chase. Gabriel's first-person narrative allows the reader to share his feelings about letting his father and Mr. Giles down; racism he finds in the North; being framed and accused of setting a fire in the stalls at the track; winning the race; and his feeling of truly being free. In the third book in the trilogy, *Gabriel's Journey* (2007), Gabriel leaves horse racing and joins his father in the fifth U.S. Colored Cavalry. Social Studies, Physical Education LA1, SSII, SSIII, SSIV, SSV, SSVI African Americans

The Reconstruction Era. Drama of African-American History
By Bettye Stroud and Virginia Schomp. 2007. Illus.
70 pages. Marshall Cavendish Benchmark. (NF) **Grades 5–9**

From the end of the Civil War to 1877, fiercely fought battles were waged to provide freed slaves with aid and ensure their rights as freed men and women. A wide array of topics is covered here: bitterness felt by the newly defeated Southerners; arguments between President Lincoln and congressional leaders over Reconstruction policies; work of the Freedmen's Bureau, a federal agency created to help former slaves make the transition to freedom; Black Codes created by Southern governments to ensure African Americans continued to work under strict white control; and Reconstruction governments that included many African Americans before being dismantled politically. When Rutherford B. Hayes withdrew federal troops from Southern capitals in 1877, new Southern Democratic governments took advantage of their free rein to roll back the advances of Reconstruction. For details on this series' format and style, see *Africa: A Look Back,* page 153. Social Studies LA1, SSIII, SSV, SSVI, SSVII African Americans

Riot
By Walter Dean Myers. 2009. 164 pages. Egmont. (F) **Grades 6–10**

For 15-year-old Claire and her best friend, Priscilla, life in the Five Points area of New York City had been good; but simmering tension erupts on July 11, 1863, and changes things. Claire is biracial—her father is black, her mother is Irish, but she considers herself "just" a person. Priscilla is black, and up to this point, that hasn't been a problem. However, poor Irish immigrants perceive things differently. They think they are being drafted into the Union army to fight to free African Americans while African Americans take jobs the Irish think should be theirs. In the four-day New York City Draft Riots, the angry Irish taunt blacks and destroy, loot, and burn businesses, homes, and the Colored Orphan Asylum. Using fictional characters, Myers writes a play about this little-known event and gives voice to the various sides, leaving readers to wrestle with the outcome of the issue. He includes a timeline of events leading to the riots, gives a detailed author's note about them, and provides primary source photos related to the event. Social Studies LA1, LA9, H2, H5, SSII, SSIII, SSIV, SSV African Americans, Mixed-Race Americans

Sojourner Truth's Step-Stomp Stride
By Andrea Davis Pinkney. 2009. Illus.
No page numbers. Disney/Jump at the Sun. (NF) **Grades K–5**

Her master named her Isabella, but her parents called her Belle. By age 6 she was over six feet tall with size-twelve feet. Even while serving three slave masters, Belle had a determination that one day she would be free. When her master, John Dumont, wouldn't allow her to buy her freedom, she ran. She reached Quaker Isaac Van Wagener's house, but Dumont caught her. Van Wagener purchased Belle and immediately freed her. Celebrating her freedom, she went to work to free others. She changed her name to Sojourner Truth and began her many trips into slave territory to free both her family and strangers. She couldn't read or write, but she could talk; and talk, she did! In 1850, she told her own story to Olive Gilbert who wrote it as *The Narrative of Sojourner Truth: A Northern Slave*. She step-stomped to a women's rights convention in Akron, Ohio, and after hearing men preachers decry the role of women, she marched to the pulpit and delivered a fiery, impassioned speech about the rights of women. Andrea and Brian Pinkney join their talents to present an almost "tall tale" version of Sojourner's life. They also provide a short biography, photographs, and further readings. Language Arts, Social Studies LA1, LA9, SSIII, SSIV, SSV, SSVI, VA 4, VA6 African Americans

Stella Stands Alone
By A. LaFaye. 2008. 245 pages. Simon & Schuster. (F) **Grades 5–9**

Fourteen-year-old Stella has two problems: she is an orphan, and the bank has foreclosed on the family property and plans to hold a public auction. She wants to honor her dead father's wish to free their slaves and give them the plantation. However, with the deadline looming, Stella must find her father's will to prove all his debts are paid and show that she and the former slaves are the rightful owners. Her tenacity and stubbornness don't waver, even when she has to ask a carpetbagging Yankee to bid on the property to give her more time. The fast-paced, engaging story, a strong female protagonist, and just enough mystery keep the plot moving. Social Studies LA1, SSII, SSIII, SSIV, SSV, SSVI African Americans

A Sweet-Sounding Place: A Civil War Story of the Black 54th Regiment
By Nancy Johnson. 2007. 128 pages. Down East. (F) **Grades 4–7**

Sixteen-year-old Moses sneaks onto the boat carrying the Fifty-Fourth Massachusetts Regiment. He hopes to join up and find his birth family. Uncle Daniel has raised him as a freedman in Boston. He's too young to fight, so he helps Cook and cares for three scared young slaves who have made it across the Union lines. While fishing to augment the regiment's meager dinner, an alligator attacks him. A young black Indian girl rescues him. The story only touches on the maneuvers of the Fifty-Fourth; however, it gives a warm picture of a young man searching for his roots, but finding family with his fellow soldiers who love him. Social Studies LA1, SSII, SSIV African Americans, American Indians, Mixed-Race Americans, Seminoles

They Called Themselves the K.K.K.:
The Birth of an American Terrorist Group
By Susan Campbell Bartoletti. 2010.
Illus. 172 pages. Houghton Mifflin. (NF) **Grades 7–12**

In 1886, six former Confederate offices began meeting weekly in Pulaski, Tennessee. The speculated purpose of their meetings was to discuss the political situation in the South. As time passed, more men joined the group; similar groups formed in neighboring towns. In 1867, in Nashville, Tennessee, they met to "create a secret empire powerful enough to overthrow Republican rule." Between 1867 and 1876 the Ku Klux Klan grew and expanded into most Southern states. The purpose of their midnight rides was to scare African American families and communities. Looting, lynching, beating, and burning became their hallmark. Toward the end of the 1800s, the Klan's activities waned; however, as nostalgia about the Civil War became the norm in the early 1900s, they became active again. During the Civil Rights era, they murdered and killed in the name of white supremacy. In her lengthy author's note, Bartoletti describes her visit to a Klan Congress held in the mountains of north Arkansas. Her description of this meeting is as chilling as any other part of the book—and shows the undercurrent of radical white hate groups in America. Includes primary source

documents and photographs, a Civil Rights timeline (beginning in 1863), quote attributions, a bibliography and source notes, acknowledgments, and an index.
Social Studies LA1, SSII, SSIII, SSIV, SSV African Americans

United No More! Stories of the Civil War
By Doreen Rappaport and Joan C. Verniero. 2006. Illus.
132 pages. HarperCollins. (NF) **Grades 5–8**

The first short chapter describes the beginning of the war; each remaining chapter focuses on individual people who, for various reasons, are important to the Civil War. When Jefferson Davis commands farmers to sell food to soldiers for half-price, Mary Jackson leads women in a march called "Bread or Blood" because their children are starving. William H. Carney, a member of the Massachusetts 54th Colored Infantry, never lets the Union flag fall in a fierce battle and is the first African American to receive the Congressional Medal of Honor. At the end of each story, the authors give further explanation about the people. The book includes a pen-and-ink drawing, a map, or both with each story. The back matter includes a timeline from 1787 when slavery became legal to 1865 when the Thirteenth Amendment was ratified; the text to Lincoln's Second Inaugural Address; acknowledgments for each story; selected research sources; books and websites for young readers; and a detailed index. Social Studies LA1, SSII, SSIII, SSIV, SSV, SSVI African Americans

When I Crossed No-Bob
By Margaret McMullan. 2007. 209 pages. Houghton Mifflin. (F) **Grades 4–8**

Abandoned 12-year-old Addy O'Donnell finds a new way of living when Frank and Irene Russell take her in. She likes learning, enjoys helping them, and makes two new friends. For the first time, she sees a life of promise ahead of her. Then she witnesses a terrible event, and her vicious father, absent for years, comes to claim her. Not wanting to bring the wrath of the O'Donnell clan down on Frank and Irene, Addy goes back to the isolated community of No-Bob. When she pieces together her father's plans, she knows she must take action. But how? Addy's first-person narrative immerses the readers in Reconstruction-era Mississippi: the actions of the Ku Klux Klan, the dilemmas of Choctaw residents, and the struggles of a small town. Social Studies LA1, SSII, SSIII, SSIV, SSV, SSVI African Americans, American Indians, Choctaw

EARLY WAVES OF IMMIGRATION

At Ellis Island: A History in Many Voices

By Louise Peacock. 2007. Illus. 44 pages. Atheneum. (F) **Grades 3–6**

Peacock intertwines two fictional stories (one of a modern girl touring Ellis Island and one of a fictional 10-year-old Armenian girl, Sera, coming to America through Ellis Island in 1910 to join her father) with informational blocks about immigration and actual quotes from immigrants and immigration officials. Sera's letter to her dead mother describes her experiences on the voyage and in the processing center of Ellis Island. Archival photographs and Walter Krudop's insightful gouache paintings lend authenticity to Peacock's fictional work. Because of the layout of the book, younger students may need help ciphering fiction from factual information. Includes further suggested readings and websites.   Social Studies, LA1, SSI, SSII, SSIII, SSIV AOD, Armenians

Denied, Detained, Deported: Stories from the Dark Side of American Immigration

By Ann Bausum. 2009. Illus. 111 pages. National Geographic. (NF) **Grades 6–12**

Bausum presents startling accounts, questions, and facts about treatment of those who come to the United States seeking a better life. She presents five poignant chapters, using these headings: "Excluded" (Chinese in the 1880s), "Deported" (Jews deported on December 20, 1919), "Denied" (937 Jews not granted entry in May, 1939), "Detained" (Japanese immigrants and Japanese Americans herded into internment camps during WWII), and "Exploited" (Mexican immigration today). She raises hard questions with no easy answers that give pause for consideration and debate. The book includes primary source photographs, resource guide, a lengthy bibliography, a detailed list of resource notes, citations, illustrations credits, and an index.   Social Studies LA1, SSII, SSIII, SSIV, SSV, SSVI, SSIX Chinese, Japanese, Jews, Mexicans

Good Fortune: My Journey to Gold Mountain

By Li Keng Wong. 2006. 136 pages. Peachtree. (NF) **Grades 4–7**

Li Keng's father lived and worked in America, called "Gold Mountain." He sent money home to his family in their small Chinese village, but he'd been gone so long, Li Keng couldn't remember him very well. In the spring of 1933 about the time of her seventh birthday, a letter from her father arrived. He would come home in nine months to bring his family to America, but to get through immigration at Angel Island, Mama and the three girls would have to pretend she was their aunt. Wong uses first person to tell of her family's experiences (some joyous, some harrowing) beginning with their 1933 journey from the village through receiving citizenship on December 2, 1941. The Depression affected Baba's illegal lottery business and brought the police several times. Wong's sparse text gives a good picture of the hard life of Chinese immigrants but leaves room for the reader to share in their emotional journey. In her author's note, she concludes the account of her family's life and gives a photo taken in 1944 when she graduated from high school. Social Studies LA1, SSI, SSIII, SSIV, SSVI Chinese Americans

Ice Cream Town
By Rona Arato. 2007. 204 pages. Fitzhenry & Whiteside. (F) **Grades 4–6**

When he and his older sister, Malka, finally leave Ellis Island to move in with their father in the Lower East Side of New York City, 10-year-old Sammy Levin is filled with excitement. As he adjusts to life in their crowded tenement, explores the neighborhood, and begins to learn English at school, Sammy must decide how he will live in this new country. He knows he doesn't want to become like his snooty, wealthy Aunt Pearl, who looks down on his "greenie" family. But he also doesn't agree with Papa, who forbids Malka to see a young man who chooses to work on the Sabbath rather than lose his job. Sammy's hardest decision, however, involves joining Herschel's gang. He loves their stickball games and knows he needs protection from the bully Luigi, but at what cost? Filled with the hustle and bustle of 1920s immigrant life, this could introduce a number of topics in the social studies classroom. Social Studies LA1, H2, H5, SSIII, SSIV, SSVII Jewish Americans, Jewish Poles

In the Promised Land: Lives of Jewish Americans
By Doreen Rappaport. 2005. Illus. 32 pages. HarperCollins. (NF) **Grades 5–8**

With her Jewish grandparents having fled Poland and Russia because of persecution Rappaport has a personal interest in exploring the lives of Jewish Americans. Here she presents life sketches of thirteen men and women who succeeded in the United States. Some are well known, others are not; but their contributions to American life are significant. Beginning with Asser Levy (1628–1682) and ending with Steven Spielberg (1946–), the author introduces one defining moment in each person's life. The textual sketch is combined with a full-page (and one-third of another) picture of the person. The expressionist art style used by illustrators Cornelius Van Wright and Ying-Hwi Hu is reminiscent of that of Emily Arnold McCully or Jerry Pinkney. The book fills a niche that enriches biographical collections.   Social Studies LA1, SSII, SSIII Jewish Americans, Jews

A Kid's Guide to Latino History: More than 70 Activities
By Valerie Petrillo. 2009. Illus. 208 pages. Chicago Review Press. (NF) **Grades 4–8**

Petrillo begins with a timeline from 1492 to 2006. She divides the book into ten chapters, each with historical background, crafts, and foods representative of the group discussed in the chapter. The first three chapters describe the spread of the Spanish from San Salvador into the Mexican Southwest. Chapters 4 through 9 each focus on a particular group of peoples: Mexican Americans, Puerto Ricans, Cuban Americans, Central Americans, Dominican Americans, and South Americans. Chapter 10 looks at "Latinos: Past, Present and Future." The book includes a bibliography of books for children and another for adults; websites for kids and websites for adults; a list of Latino museums with a description of each with contact information; a list of suggested reading for kids; Latino movies and videos; a teacher's guide with activities by grade level, K–8; history standards; and a detailed index. Other Kid's Guides from Chicago Review Press include *Kid's Guide to African American History* (2007), *Kid's Guide to Asian American History* (2007), and *Kid's Guide to Native American History* (2009). Social Studies, Visual Arts LA1, SSII, SSIII, SSIV, SSV, SSVI, SSVIII, SSIX, VA1, VA4, VA6 Latinos

The King of Mulberry Street
By Donna Jo Napoli. 2005. 245 pages. Wendy Lamb. (F) **Grades 6–8**

In 1892, after receiving new shoes from his mother and visiting all the people he knows in Naples, 9-year-old Dom awakens one morning to his mother's soft touch. She dresses him in his best pants and new shoes and they walk quickly to the Naples dock. Dom is confused when his mother makes him promise to be careful and get an education. They board a ship and his mother bargains with a sailor to hide Dom until they arrive in America. The remainder of the book is a survival and success story. Getting through immigration at Ellis Island without an adult is tricky, but with some help Dom succeeds. After spending his first night in New York in a barrel, he knows his shoes are a prized possession. He guards them almost with his life. As an Italian Jew, Dom faces prejudice, but he now understands why his mother wanted him to get an education. Napoli bases the story on the lives of both her grandfathers who emigrated alone from Italy as young children.   Social Studies LA1, LA9, SSII, SSIII, SSIV Jewish Americans, Jewish Italian Americans

Landed
By Milly Lee. 2006. Illus. 40 pages. Farrar, Straus and Giroux. (F) **Grades 4–6**

The picture-book format with Yangshook Choi's moving oil paintings belies the book's content. Most children learn about Ellis Island, but rarely do they learn about Angel Island and Chinese immigrants. Twelve-year-old Sun is joining his merchant father in San Francisco. In preparation for his immigration Sun studies arduously for months; he must know even the minutest details about his house and village in China. On the voyage, he studies his "coaching book" that helps him remember these details, but he destroys the book before he disembarks. Sun goes before the immigration board three times because he can't remember the direction his bedroom in China faces! Finally, he gives the correct answer and learns he is "landed." In her author's note, Lee gives further details about the difficulties the Chinese faced coming to America. She based her story on the life of her father-in-law, Lee Sun Chor.   Social Studies, Visual Arts LA1, SSII, SSIII, SSIV, SSV, SSVI, SSVII, SSIX, VA1, VA4, VA6 Chinese, Chinese Americans

Paper Daughter
By Jeanette Ingold. 2010. 215 pages. Harcourt. (F) **Grades 6–9**

Maggie is set to begin her internship with *The Herald*, her father's newspaper. As she assists a reporter in uncovering corruption in city hall, she learns more about her father, Steven Chen, a well-recognized journalist killed in a hit-and-run accident a few weeks earlier. Threads of information about her father don't add up—Maggie wonders who he really was. As Ingold weaves the story of Steven Chen's extended family into this captivating story, readers learn about Fai-Yi Li and how he and his sister immigrated to America in 1932. Due to the Chinese Exclusion Act, they came as "paper children" of Li Dewei, the owner of a laundry in Seattle. Maggie's journalistic skills help her begin to unravel a string of events connected to her own life. In an author's note, Ingold gives further information about the Chinese Exclusion era and immigration, and other resources for information. Social Studies H2, H5, LA1, SSII, SSIII, SSIV, SSV Chinese, Chinese Americans

Puzzle of the Paper Daughter: A Julie Mystery (American Girl Mysteries series)
By Katheryn Reiss. 2010. 181 pages. American Girl. (F) **Grades 4–6**

As Julie helps her mother in her resale shop, she discovers a tiny, carefully folded note in the pocket of a coat that Ivy's grandmother had when she was a girl. The note, written in Chinese, confuses Julie and Ivy; what did Grandmother Jiao Jie's mother mean by "*give Kai to Father when you arrive: she will bless you both with riches until we meet again, my dear Jiao Jie.*" Grandmother only remembers giving her doll to another girl on the ship. In solving the mystery of the note and the missing doll, they learn about the Chinese Exclusion Act of 1882 and how Chinese parents sent their children to America under the pretense of belonging to someone else. They are surprised at how much trivial information Chinese children had to memorize to prove they should legally enter the U.S. In e-mail correspondence with Reiss, we learned the depth of her research (we only wish the publisher had included more of it). Social Studies H2, LA1, SSII, SSIII, SSIV, SSV Chinese, Chinese Americans

HUMAN RIGHTS DURING THE
TIME OF THE INDUSTRIAL REVOLUTION

Black Elk's Vision: A Lakota Story
By S. D. Nelson. 2010. 47 pages. Abrams. (NF) **Grades 4–8**

Through a first-person narrative by revered medicine man Black Elk, readers become immersed in the history and life view of the Lakota. Born in 1863, Black Elk witnessed the brutal destruction of his people's way of life. At age 9, a fever-induced dream connected him with the Six Grandfathers, "the ancient ones—the Powers of the World." Eventually he shares his Great Vision, bringing hope to many. While he cannot change the events that cause so much suffering at the hands of the Wha-shi-choos, or white people, his worldview remains positive. Nelson, a member of the Standing Rock Sioux tribe of the Dakotas, illustrates events here in vivid acrylics and drawings in black pencil. Page borders are based on traditional Lakota geometric patterns. Numerous period photographs help connect the story to historic events. Includes an in-depth author's note, a select timeline from 1541–1950, source notes, a bibliography, an index, image credits, and author information. The end pages present a map showing various territories, villages, forts, trails, and battlegrounds.   Social Studies, Visual Arts LA1, SSII, SSIII, SSIV, SSVI, SSVII, SSVIII, VA4, VA6 Lakota, Sioux

Frederick Douglass: A Noble Life
By David A. Adler. 2010. 138 pages. Holiday House. (NF) **Grades 7–12**

Born into slavery in 1818 and taken away from his mother while still a baby, Frederick was owned by a series of hard-hearted men. Along the way, he secretly learned to read and write. Finally in 1838, he escaped and made his way to New Bedford, Massachusetts. Crossing paths with William Lloyd Garrison, editor of the antislavery paper *The Liberator*, led to Douglass's becoming a speaker on the lecture circuit and writing his autobiography, *Narrative of the Life of Frederick Douglass, An American Slave*. An outspoken abolitionist, Douglass wasn't afraid to speak his mind. Douglass ended his life in service to the U.S. and Haitian governments, but he continued to fight for the rights of African Americans until his death, February 25, 1895. Includes numerous primary photographs, a timeline, chapter notes, a selected bibliography, picture credits, and detailed index.   Social Studies LA1, SSIII, SSIV, SSV African Americans

Onward: A Photobiography of
African-American Polar Explorer Matthew Henson
By Dolores Johnson. 2006. Illus. 64 pages. National Geographic. (NF) **Grades 5–9**

Orphaned at 13, Matthew Henson went to sea as a cabin boy. His captain taught him "reading, writing, geography, history, carpentry, and how to navigate the stars." He used the knowledge when, at age 21, he began working as a man-servant for a young naval lieutenant, Robert Peary. His relationship with Peary grew as they shared the dream of reaching the North Pole. Filled with arresting black-and-white photographs and maps, this photobiography emphasizes Henson's pivotal role in their expeditions. His warmth, his skills, and his ability to learn the customs and language of the Inuit people who assisted them made him a key member of each Arctic team. Unfortunately, while back in the U.S., Henson battled the prevalent racism. Finally, years later, he was officially recognized as a true colleague. Well researched, with quotes from primary sources, a timeline, a bibliography, some web resources, and an index, this is a fascinating read. An afterword discusses Henson's Inuit son, Anaukaq, and his descendants. The focus remains on Henson and the white explorers, but the skills and assistance of the Inuit are acknowledged.   Social Studies LA1, SSII, SSIII, SSIV, SSV, SSVI, SSVII, SSVIII, SSIX African Americans, Inuits

Reparations for Slavery (Lucent Library of Black History series)
By Cherese Cartlidge. 2007. Illus. 104 pages. Lucent. (NF) **Grades 7–12**

This provides a wealth of information on reparations for slavery in the United States. Beginning with chapters that give an overview of slavery and its aftermath, this looks at the attempts made for reparations immediately after emancipation and into the early part of the twentieth century. While these failed, they spurred organizations committed to the civil rights movement. Reparation efforts from the 1960s to the present include the thoughts of Martin Luther King Jr., Malcolm X, and Lyndon B. Johnson, as well as other documents. The complexities and the controversy over reparations in both black and white communities round off this dense yet informative book. Black-and-white photographs and illustrations as well as gray text boxes help break the text. Chapter notes, a chronology, a listing of further resources, an index, and picture credits are provided.   Social Studies LA1, SSII, SSIII, SSV, SSVI, SSVII, SSIX African Americans

Sarah Winnemucca: Scout, Activist, and Teacher (Signature Lives series)
By Natalie M. Rosinsky. 2006. Illus. 112 pages. Compass Point. (NF) **Grades 6–10**

Sarah Winnemucca, named Thocmetony, or "Shell Flower," grew up in the Great Basin of western Nevada. As whites flooded the area when gold was discovered in the Comstock Lode, her people's lifestyle changed drastically. Her grandfather believed whites and Paiute could coexist, so Sarah was educated in white culture. She became a spokeswoman for her people, who were herded from their land to various Bureau of Indian Affairs reservations. Sarah's protests over these injustices led her from the vaudevillian stage to the homes of influential suffragettes. She eventually wrote a book detailing her criticisms of corrupt Indian agents and the reservation system. Rosinsky tells Sarah's story through a well-written and easy-to-follow narrative peppered with quotes from documented primary and secondary sources. For details on this series' format and style, see *George Washington Carver*, page 85. Social Studies LA1, LA9, SSII, SSIII, SSV, SSVI American Indians, Northern Paiutes

She Sang Promise: The Story of Betty Mae Jumper, Seminole Tribal Leader
By Jan Godown Annino. 2010. Illus. 33 pages. National Geographic. (NF) **Grades 2–5**

Born in 1923, Betty Mae Tiger grew to be a strong leader for her Seminole people. When she was 5, men came to "throw her bad spirits into the swamp" because her father was French and her family had adopted some of the white man's religion. Her family moved to protect their daughter. At 13, she began school. With her academic skills and her nurse's training, Betty Mae served her people in many ways. With Annino's free-verse poems and Lisa Desimini's brightly colored, elegantly detailed traditional-art oil paintings, this book is appropriate for a variety of curricular areas. The author's note gives additional details of Jumper's life. Includes an afterword by Moses Jumper Jr. (Betty Mae's son), a timeline, a glossary, a bibliography of sources, further readings, websites, a note about why she wrote the book, and detailed thanks to contributors. Social Studies, Visual Arts LA1, SSII, SSIII, SSV, VA1, VA4, VA6, American Indians, Seminoles

A Stranger in My Own House: The Story of W. E. B. Du Bois
By Bonnie Hinman. 2005. Illus. 176 pages. Morgan Reynolds. (NF) **Grades 7–12**

The whole town of Great Barrington, Massachusetts, came together to send their star pupil to Fisk University in Tennessee after his mother's death in 1885. William Du Bois went on to Harvard, pursued graduate studies in Germany, and left academics to help found the National Association for the Advancement of Colored People (NAACP). Hinman effectively traces Du Bois's concept of "voluntary segregation" and the "talented tenth" (his opposition to Booker T. Washington's "Tuskegee Machine"), his belief in education as the preeminent means to change society, and his rocky relationship with the NAACP. The chronological narrative presents Du Bois's opinions and life, the Jim Crow laws in effect, the political landscape within the U.S., and the frustration of African

Americans attempting to achieve parity. Numerous black-and-white and color photographs and illustrations, a timeline, source notes (mainly from Du Bois's autobiography), a bibliography, websites, and an index are provided. While dense, this is a well-written, rewarding source. Social Studies LA1, SSIII, SSIV, SSV, SSVI, SSVII, SSIX, SSX African Americans

Sweetgrass Basket
By Marlene Carvell. 2005. 243 pages. Dutton. (F) **Grades 5–8**

After their mother's death in the early 1900s, Sarah and her older sister, Mattie, are sent to the Bureau of Indian Affairs Carlisle School in southern Pennsylvania. Headed by the hate-filled Mrs. Dwyer, the girls get a rudimentary education and learn basic tasks. A mean older girl makes Mattie's life difficult, and the drudgery of the daily routine wears on all the children. After being falsely accused of theft, Mattie runs away, leading to the tragic ending to a bleak, yet highly moving tale. In free verse through each girl's voice, chapters alternate in different typeface describing the harsh conditions and cruel attitudes they encounter daily. Mohawk words scattered here and there convey the girls' longing for home, while their inner thoughts poignantly reveal their love for each other, their grief over their mother's death, and their loneliness as they endure life in a strange and hostile culture. Social Studies LA1, SSIII, SSIV, SSV, SSVI, SSVII American Indians, Mohawks

WORLD WAR I, THE 1920S, AND GREAT DEPRESSION

Celeste's Harlem Renaissance: A Novel
By Eleanora E. Tate. 2007. 279 pages. Little, Brown. (F) **Grades 5–8**

Life keeps changing for 13-year-old Celeste. Her mother and baby brother have died; now her father has tuberculosis. Poppa wires Aunt Valentina to inquire if Celeste might come live with her in Harlem because on her last visit home, Valentina convinced people she was a star in Harlem. What a surprise awaits Celeste—none of what Valentina said was true! Celeste and her aunt live in a windowless boardinghouse room and help sweep, mop, and scrub floors in a theater, but even these are tolerable because it's 1921 in Harlem. Celeste loves Harlem but misses her father and friends back in Raleigh. In this coming-of-age novel, she learns an important lesson about the meaning of family and promise. In her author's note, Tate explains how she researches historical fiction and how she integrates fictional characters and real people into a story true to time and place.   Social Studies LA1, SSII, SSIII, SSIV, SSV, SSVI African Americans

Children of the Great Depression
By Russell Freedman. 2005. Illus. 118 pages. Clarion Books. (NF) Grades 5–12

Freedman's account of the Great Depression draws on a variety of primary sources to present the impact it had on children and teens throughout the country. Facts and figures are woven into the narrative in a seamless manner, giving essential background with quotes from the Depression: "One child who looked ill when she arrived at school was told by her teacher to go home and get something to eat. 'I can't,' she replied. 'It's my sister's turn to eat.'" Freedman focuses on events significant to young people: school (or the inability to go to school), work (spending all daylight hours in a field, looking for a job, feeling helpless to contribute to the family), and often losing one's home, family, and sense of security. He includes some information on African American children and teens. The book itself is arresting: every double-page spread in this oversize book includes moving photographs that capture the reader's attention. Documentation includes chapter notes of quoted material, an excellent bibliography, picture sources, and index. Despite its sometimes grim subject, the book ends on a hopeful note, giving information on movies, music, and radio programs of the times, two world's fairs, and the strength of the generation of children who lived through this time.   Social Studies LA1, SSII, SSIII, SSV, SSVI, SSVII African Americans

El lector (The reader)
By William Durbin. 2006. 195 pages. Wendy Lamb. (F) Grades 5–8

Thirteen-year-old Bella loves her grandfather's stories and desperately wants to become a lector, just like him. Every day, Grandfather is paid to read in Spanish to the cigar factory workers. From classics such as *Don Quixote* to national and international newspapers, his resonant voice entertains and informs—especially about union issues. Factory owners in Florida's Ybor City want to crush the tobacco union and its impending strike, so they fire Grandfather. Bella's school career ends and she begins working with her aunt in the cigar factory. The third person singular narrative allows Durbin to give background information necessary to understanding Bella's life. While at times this slows the story's pace, it effectively describes the hot Depression-era Florida town in which Bella's widowed mother is trying to raise her two children. Bella's character is convincing as we learn of her aspirations, her frustration with her out-of-control brother, her fear when her Tía Lola is unjustly arrested and jailed, and her eventual plan to get her family back on its feet. This solid historical fiction, based on true events, explores racism, the Depression, the labor movement, and the role of Spanish, Cuban, and Latin American immigrants.   Social Studies LA1, SSII, SSIII, SSVI, SSVII Cuban Americans, Latinos

The Harlem Hellfighters: When Pride Met Courage
By Walter Dean Myers and William Miles.
2006. Illus. 150 pages. HarperCollins. (NF) **Grades 7–12**

In 1916 America still carried the wounds of slavery; African American poverty was a reality; equality was only a dream. For some, joining the military seemed a way to address all three. For African Americans, proving themselves worthy to serve their country was important. However, the Army was still mostly whites-only. The first totally black regiment, the Fifteenth New York National Guard, was formed in mid-1916. The 359th Infantry Regiment evolved out of the Fifteenth; and, after their heroic efforts fighting alongside the French in a bloody battle of World War I, the men became known as the Harlem Hellfighters. Myers and Miles have compiled an excellent history of the role of African American soldiers in all U.S. wars, but particularly in World War I. Using primary source documents and photographs they take readers through the long struggles African Americans faced in America. They present the horrors of war and the heroics of these soldiers, but an index would have made it much more useful.
Social Studies LA1, SSII, SSIII, SSIV, SSV, SSVI African Americans

The Harlem Renaissance
(Drama of African-American History series)
By Dolores Johnson and Virginia Schomp. 2008.
Illus. 80 pages. Marshall Cavendish. (NF) **Grades 5–10**

For a description of this book and the book, *The Harlem Renaissance: An Explostion of African-American Culture,* see page 182.

The Harlem Renaissance: An Explosion of African-American Culture
(America's Living History series)
By Richard Worth. 2009. 128 pages. Enslow. (NF) **Grades 6–12**

Following the same general pattern, these two books give background events that led to the rise of Harlem as a neighborhood that provided ferment for the Harlem Renaissance movement in literature, music, and art; short biographical information about the role of giants in each of these areas; and events that led to the decline and death of the movement. Johnson's book is geared toward a bit younger audience; the text, layout, and design are cleaner with more white space. While Worth's text is clear, it is obviously designed for a slightly more advanced audience. Both books contain numerous documented archival photographs (often the same photos). Each book has further readings; each has chapter notes; each has a glossary and index. One added benefit of Worth's book is the timeline of the rise and fall of the Harlem Renaissance. Language Arts, Music, Social Studies, Visual Arts LA1, LA9, MU8, MU9, SSI, SSII, SSIII, SSIV, SSV, SSVI, VA4, VA6 African Americans

Langston Hughes (Poetry for Young People series)
By Langston Hughes. Edited by Arnold Rampersad and David Roessel. 2006.
Illus. 48 pages. Sterling. (NF) **Grades 6–12**

Roessel and Rampersad have collected twenty-six of Langston Hughes's most famous poems, here illustrated with Benny Andrews's bright, incredible collage-and-watercolor paintings. Probably Andrew's art will be the real appeal for children. The introduction to the volume gives a short but detailed biography of Hughes. Accompanying each poem is a brief introduction and explanation of unfamiliar terms or people mentioned. Language Arts, Visual Arts LA1, LA9, SSII, SSIV, VA1, VA4, VA6 African Americans

Surprising Cecilia
By Susan Gonzales Abraham and Denise Gonzales Abraham.
2006. 220 pages. Cinco Puntos. (F) **Grades 5–8**

Although embarrassed by wearing her brother's boots the first day of high school, Cecilia doesn't complain. After all, Mamá thinks she should stay home to learn to be a good farmwife! Peppered with her aunt's *dichos*, or proverbs, Spanish phrases, and the authors' family photographs, this warm family story highlights the struggles of a young southern New Mexico girl in the 1930s who dreams of an education. Episodic chapters recount her struggles to fulfill her household chores, adjust to the different culture of the town kids, help care for new twins in her family, *and* keep an A average at school. Sequel to *Cecilia's Year* (2004).   Social Studies LA1, SCI, SCV, SSIII, SSIV, SSV Latinos

Tough Times
By Milton Meltzer. 2007. 168 pages. Clarion. (F) **Grades 6–10**

Life in the Great Depression is hard—people are out of work, people are hungry, and World War I vets can't get the bonus pay the government promised. Joey Singer's family is no different from thousands of others. His father's window-washing business is shrinking, so Joey works on a 2 a.m. milk delivery run. He is trying to finish high school, and his hopes for a college scholarship seem dim. As the veterans' march on Washington escalates, Joey accompanies his father to Washington for the protest; tragedy occurs, and Joey feels guilty. How he overcomes this guilt and moves on with his life brings the story to a satisfying conclusion. Meltzer loosely bases the story on his own experiences, and although Joey's character moves the story along, he is less important than the depiction of life in the Great Depression. Includes an author's note.   Social Studies LA1, SSIII, SSIV, SSVI Jewish Americans

THE 1940S AND WORLD WAR II

Annie's War
By Jacqueline Levering Sullivan. 2007. 183 pages. Eerdmans. (F) **Grades 4–7**

In 1946, 10-year-old Annie Leigh is sent to live with her grandmother in Walla Walla, Washington, to recover from a burst appendix. She looks forward to helping in Grandma's small neighborhood grocery. What she doesn't expect is the tension caused when Grandma rents to an African American woman, Miss Gloria. Furthermore, Annie misses her father, a soldier declared missing in action, and doesn't understand why her once-cheerful Uncle Billy has turned so mean. Her imaginary conversations with President Truman reveal her anxieties as she gets to know Miss Gloria and tries to piece together why folks act the way they do. Annie's first-person narrative is smart and sassy, and there is plenty of humor in her view of the world despite the trials she faces.   Social Studies LA1, SSII, SSIII, SSIV, SSV, SSVI, SSVII African Americans

The Baptism
By Shelia P. Moses. 2007. 130 pages. Margaret K. McElderry. (F) **Grades 5–8**

Twelve-year-old twins Leon and Luke Curry must clean up their "sinning ways" before being baptized on Sunday. What a difficult time they have being good! They've had to adjust to a new stepfather they call "Filthy Frank" and deal with their older brother, "Joe Nasty." Twin Leon, who narrates the story, often finds himself in trouble with his ma. His twin, Luke, is good, minds Ma, and gets along with Frank. The story takes place in one week, from Sunday to Sunday, with each chapter sequentially following each day. The week is filled with fun, trouble, sadness, love, and revelations about the extended white side of the family. Leon says he will never be ready for the "mournin' bench" or the baptism. Will he? Moses has a way of weaving characters from her other books into this one to give readers connections.   Social Studies LA1, LA9, SSIII, SSIV, African Americans

Best Friends Forever: A World War II Scrapbook
By Beverly Patt. 2010. Illus. 92 pages. Marshall Cavendish. (F) **Grades 4–7**

Louise and Dottie, both 14, have grown up together, but their lives are disrupted when Japan bombs Pearl Harbor on December 7, 1941. All persons of Japanese ancestry in the western U.S. are rounded up and shipped to internment camps. Dottie's family is taken to the Puyallup Assembly Center in Washington State. Louise decides to keep a scrapbook while Dottie is gone. She writes long diary entries and includes newspaper clippings, letters from Dottie, personal memorabilia—anything to keep a record of these years. The appealing scrapbook style adds authenticity to the fictional story of friendship. We contacted the author to ask why she and her editor decided, contrary to historical fact, not to censor the parts of Dottie's letters in which she describes or complains about conditions in the camp; she said they felt this would confuse young readers. We, however, recommend discussing censorship with students when using the book.   Language Arts, Social Studies LA1, LA9, SSII, SSIII, SSIV, SSV, SSVI Japanese Americans

Code Talker: A Novel about the Navajo Marines of World War Two
By Joseph Bruchac. 2005. 231 pages. Dial. (F) **Grades 7–12**

Sixteen-year-old Ned Begay hates the Navajo mission school. Teachers tell him to forget his Navajo ways and never to speak the Navajo language. In a great irony of World War II, the Marine Corps suddenly places great value on the Navajo language. Young Navajo men are recruited to use their language to create an unbreakable code. (Navajo is one of the most difficult of all American Indian languages to learn; only Navajo people speak it fluently.) Ned joins this select group of Navajo who create a code the Japanese can't break. As he shares his memories with his grandchildren, he tells them about school, his military training, and his time in the Pacific during the war. Navajo code talkers bravely served their country but couldn't even discuss their role until the late 1960s. The author interviewed code talkers for this novel. He includes three bibliographies, on the Navajo nation, code talkers, and World War II.   Social Studies LA1, SSII, SSIII, SSV, SSVI, SSIX American Indians, Navajos

Counting Coup: Becoming a Crow Chief on the Reservation and Beyond
By Joseph Medicine Crow and Herman J. Viola.
2006. Illus. 128 pages. National Geographic. (NF) **Grades 6–9**

With a traditional storyteller's sense of timing, joie de vivre, and sense of humor, this autobiography gives a fresh look at Absarokee tribal life and life within the white world. Joseph Medicine Crow is a member of the Whistling Water Clan, one of ten clans of the Crow nation. Born in 1913, he spent much time as a child with his many grandparents on the reservation in Montana: "Although times were tough for the old people, for us kids, life was good. We played lots of games and had no worries." As he progresses through his story, Joseph Medicine Crow shares anecdotes, history, conditions of the times, and descriptions of people to give a rounded view of his world. The first-person narrative brings the story alive, and the framing element of counting coup (the elders counted his successful completion of leading his men on a harrowing assignment in World War II as his first war deed) sets the tone for learning about the Crow traditions described throughout the book.   Social Studies LA1, LA9, SSIII, SSIV, SSV, SSVI American Indians, Crows

The Fences between Us: The Diary of Piper Davis (Dear America series)
By Kirby Larson. 2010. 313 pages. Scholastic. (F) **Grades 4–7**

Thirteen-year-old Piper Davis reveals her innermost thoughts to her diary—thoughts she cannot express to others. Her brother, Hank, is in the navy, and her family never knows where his ship is—or if he is alive. Now the government is rounding up all their Japanese neighbors; and Piper, whose father is a Baptist minister with a Japanese church, watches in dismay as people she loves are taken away. When her father decides to minister to his Japanese congregation in the Minidoka War Relocation Center in Eden, Idaho, Piper finds herself living in Minidoka and attending school with her best friend, Betty. Readers see the hope and despair, resilience and resignation, of those in the camp through Piper's eyes. Many details of life during World War II are included, making the tensions in the U.S. ring true: the information blackouts on troop movements, the delays in letters from the troops, boys missing in action, and the racism directed at American citizens of Japanese ancestry. The author includes a historical note, photos, maps, a copy of Franklin D. Roosevelt's speech to the U.S. Congress after Pearl Harbor was hit, and a short history of the pastor on whom Piper's father is modeled.   Language Arts, Social Studies, LA1, SSIII, SSIV, SSV, SSVI, SSIX Japanese Americans

Fighting for American Values, 1941–1985 (Latino American History series)
By Robin S. Doak. 2007. Illus. 106 pages. Chelsea House. (NF) **Grades 5–9**

In the preface by consulting editor, Mark Overmyer-Velázquez, readers first learn that Latino "refers to immigrants (and their descendants) who originally came to the United States from the Spanish-speaking countries of North, Central, and South America, as well as from countries in the Caribbean." The decades covered here are filled with both strife and advancement as Latinos sign up en masse to fight in World War II; return home to face institutionalized discrimination and tough employment options; are deported and then re-invited to work as *braceros* in fields and factories; migrate from the Americas, Puerto Rico, and the Caribbean; and, struggle for civil rights. At the end of this period there is a growing influence on U.S. culture from Latino music, art, cinema, literature, and sports, and some gains in political influence. Written in a clear and organized manner with short sentences and easy-to-navigate vocabulary. Clearly subdivided, with photographs and "Fast Fact" text boxes, the book includes a timeline, a glossary, further reading, a bibliography, an index, photo credits, and author information.   Social Studies LA1, LA9, SSIII, SSV, SSVI, SSVII, SSIX Latinos

Freedom Train
By Evelyn Coleman. 2008. 140 pages. Margaret K. McElderry. (NF) **Grades 3–6**

To shore patriotism and freedom following World War II, the U.S. attorney general's office and the American Heritage Foundation collected over one hundred of the nation's most precious documents and put them on a train to traverse the forty-eight states between 1947 and 1949. Because the city agreed to host integrated viewing, Atlanta was one of the three hundred stops. Twelve-year-old Clyde Thomason is selected to say the Freedom Pledge at the exhibit opening. Clyde has three problems: he stutters; he is bullied; and he has a secret African American friend, William. Clyde's older brother, Joseph, a Marine guard on the train, writes and encourages Clyde to relax so he doesn't stutter. Racial tensions mount as white bosses incite their workers to fear and hate African Americans. Clyde begins to understand Joseph's message in his letters: "Become different, and learn to stand up for what you know is right." Can he take these words to heart?   Social Studies LA1, LA9, SSII, SSIII, SSIV, SSV, SSVI African Americans

House of the Red Fish
By Graham Salisbury. 2006. 291 pages. Wendy Lamb. (F) **Grades 5–9**

Continuing the story of Tomi Nakaji told in *Under the Blood-Red Sun,* this details Tomi's efforts to restore his father's fishing boat. Sunk by the U.S. Army after Papa was arrested, it lies in the Ala Wai canal. How can a 14-year-old possibly raise it? Tomi is determined to have the boat afloat by the time his father gets home—whenever that will be. Salisbury richly details the impact of the attack on Pearl Harbor, from nighttime curfews and blackouts to the need to carry a gas mask and identification at all times. The first-person narrative allows Tomi to give background on his friends and family in a seamless fashion, giving the cast of characters depth. The dialogue includes Hawai'ian and Japanese words (a glossary is appended), and Tomi and his friends switch from "proper" English to their own type of street language. Most important, Tomi's determination and his friends' loyalty in the face of racism engendered by the war bring home the theme that seeing past the surface is the way to keep a community safe.   Social Studies LA1, LA9, SSII, SSIII, SSV, SSVII, SSIX Japanese Americans

Missing in Action
By Dean Hughes. 2010. 228 pages. Atheneum. (F) **Grades 5–9**

When his father goes missing in World War II, 12-year-old Jay hopes to make a fresh start in his mother's hometown of Delta, Utah. His hopes are dashed when cheerful and popular Gordy dubs him "Chief" upon learning Jay's dad is Navajo. Things worsen as Jay learns the teen he'll work with at his grandfather's farm is Japanese American. However, Ken seems as American as anyone, and Gordy is friendly and cheerful; Jay slowly begins to see how prejudice can be overcome through personal relationships. The third-person limited point of view allows the reader to trace Jay's progressively widening understanding of his world and his gradual acceptance that life with his abusive father wasn't the idealized life he wishes it had been. Plenty of action and dialogue keep this relevant, insightful book flowing.   **Physical Education, Social Studies LA1, PE6, SSIII, SSIV, SSV, SSVI Japanese-Americans, Navajo, Mixed Race Americans**

The Return of Buddy Bush
By Shelia P. Moses. 2006. 143 pages. Margaret K. McElderry. (F) **Grades 5–8**

Pattie May's grandfather died at the end of *The Legend of Buddy Bush* (2004). Everyone, particularly Pattie May, is sad that Buddy Bush wasn't at the funeral. Buddy had recently escaped from jail as the Klan broke in to try to hang him. As 12-year-old Pattie May puts Grandpa's obituary in the wooden chest with the obituaries of previous generations, she wonders about her Uncle Buddy and hopes he really is safe. Pattie May goes to Harlem with her older sister after the funeral and begins her sleuthing. She learns that Uncle Buddy was at Grandpa's funeral, dressed as a gravedigger. Uncle Buddy visits her in Harlem and tells her he is going back to see Ma Jones and face whatever trial awaits him. Moses explains in her author's note that after leaving readers hanging at the end of *The Legend of Buddy Bush*, she had to finish the story her grandmother told her. Through research, she learned the rest of Buddy Bush's story.   **Social Studies LA1, LA9, SSII, SSIII, SSIV, SSV, SSVI African Americans**

The Tragic History of the Japanese-American Internment Camps (From Many Cultures, One History)
By Deborah Kent. 2008. 128 pages. Enslow. (NF) **Grades 7–12**

Kent's book is a good addition to a collection about the internment of Japanese during World War II. In the frenzied aftermath of the bombing of Pearl

Harbor, white American leaders, including President Roosevelt, felt that people of Japanese descent living on the western coast of the U.S. should be moved to isolated places until the war ended. In haste, people with Japanese heritage were ordered to leave behind their homes, businesses, farms, and pets, and report to relocation centers. With little thought for these loyal people, the government put them in makeshift barracks surrounded by barbed-wire fences. Kent shows their determined nature and their desire to resume a normal life. She also compares treatment of the Japanese Americans to that of Arab Americans following 9/11. Includes a timeline from 1849 to 1988, chapter notes, a glossary, further readings, websites, and an index. Social Studies LA1, SSII, SSIII, SSIV, SSV, SSVI, SSIX Japanese Americans

Weedflower
By Cynthia Kadohata. 2006. 260 pages. Atheneum. (F) **Grades 5–8**

Sumiko and her younger brother live with their extended family on a carnation farm in southern California. Her story begins on Friday, December 5, 1941, when she receives an invitation to a classmate's birthday party. She arrives at the party the next day, but the girl's mother won't let her in the house. Devastated, Sumiko asks for her gift back and flees. She doesn't realize how her life is about to change. In mid-May 1942, Sumiko's family is ordered to leave their farm and eventually are relocated to an internment camp near Poston, Arizona. There Sumiko meets her first real friend, a Mohave Indian boy. The remainder of the story takes the reader through the daily routine the Japanese Americans followed to endure their time in the camp. Kadohata makes the sad, lonely Sumiko come alive, showing the hope that keeps her and the other detainees pressing onward. Social Studies LA1, LA9, SSII, SSIII, SSIV, SSVI American Indians, Japanese Americans, Mohaves

FIGHTING FOR CIVIL RIGHTS: THE 1950S AND 1960S

America Dreaming: How Youth Changed America in the Sixties
By Laban Carrick Hill. 2007. 165 pages. Little, Brown. (NF) **Grades 7–12**

Beginning with a look at the changes wrought in the United States in the 1950s, this excellent resource covers culture-changing movements of the 1960s that were spearheaded by youth. This looks at the beat generation, the women's and environmental movements, and the many civil rights efforts across the decade, including black nationalism, Native American rights, and the Chicano Power movement. This comprehensive introduction to the era is graphically exciting, utilizing artwork and photographs of the times in a packed but page-turning format. Students delving into this popular decade will find a wealth of information and starting points for research; more astute readers might pick up the occasional authorial bias. Includes a timeline, an index, websites, and illustration credits, with author information on the cover flap.   Social Studies, LA1, SSII, SSIII, SSV, SSVI, SSVII, VA4 African Americans, American Indians, Latinos

Birmingham, 1963
By Carole Boston Weatherford. 2007. Illus. 39 pages. Wordsong. (NF) **Grades 5–12.**

Told from the first-person perspective of a fictional girl celebrating her 10th birthday, the free-verse poems introduce the reader to the bombing of the Sixteenth Street Baptist Church in Birmingham, Alabama, on September 15, 1963, that kills four young girls. The narrator describes events in her life leading up to the fateful Sunday morning when she is to sing a birthday solo in church. She never gets to sing. A black-and-white primary source photograph and a well-placed red graphic on each two-page spread give the reader a sense of presence and a sense of the horror of this hate crime. Photos and short biographies of the four girls are included at the back of the book. An excellent introduction or complement to the study of the civil rights movement.   Language Arts, Social Studies LA1, SSII, SSIII, SSV African Americans

Birmingham Sunday
By Larry Dane Brimner. 2010. Illus. 48 pages. Calkins Creek. (NF) **Grades 5–8**

Sunday, September 15, 1963, was Youth Sunday at Sixteenth Street Baptist Church, Birmingham, Alabama. The service didn't happen because at 10:22 a.m., a bomb ripped out a church wall killing, four girls in a restroom as they made last-minute touches to their hair and makeup. Two boys died later that day from police shootings. Using primary source photographs and quotes, Brimner pieces together the background of Birmingham (known as "Bombingham") as white actions toward African Americans escalate, sets the stage for the morning's activities, and describes events in the days to come. The church bombing and the deaths of the children on the bloody Sunday began to bring change to Birmingham. Includes text box inserts, short biographical sketches of the six children, further readings, an author's note, acknowledgments, source notes, and picture credits.   Social Studies LA1, LA9, SSIII, SSIV, SSV, VA4, VA6 African Americans

César Chávez: A Voice for Farmworkers (Latino Biography Library series)
By Bárbara Cruz. 2005. Illus. 128 pages. Enslow. (NF) **Grades 6–9**

In 1937, at the height of the Great Depression, César Chávez's family lost their farm, thus ending their middle-class life. César was 10. Poverty-stricken, the family joined the ranks of migrant farmworkers. As did other workers, the family endured great discrimination and adversity. When he was 25, César joined the Community Service Organization, a group that fought for civil rights. His work led to the 1962 creation of the National Farmworkers Association (later the United Farmworkers). Using nonviolent methods, the union eventually gained better working conditions for farm laborers. This book is well-researched, uses a wide range of primary and secondary sources, and weaves together a rich narrative about the union with quotes from participants and observers. Photographs and insets help break the text, giving in-depth information on a topic or highlighting specific quotes. Includes a timeline, chapter notes, resources, illustration credits, and an index.   Social Studies H2, LA1, SSII, SSIII, SSIV, SSV, SSVI, SSVII Latinos

The Civil Rights Act of 1964 (We the People series)
By Jason Skog. 2007. Illus. 48 pages. Compass Point. (NF) **Grades 7–10**

To underscore the need for the Civil Rights Act, Skog begins by describing life before 1964: the segregation in the South, and the Jim Crow laws in both the North and South that "controlled what kind of work African-Americans could do, where they could meet, and how they could talk to white people." He then covers the demonstrations, sit-ins, acts of civil disobedience, and other efforts of the 1950s and 1960s that helped make the Civil Rights Act into law. Included are President Kennedy's speech in June 1963, to gain support for a broad civil rights bill; the August Freedom March on Washington, DC; the church bombing and death of four young girls in Birmingham; and Kennedy's death. A lot of information is packed into this small volume, and the fact that it is not strictly chronological at times confuses. The overall effect, however, gives the reader a strong sense of why this act was so important. For details on this series' format and style, see *The Dred Scott Decision*, page 154.   Social Studies LA1, SSII, SSIII, SSV, SSVI, SSVII African Americans

Coretta Scott King: Civil Rights Activist (Black Americans of Achievement series)
By Lisa Renee Rhodes and Dale Evva Gelfand.
2005. Illus. 136 pages. Chelsea House. (NF) **Grades 7–12**

Born in rural Alabama to supportive, hard-working, successful parents who wanted more for their daughters, Coretta and her older sister, Edythe, believed they could succeed. This is not to say they didn't experience isolation, fear, and prejudicial acts—they did. Coretta earned degrees in music and elementary education from Antioch College and was accepted into New England Conservatory of Music in Boston. Shortly after beginning her studies, however, she met Martin Luther King Jr. They were soon engaged and married, but both finished their studies. Coretta balanced being a full-time stay-at-home mother to their small children with her behind-the-scenes organization of the activities. Her quiet work during the Montgomery bus boycott was crucial to its success. After Martin was killed, Coretta picked up his work. The children were still young, yet her strong support for equality and justice led her to expand her fight to include women's rights and world peace. Enough photographs and text boxes are interspersed to break up, but not distract from, the readable, interesting text. The book includes a chronology of her life, further readings, websites, a detailed index, and picture credits. Despite the lack of source notes, the book appears to be well researched.   Social Studies LA1, SSII, SSIII, SSIV, SSV, SSVI, SSX African Americans

Fire from the Rock
By Sharon M. Draper. 2007. 240 pages. Dutton. (F) **Grades 6–9**

In 1957, the school board of Little Rock, Arkansas, decides to comply with federal law and integrate all-white Central High School. Elaborate hurdles dissuade African American students from enrolling. Racial tensions run high; the black community fears for their children. Based in solid historical facts, this fictional story of Sylvia Patterson represents the hopes and the fears of black students wishing to attend Central High School. Told through a third-person narrator and through Sylvia's personal journal entries, the story spans the nine months leading to the beginning of the school year. Sylvia's parents offer their support but allow her the choice of enrolling at Central High or returning to her all-black school. The story continues for another month as the Little Rock Nine work to be allowed in the school. Concluding with historical facts, Draper paints a realistic picture of the nine students' courage in the face of white hatred.
Language Arts, Social Studies, LA1, LA9, SSII, SSIII, SSIV, SSV, SSX African Americans

Freedom Riders: John Lewis and Jim Zwerg
on the Front Lines of the Civil Rights Movement
By Ann Bausum. 2006. Illus. 79 pages. National Geographic. (NF) **Grades 5–8**

During the early years of the civil rights movement, young people galvanized themselves and traveled by bus into the segregated South to participate in peaceful protest activities. Bausum presents more than a biography of John Lewis and Jim Zwerg, key players in the Freedom Rides; she gives a realistic picture of the hatred and dangers brave people faced each time they got on a bus. The format of the book with primary source photographs and clear text will engage the reader enough to read it from cover to cover. Includes a partial roster of riders, a timeline of key moments in civil rights movement, a history of the Freedom Rides, short biographies of John Lewis and Jim Zwerg, chapter source notes, a bibliography, an index, and illustration/photograph credits. **Social Studies LA1, SSII, SSIV, SSX African Americans**

Freedom Walkers: The Story of the Montgomery Bus Boycott
By Russell Freedman. 2006. Illus. 114 pages. Holiday House. (NF) **Grades 6–12**

Tension mounted in Montgomery, Alabama, in 1949, particularly on city buses. When blacks wouldn't give their seats to whites, bus drivers would verbally abuse black riders, even if they were sitting in "their section" of the bus. Things get worse. Thursday, December 1, 1955, becomes a day of beginnings as Rosa Parks refuses to give her seat on the bus to a white person. She says, "The only tired I was, was tired of giving in." For 381 days and nights, nearly forty thousand blacks boycott the buses. With Parks as the symbol and Martin Luther King Jr. as their leader, they walk, form carpools, take black taxis; but they don't take Montgomery buses. Life is hard, but resolution holds them together. During this time, whites in Montgomery and in Birmingham commit acts of violence. They murder; they shoot at and severely damage King's house; they bomb a church, killing four young black girls. In his typical narrative style, Freedman presents this account with great skill and engaging text, accompanying it with black-and-white primary source photographs. Includes detailed chapter notes, a selected bibliography, acknowledgments, and an index. **Social Studies LA1, LA9, SSII, SSIII, SSIV, SSV, SSVI African Americans**

A Friendship for Today
By Pat McKissack. 2007. 172 pages. Scholastic. (F) **Grades 4–7**

"Our backyards are joined, but we don't go to the same school. We don't play in the same places. We've not been to each other's houses, and I can't imagine the two of us ever sharing a secret." But in her 12th year, Rosemary Patterson sees a lot of changes. Her segregated school closes, and she is the only black student in a class in an integrated school. Her best friend contracts polio and moves to a clinic in another state. Her parents divorce, but Rosemary stays on an even keel with the help of her kind teacher, a stray cat she rescues and names Rags, and her unlikely friendship with Grace, a white girl from a racist family. Filled with day-to-day scenes that highlight life in a suburban St. Louis community in 1954, this semiautobiographical novel looks at racism through the lens of a bright girl with a strong support network. McKissack creates a unique voice filled with humor and insight.   Social Studies LA1, SSIII, SSIV, SSV, SSV African Americans

MLK: Journey of a King
By Tonya Bolden. 2006. Illus. 41 pages. Abrams. (NF) **Grades 5–12**

This engagingly written photobiography of Martin Luther King Jr. is filled with primary source photographs from both his private and public life. Each has a detailed caption or description. Some photographs are disturbing and show the violence waged against Dr. King and the participants in the nonviolent civil rights movement. The book includes an eight-page detailed timeline of King's life, detailed source notes, selected print sources, photography credits, acknowledgments, and an index.   Social Studies LA1, SSII, SSIII, SSIV, SSV, SSVI, SSX African Americans

Nobody Gonna Turn Me 'Round: Stories
and Songs of the Civil Rights Movement
By Doreen Rappaport. 2006. Illus. 63 pages. Candlewick. (NF) **Grades 5–12**

Presents songs, stories, poems, quotes, and art covering the period from 1954 to 1965. Each two-page spread focuses on one person, event, or song and includes both text and a painting by artist Shane Evans. Some of the paintings are intense and starkly haunting. At the end of the book are drawings of each of the eight people featured in the book with a one-sentence description of what they are now doing, or did before their death. The book includes a chronology of important events, both author's and artist's notes, acknowledgments, source notes and permissions, further readings, websites, and an index. Earlier and equally solid books in the trilogy are: *No More! Stories and Songs of Slave Resistance* (2002) and *Free at Last! Stories and Songs of Emancipation* (2004). Music, Social Studies LA1, MU8, MU9, SSII, SSIII, SSIV, SSV, SSVI African Americans

Red Power: The Native American Civil Rights Movement
(Landmark Events in Native American History series)
By Troy R. Johnson. 2007. Illus. 112 pages. Chelsea House. (NF) **Grades 8–12**

This begins with a short introduction to the roots of American Indian activism. Earlier atrocities committed against Native Americans are better covered by other books in the series; this volume looks at the beginnings of "Red Power" and the rise of protest groups who "sought redress against the federal government for wrongs committed against Indian nations and people." It specifically looks at the "reign of terror" and unsolved murders of Lakota Sioux on the Pine Ridge Reservation. When members of the American Indian Movement (AIM) were asked to protest to publicize and thus try to stop these atrocities, events culminated in a seventy-one-day armed occupation of Wounded Knee in 1973. Seen as a watershed event in American Indian activism, Wounded Knee focused attention on the plight of Native Americans throughout the country. Source notes, a chronology, a bibliography, a list of further reading and websites, picture credits, an index, and author information are provided. Detailed and scholarly, this series could serve as a reference work for middle schools; individual titles are recommended for highly motivated researchers. Social Studies LA1, SSIII, SSIV, SSV, SSVI, SSVII American Indians

Remember as You Pass Me By
By L. King Pérez. 2007. 184 pages. Milkweed. (F) **Grades 6–9**

Silvy and Mabelee have been best friends from childhood, so Silvy is unhappy when Mama won't let her invite Mabelee to her 12th birthday party. It's 1954, and talk of a new Supreme Court ruling to integrate the schools has her small Texas town reeling. Silvy's family, too, has its troubles. With her father beginning a new job, her parents seem to quarrel more than usual. Mabelee is busy working with the new youth pastor to raise funds for the Negro school, so when the girls see each other, their words are strained. Silvy finds solace in the friendship of newcomer Allie Rae, but Allie Rae's racist comments throw her. Silvy's exuberant and candid first-person narrative moves at a fast clip and skillfully shows both overt and covert racism within her community. Students studying the civil rights movement and Brown vs. Board of Education of Topeka will find this contains excellent background.   Social Studies LA1, LA9, SSII, SSIII, SSIV, SSV, SSVI, SSVII African Americans

Remember Little Rock: The Time, the People, the Stories
By Paul Robert Walker. 2009. Illus. 61 pages. National Geographic. (NF) **Grades 5–9**

This presents the personal stories of many high school students (black and white) who braved racist mobs to attend Central High School in Little Rock, Arkansas, in 1957. This begins with the experiences of junior Elizabeth Eckford, the first black student to arrive on September 4, who was soon surrounded by a mob of screaming whites. Three hundred National Guardsmen prevented the African American students from entering the school, leaving them on their own to face a jeering, dangerous mob. Along with the students' personal experiences, the book presents basic information on life in the Jim Crow South and discusses how Arkansas' governor came to breach the federal law to integrate schools. The main focus, however, is on the students—the hatred they faced daily in the school, as well as the acts of kindness from some white students and teachers. It includes arresting photographs and illustrations, thorough source notes, a timeline of the civil rights movement, a bibliography, an index, and a list of the educational and work achievements of the Little Rock Nine. Excellent introduction to this pivotal event.   Social Studies LA1, LA9, SSII, SSIII, SSIV, SSV, SSVI African Americans

Rosa Parks: Freedom Rider
By Keith Brandt and Joanne Mattern.
2006. Illus. 54 pages. Scholastic. (NF) **Grades 4–6**

Soft pencil drawings on every double-page spread of this short, paperback chapter book add interest to the story of Rosa Parks and the successful boycott she helped lead in Montgomery, Alabama. However, it is the authors' flowing prose that moves along quickly and clearly to make this a page-turner. In eight short chapters, they detail the boycott and describe Rosa's life from childhood through her retirement.   Social Studies LA1, SSII, SSIII, SSV, SSVI, SSVII African Americans

Rosa Parks: "Tired of Giving In." (African-American Biography Library series)
By Anne E. Schraff. 2005. Illus. 128 pages. Enslow. (NF) **Grades 5–8**

The readability and the use of primary source photographs (with credits) makes the book appealing. Detailed chapter notes acknowledge sources and provide an impressive record of in-depth research. Besides the comprehensive chapter notes, the book includes a chronology of Parks's life, further readings, reputable websites, and an index. Although not a book just for pleasure reading, this is an excellent resource for student research.   Social Studies LA1, LA9, SSIV, SSV, SSVI African Americans

Simeon's Story: An Eyewitness Account of the Kidnapping of Emmett Till
By Simeon Wright and Herb Boyd. 2010.
144 pages. Lawrence Hill. (NF) **Grades 7–12**

After fifty-five years, no one has ever been punished for the kidnapping or murder of Emmett Till. Stories abound about the incidents of August 24–25, 1955—most are just that, stories. Some have a grain of truth, but others are falsifications. Simeon Wright finally agreed to give his eyewitness account to set the record straight. For those who have read the many accounts, hearing Wright's recollections brings as satisfying-as-possible closure to the senseless murder of a 14-year-old boy. Simeon's story may not match the excitement of Chris Crowe's fiction and nonfiction accounts of the trial, but he leaves a serious statement for young people to follow: "If you want an accurate account of any story, go to the primary sources. They know what really happened."   Social Studies LA1, LA9, SSIII, SSIV, SSV, SSVI, SSX African Americans

Sources of Light
By Margaret McMullan. 2010. 233 pages.
Houghton Mifflin Harcourt. (F) **Grades 6–10**

In 1962, when 14-year-old Sam and her mother move to Jackson, Mississippi, all Sam wants is to fit in. She desperately misses her father, who died a hero's death in the Vietnam War the previous year. When her mother brings home Perry, a news photographer who teaches at her college, Sam is wary. But Perry gives her a camera and tells her to shoot "anything you look at or wonder about or want to know more about." There is a lot Sam doesn't know—the unspoken Jim Crow rules of the town, whether or not her new boyfriend is like his clearly racist parents, and how Christians can gang up on peaceful black protestors who simply want the right to vote. Sam captures events of the tumultuous times with her camera. The first-person narrative gives the reader food for thought as Sam struggles with her place in the white social structure of Jackson and with the difference between right and wrong.   Social Studies LA1, LA9, SSIII, SSIV, SSV, SSVI, VA4, VA6 African Americans

A Summer of Kings
By Han Nolan. 2006. 334 pages. Harcourt. (F) **Grades 7–10**

Fourteen-year-old Esther Young wants the summer of 1963 to be different, and with the arrival of King-Roy Johnson she is certain her life will be transformed. King-Roy, taking refuge with Esther's family after being accused of murdering a white man in Alabama, is an angry young man, uncomfortable living with Esther's wealthy family but determined to follow his mother's wish for his safety. An outcast in her own picture-perfect family, Esther works relentlessly to become friends with King-Roy, who understands much better than she the ramifications of their developing relationship. Fighting his own demons, King-Roy is drawn to the ideas of black revolution espoused by Malcolm X, and as the summer progresses both teens find themselves struggling to understand and change their worlds. Complex and compelling, this richly written novel illuminates the tumultuous times and the difficulties teens face as they find their own place in the world.   Social Studies LAI, LA9, SSII, SSIII, SSIV, SSV, SSVI African Americans, Muslims

A Thousand Never Evers
By Shana Burg. 2008. 301 pages. Delacorte. (F) **Grades 5–8**

In the early 1960s railroad tracks divided Kuckachoo, Mississippi, along racial lines. Wanting to make a honey cake causes trouble for 12-year-old Addie Ann Pickett and her family. Elias accompanies his sister to the general store and fights a white boy so Addie Ann and her cat can escape. Elias goes missing and is presumed drowned. Addie Ann believes he's alive—and believes his spirit gives her strength. When aged Mr. Adams dies, he wills his six-acre garden to the community—both black and white. The whites plan and plant the garden, but they don't go back till harvestime because they assume Addie Ann's Uncle Bump has been hired to tend it. What a surprise when they find the garden overgrown with butter bean vines! In anger, the whites torch Uncle Bump's house and shed, causing further upheaval in Addie Ann's family. Burg's solid research and engaging story give a realistic picture of how life in the segregated South continued even after Brown v. Board of Education.   Social Studies LA1, LA9, SSII, SSIII, SSIV, SSV, SSVI African Americans

We Are One: The Story of Bayard Rustin
By Larry Dane Brimner. 2007. Illus. 48 pages. Calkins Creek. (NF) **Grades 5–9**

Raised by his grandmother in a racially mixed area of West Chester, Pennsylvania, Rustin was influenced by her Quaker beliefs. These beliefs set the course for Rustin's entire life. He eventually worked with almost all the leaders of the civil rights movement, even teaching Martin Luther King Jr. Gandhi's philosophy and methods, and organizing the March on Washington for Jobs and Freedom in August 1963. Every double-page spread contains black-and-white photographs with headings and captions underlaid with bright blue or brown strips of color. This short book is an excellent resource about "the 'intellectual engineer' of the Civil Rights Movement." Although the book has no index, it has source notes, picture sources, and an author's note with further resources.   Social Studies, LA1, SSII, SSIII, SSIV, SSV, SSVI, SSVII African Americans

A Wreath for Emmett Till
By Marilyn Nelson. 2005. 34 pages. Houghton Mifflin. (NF) **Grades 7–12**

In her note at the beginning of the book, Marilyn Nelson says the impact Emmett Till's death had on her as a child led her to write this book; she also explains why she wrote the book as a heroic crown of sonnets and gives a thorough definition of this type of poetry. Her powerful text and Lardy's equally powerful black-and-white tempera on cardboard drawings with a touch of red combine to produce beauty out of despair. In notes at the end, Nelson provides explanations of each sonnet, and Philippe Lardy provides explanations on his choice of illustrations. Also includes related books and a related website on this hate crime. Language Arts, Social Studies, Visual Arts LA1, LA9, SSII, SSIII, SSV, SSX, VA4, VA6 African Americans

VIETNAM TO 1990

10,000 Days of Thunder: A History of the Vietnam War
By Philip Caputo. 2005. 128 pages. Atheneum. (NF) **Grades 7–12**

Caputo, having served in the Vietnam War, initially brings his personal experiences to bear in this dense, but readable account of the "war most Americans would like to forget." U.S. soldiers served in various capacities in Vietnam from 1959 to 1975, but intense guerilla fighting lasted from 1964 to January 1975. To date, it is the only war the U.S. has lost. Each two-page spread incorporates full-page photographs, smaller photographs, and "Quick Fact" boxes and holds the interest of readers. Includes a timeline on the end-pages, a glossary, a bibliography, Vietnam War websites, a detailed index, and photo credits. Social Studies LA1, SSII, SSIII, SSIV, SSV, SSVI, SS IX Vietnamese

All the Broken Pieces: A Novel in Verse
By Ann E. Burg. 2009. 218 pages. Scholastic. (F) **Grades 5–9**

Matt Pin's mother pushes him onto a helicopter and sends him away from the war raging around them in Vietnam. Even though adopted by Americans, 10-year-old Matt can't forget the brother he left behind with their mother— the tiny brother he loved dearly. He also wonders why his birth father, an American soldier, never returned to his Vietnamese family. Matt's first-person narrative poems let the reader into his deepest thoughts. He struggles with his past, with the hatred of one of his new baseball teammates, and his fear that his adoptive mom will push him away just as his mother did. When he meets Chris Williams, a Vietnam War vet confined to a wheelchair, Matt thinks Chris must blame him for his injury. As the story comes together, Coach Robeson works to reduce the prejudicial feelings on the team, and Matt slowly comes to terms with the many conflicts in his life. Deeply moving and wholly realistic, this give a new face to ways prejudice and fear can alter lives—and how true understanding only comes when people share their stories, hopes, and fears. **Health, Physical Education, Social Studies H2, H4, H5, LA1, PE5, PE6, SSIII, SSIV, SSV, SSIX Vietnamese, Mixed-Race Americans**

Finding My Place
By Traci L. Jones. 2010. 181 pages. Farrar, Straus and Giroux. (F) **Grades 6–10**

Tiphanie Baker is scared. She's moved away from Denver and is starting high school in a tony suburb where there is only one other African American student. It's 1975, and the one person who really talks to her is Jackie Sue, a white girl from "the other side of Sheridan Boulevard." Jackie Sue lives in a trailer, a world far from Tiphanie's wealthy suburb, and is refreshingly honest. As Tiphanie begins to navigate her way into friendships with her white classmates and keep up with her parent-driven social schedule, Jackie Sue is the one constant in her life. The divide between their worlds is deep; Tiphanie's upwardly mobile and caring family contrast sharply with Jackie Sue's alcoholic, borderline mother. Can the girls remain friends? Delving deeply into the changing world of suburban America in the 1970s, Tiphanie's first-person narrative explores the meaning of friendship, the uncomfortable social borders of a newly integrated school, and the shifting divides between social classes, race, and gender. **Social Studies H2, LA1, SSIII, SSIV, SSV African Americans**

Primary Source Accounts of the Vietnam War
(America's Wars through Primary Sources series)
By Kim A. O'Connell. 2006. 128 pages. Enslow. (NF) **Grades 5–8**

Following a definition of *primary sources*, a timeline, and a map of major battle sites, the author introduces the Vietnam War through American soldiers' letters describing the Tet Offensive. A chapter giving the political history of the war leads to first-person accounts by American, South Vietnamese, and North Vietnamese soldiers that give their personal perspectives. The book also covers antiwar protests, the effects of press coverage, civilians' observations, and even songs that gained in popularity both in the U.S. and in South Vietnam. Numerous websites presented throughout lead students to further information and more primary sources. The busy but not text-heavy format has clear subheadings, photographs, and insets of primary source writings. Includes websites, a glossary, chapter notes, a bibliography, an index, photo credits, and brief author information. **Social Studies LA1, SSIII, SSV, SSVI, SSIX Vietnamese**

A Song for Cambodia

By Michelle Lord. 2008. Illus. No page numbers. Lee & Low. (NF) **Grades 4–6**

Torn from his family when the Khmer Rouge seize control of Cambodia in 1975, Arn is put into a grueling children's work camp. He and five others are chosen to play the *khim,* a traditional string instrument. Two of the players survive the final test; the others are shot. Now Arn plays music while the other children work. At age 12, all are sent to the border to fight the South Vietnamese. Arn flees and makes it to a refugee camp in Thailand. Large gouache illustrations on each double-page spread focus on Arn, showing his worried expression rather than depicting the effects of the violence described in the story. At first, the book seems too young for middle grades, but the story of Arn Chorn-Pond's life provides a compelling overview of a dark period of war. **Music, Social Studies LA1, MU8, MU9, SSII, SSIII, SSIV, SSV, SSVI, SSVII, SSIX Cambodians, East Asians**

The Trouble Begins

By Linda Himelblau. 2005. 200 pages. Delacorte Press. (F) **Grades 4–6**

"I'm angry because my dad finds something bad about everything I do, and I'm sad because I know he's disappointed in me." No matter what he does, fifth grader Du always finds trouble. He has just come from a Vietnamese refugee camp in the Philippines, where he and his grandmother lived since he was a baby. There his street smarts and active ways helped them survive. In America he can't seem to fit in and doesn't have quick comebacks to bullies' taunts; only his school counselor and grandmother believe in him. The first-person narrative brings home Du's many predicaments, and a cast of wholly believable characters—from the grouchy old man next door who ends up a friend, the nice kids in school who involve him in soccer, and the classmate who falsely accuses him of stealing a bike—keeps the plot moving briskly. Du's lack of English and subsequent mishaps as well as the tensions within his family may help readers understand more about the immigrant experience. **Social Studies LA1, LA9, SSIII, SSIV, SSVI, SSVII Vietnamese Americans**

1990 TO THE PRESENT

African-American Holidays, Festivals, and Celebrations: The History, Customs, and Symbols Associated with Both Traditional and Contemporary Religious and Secular Events Observed by Americans of African Descent
By Kathlyn Gay. 2007. 569 pages. Omnigraphics. (NF) **Grades 6–12**

This eminently readable reference work should be on all library shelves. Covering 109 events that take place across the U.S., entries include the background of the occasion or person celebrated, how the celebration was created, and descriptions of the customs and symbols of the event. Contacts and websites are included along with short lists of further reading. Numerous black-and-white photographs break the text, as do gray text boxes with further information, lyrics, or primary sources such as the Emancipation Proclamation. Printed on glossy paper, this is a browsable, useful reference source. From Bessie Smith and Charlie Parker to Juneteenth and the Odunde Festival, this is chock full of interesting and useful information. Appendixes include a chronology of significant historical events commemorated by the African American celebrations listed, a geographical list of events, a complete list of books and articles consulted for this book, and contact information and websites for all organizations represented.
Social Studies Reference LA1, SSIII, SSV African Americans

Michelle Obama: An American Story
By David Colbert. 2009. Illus. 151 pages. Houghton Mifflin. (NF) **Grades 4–8**

This biography details Michelle Obama's family history, childhood, and teenage years to bring her story to life. Her father, Fraser Robinson III, managed a city water filtration plant despite daily pain caused by multiple sclerosis. Her mother, Marian, taught her children to read at an early age, and with her husband encouraged academic achievement. The influence of her brother and her parents' commitment to have their children speak their minds and not hesitate to question authority led to Michelle's determination to excel in school and her work. Her story is told through vignettes and primary source quotes. The author delves into the Robinson's family roots in the low country of South Carolina. The book has extensive source notes, color photographs with sources, and an author note, but no index. Social Studies LA1, SSIII, SSIV, SSIV, SSV, SSVI, SSVII, SSX African Americans

Racism and Intolerance (Man's Inhumanities series)
By Charles E. Pederson. 2009. Illus. 64 pages. Erickson. (NF) **Grades 7–12**

Pederson introduces racism, prejudice, stereotyping, and intolerance in a clear, concise manner. He provides definitions and examples of each at the beginning of a chapter, and follows with in-depth discussion and examples. For the most part, his emphasis is on the U.S., although he briefly mentions the Holocaust and genocide in Yugoslavia and Rwanda. The text is broken up with a photograph, map, or text box on each page. Chapters are short and have many subheadings. Includes a glossary, more readings, websites, chapter source notes, an index, photo credits, and brief information about the author. The chilling photographs in the other books in the series could be disturbing for middle schoolers; this one, however, would suit most middle school collections.
Social Studies LA1, SSII, SSV, SSVI, SSIX AOD, Global

Sonia Sotomayor: First Hispanic U.S. Supreme Court Justice
By Lisa Tucker McElroy. 2010. Illus. 48 pages. Lerner. (NF) **Grades 4–6**

A girl growing up in the Bronx wasn't likely to become a Supreme Court Justice, but no one told Sonia that! Her mother always said, "I do not care what you do, but be the best at it." From age 10, Sonia knew she wanted to be a judge, and she knew she had to work hard to achieve that goal. Graduating first in her class at Spellman High School, receiving a full scholarship for her undergraduate studies at Princeton, and receiving a full scholarship from Yale University to study law led to her following her dream. She became a federal district judge in 1992 and heard the famous 1994 Major League Baseball case. In 1998 she became a federal appeals judge and then was confirmed by the Senate to become a Supreme Court Justice in 2009. Throughout the book, McElroy portrays Sotomayor as one who loves life and her family, respects those with whom she works, and champions peoples' rights. The photographs are either primary ones or current ones of buildings for which no archival one was appropriate. Includes "Fun Facts" about Sotomayor, important dates, a glossary, source notes, a selected bibliography, further readings, and an index. Social Studies LA1, SSIII, SSIV, SSV Latinos

IMMIGRATION

Ask Me No Questions

By Marina Tamar Budhos. 2006. 162 pages. Atheneum. (NF) **Grades 7–10**

When her family is turned away while seeking asylum in Canada after the U.S. crackdown on Muslim families, Nadira's father (Abba) is taken into custody. She and her older sister, Aisha, return to their New York City neighborhood to continue high school while their mother waits at the border for father's release. They can tell no one of their plight, for they are illegal aliens. Although their parents have pursued legal residency since their visas from Bangladesh expired, their papers have never made it through immigration. From their tight-knit Bangladesh community, the girls learn father's contributions to a local mosque implicate him in a suspect political affiliation. Star student Aisha, always the one with answers, goes into a tailspin of worry about Abba and gives up on college. Always the "average" sister, Nadira realizes she must find a solution. Her first-person narrative is tense and absorbing, and brings the reader into the heart of her family, showing their fears and hopes in the midst of an almost impossible situation. Readers will see how difficult it is to live in a country without the proper legal status—and how difficult that status can be to achieve.   Social Studies LA1, LA9, SSII, SSIII, SSIV, SSV, SSVI, SSVII, SSX **Bangladeshi Americans, Bangladeshis**

Crossing the Wire

By Will Hobbs. 2006. 216 pages. HarperCollins. (F) **Grades 7–9**

"Los Árboles is an out-of-the-way place surrounded by mountains" and offers little hope for the future. Victor Flores's father had crossed the border between Mexico and the U.S. every year to find work to support his family in Mexico, but he was killed in an accident in his last job. Now Victor is faced with the decision of making the dangerous trip for the sake of his mother and siblings. With no money for a coyote (a smuggler who assists illegal immigrants in crossing the border), Victor must go alone. He is ill prepared for the obstacles he faces, yet his drive to support his family keeps him alive. Despite the hardships, Victor manages to get to Washington State, where he finds work picking asparagus and sends his first money order to his mother. All Victor sees ahead of him is hard manual work and a healthy fear of being caught and sent back to Mexico, but he knows this will be his way of life for years to come. Hobbs deftly captures the dangers of heat, cold, dehydration, and starvation and the hope of a better life. Social Studies LA1, LA9, SSIII, SSIV, SSV, SSVI, SSVII, SSIX Mexicans

Drita, My Homegirl
By Jenny Lombard. 2006. 135 pages. Putnam. (F) **Grades 4–6**

Alternating chapters with different typefaces present this story in first person narrative from the viewpoints of its two 10-year-old protagonists, Drita and Maxie—both of whom have secrets. When Drita enters Maxie's classroom, she is a new refugee from Kosovo and speaks little English. Classroom cutup Maxie is assigned to help Drita become familiar with the school. As the two girls' lives intertwine, each reveals secrets about her home situation. Drita's mother is depressed from the trauma of life in Kosovo and the move. She sleeps all day on the couch, leaving Drita's grandmother to care for her while her engineer father drives a cab. Maxie still aches from her mother's death three years previously, but never discusses her with her friends and rarely with Grandma. Her father begins to date, which only makes things worse. Fresh and lively, the book shows the importance of friendship and of family. Maxie's upper-middle-class African American family helps counteract some stereotypes. Social Studies H2, H5, LA1, LA9, SSII, SSIII, SSIV, SSIX Albanian Americans, African Americans

How Tia Lola Came to Teach
By Julia Alvarez. 2010. 134 pages. Knopf. (F) **Grades 4–7**

Readers became acquainted with Juanita, Miguel, and their quirky Tia Lola in *How Tia Lola Came to ~~Visit~~ Stay* (2002). Now, they are back! The teachers and principal of the local school want Tia Lola to teach Spanish to the children in Juanita and Miguel's classrooms, but how can they convince Tia Lola? The children and their mother trick Tia Lola into attending the bogus "Bring a Special Person to School Day." What fun she and the schoolchildren have as she tells them about the culture of her home country. Miguel and Juanita are her translators—they don't realize how this improves their Spanish. Tia Lola endears herself to all the children. Toward the end of the book, Tia Lola has a problem—she has outstayed her visitor's visa and faces extradition to the Dominican Republic. Can the lawyer, the community, and her family convince Immigration Services to let her stay? Also see *How Tia Lola Ended Up Starting Over* (2011). Social Studies LA1, SSIII, SSIV, SSV Latinos

Indian Americans (The New Immigrants series)
By Padma Rangaswamy. 2007. Illus. 158 pages. Chelsea House. (NF) **Grades 8–12**

This comprehensive, well-documented work presents the history of Indian immigrants in North America. Beginning with a few thousand Punjabi men who came to work in lumber mills, now over 1.6 million Indian Americans call the United States home, and over 850,000 live in Canada. Rangaswamy describes laws that allowed—or barred—waves of Indian immigrants, gives a brief history of India, and explores the reasons why Indians have come to North America. She looks at socioeconomic levels, religious affiliations, tensions, and social and political action within the Indian American communities, highlighting notable achievers along the way. Photographs, charts, and study questions add interest. A chronology, a timeline, notes, a glossary, an index, and an extensive bibliography are appended. A solid introduction to Indian American communities. **Social Studies LA1, SSV, SSVI, SSVII East Indian Americans**

La Línea
By Ann Jaramillo. 2006. 131 pages. Roaring Brook. (F) **Grades 7–9**

Fifteen-year-old Miguel's father has sent money so Miguel can join his family in California. The trip across *la línea* ("the border") will be difficult, and Miguel is nervous about three things: seeing his parents for the first time in seven years, meeting his younger twin sisters, and leaving his grandmother and 13-year-old sister, Elena, in Mexico. Following his going-away celebration, Miguel takes the bus toward his first destination. However, the federals stop the bus and demand that everyone get off and be questioned. During the questioning, Miguel recognizes Elena, who has disguised herself as an Indian. The two, along with several others, are put on a bus going south rather than north. At this point the harrowing experience of crossing the border begins again. The author bases the book on stories her husband's family told and on stories she hears daily from her students. **Social Studies LA1, LA9, SSIII, SSIV, SSV, SSVI, SSVII, SSIX Mexicans, Latinos**

No Safe Place
By Deborah Ellis. 2010. 205 pages. Groundwood. (F) **Grades 7–11**

Bombs fall all around, destroying the city of Baghdad in 2003. After his family is killed and his house destroyed, 15-year-old Abdul lives with his cruel uncle.

He works for his uncle for a brief time, but one day he takes his guitar and money he has hoarded and leaves. It takes him forty days to walk from Baghdad to Calais, France. Now dirty, tired, and hungry, he is in an illegal migrant camp, looking for a way to cross the channel to England where he hopes to find safety. In a twist of events, he literally slips into the boat of a drug smuggler. Three others are already in the boat: Jonah, the young nephew of the boat's owner; Rosalia, a Romani girl; and Cheslav, a Russian teen—each hoping to escape a dismal past. Despite their lack of trust in one another, they must work together to survive the dark, stormy sea. But are they really safe? Social Studies, LA1, SSIII, SSIV, SSV, SSIX Iraqis, **Romanies, Russians**

Our New Home: Immigrant Children Speak
By Emily Hearn and Marywinn Milne.
2007. 129 pages. Second Story Press. (NF) **Grades 3–7**

Prefaced with a world map showing their countries, immigrant children share short first-person narratives that reveal their experiences in moving to Canada. Sidra, from Pakistan, remembers that in her new homeland people at school "called me names and made fun of me." Many children remember their parents encouraging them to "stay strong." And many, like Bangladeshi Nazia, still "miss my old country because of my friends and relatives." The book is divided into five sections: Leaving, Differences, Adjusting, Problems, and Feelings. Although most entries are written or drawn by upper elementary students, discussions of bullying, racism, and conditions in the students' home countries may be eye-opening to middle school students. Health, Social Studies H2, H5, LA1, SSIV, SSV **Global**

Pakistanis in America (In America series)
By Stacy Taus-Bolstad. 2006. Illus. 80 pages. Lerner. (NF) **Grades 5–8**

This begins with a lengthy and dense introduction to the geography and history of Pakistan; unfortunately, no map is given until later. The author recounts the beginnings of South Asian Indian immigration to America. The first small wave of Pakistani immigration occurred just after the partition of India in 1947 and was followed by a much larger wave beginning in 1965. The strength of this book lies in its general descriptions of close Pakistani family life, the impact of 9/11 on the Pakistani American community, and of famous Pakistani Americans. Photographs show modern Pakistanis, and the resource sections are solid;

however, the online support at www.inamericabooks.com is spotty. Social Studies LA1, SSII, SSIII, SSV, SSVI, SSVII Pakistani Americans, Pakistanis

Path to My African Eyes
By Ermila Moodley. 2007. 173 pages. Just Us Books. (F) **Grades 6–10**

Thandi Sobukwe's life has been turned on end. Her marine biologist father takes a position in California, and 14-year-old Thandi leaves her beloved South Africa to begin high school in the U.S. She makes friends, but they are white. When she meets the biracial and black teenage children of her principal and a colleague of her father, they press her to be proud of her African heritage. Thandi never spent much time thinking about her family background and puts off a writing assignment about her heritage until she and her friends laugh at her father's accent when he speak to her class. To try to reestablish a good relationship with her parents, Thandi researches her country and her parents' families. As she learns about her heritage, she realizes the importance of appreciating who she is. Readers feel Thandi's struggles in this first-person coming-of-age story. The author, a descendent of South African sugar cane plantation slave laborers, moved to California in 1987. Social Studies LA1, LA9, SSII, SSIV African Americans, South Africans

Roots and Wings
By Many Ly. 2008. 262 pages. Delacorte. (F) **Grades 7–10**

Other than speaking the language, 14-year-old Grace has no connection with her Cambodian culture. Her mother and grandmother won't talk about the family, and no other Cambodians live in Scottsville, Pennsylvania. Grandma's last wish was for a Cambodian funeral, and now Grace is in St. Petersburg, Florida, meeting relatives she never knew existed. Each new story she hears about her mother and grandmother seems to present another secret; as she unravels her family's history, she begins to understand why her mother left Cambodia years ago. Ly explores a number of themes, including immigration, acculturation, isolation, unwed mothers, family ties, and community pressures. As Grace tells her story, she uses a number of Cambodian terms (explained in the text) and brings the reader into her community. She shifts back to memories of specific events with her mother and grandmother; these slow the pace but add to the understanding of the family's inner life. Social Studies LA1, LA9, SSIII, SSIV Cambodian Americans, East Asian Americans

Shooting Kabul
By N. H. Senzai. 2010. 262 pages. Simon & Schuster. (F) **Grades 5–8**

As their family escapes from war-torn Kabul, 6-year-old Miriam slips from her brother's grasp. Now living in Fremont, California, 11-year-old Fadi can't stop blaming himself. His family has tried everything, but no one can find Miriam. Adjusting to a new language and school is difficult for Fadi—even more so after 9/11. He finds refuge with the photo club and works hard to get a winning photograph for an upcoming competition. The grand prize is a trip to India—maybe he can also go to Afghanistan to find Miriam! This moving story puts a face on war and the difficulties of immigration.   Social Studies LA1, LA9, SSII, SSIII, SSIV, SSVI Afghan Americans, Afghans

Something about America
By Maria Testa. 2005. 84 pages. Candlewick. (F) **Grades 4–6**

Badly burned during the war in Kosovo, the eighth-grade narrator of this novel in verse struggles to come to terms with her family's life as immigrants. They've lived in the small town of Lewiston for eight years. "My mother knows / I want to stay in America, / and she knows / my father dreams of home. / And I know / my mother is ready to explode." When a hate group fills her neighborhood with intimidating leaflets, the reactions of her father and her community are both unexpected and revealing. Spare verse packed with emotion makes this a page-turner.   Social Studies LA1, SSII, SSIII, SSIV, SSVI Serbian Americans, Serbians, Somalis

OTHER CONTEMPORARY ISSUES:
HOMELESSNESS, NATURAL DISASTERS, TERRORISM, AND WAR

Bird Springs
By Carolyn Marsden. 2007. 124 pages. Viking. (F) **Grades 4–6**

Living in the old motel turned homeless shelter is different from Gregory's simple life in the Navajo village Bird Springs. Two things have changed his life: the long-lasting drought that left Bird Springs with no water; and seeing his father drive off in the old truck, leaving his family with no other choice than to leave Bird Springs. Gregory doesn't want to remember his first day in his new school. He likes art class but is confused when Matt explains the class really is art therapy. Ms. Daniels, the art teacher, helps Gregory face the shadows behind the closed doors he draws—he remembers seeing and hearing his father's violent treatment of his mother, and he understands why they had no choice about coming to Tucson. The little book explores homelessness and its implications for disrupting family and cultural values.   Social Studies, Visual Arts LA1, SSIII, SSIV, VA4, VA6 American Indians, Navajos

Extra Credit
By Andrew Clements. 2009. 183 pages. Atheneum. (F) **Grades 4–7**

Abby Carson would rather be outdoors than inside doing homework, which is why she's going to flunk sixth grade if she doesn't follow her teachers' instructions. Part of her assignment includes writing letters to a pen pal. Because she loves mountains, she chooses to write to someone in Afghanistan. Eleven-year-old Sadeed Bayat has been chosen by his teacher, with the approval of the village elders, to respond to Abby's letters. He is the most skilled of all the students in the English language, and while it would be inappropriate for him to write to a girl, the elders expect him to uphold the village's honor by writing for his sister, Amira. The story alternates between Abby's life in Illinois and Sadeed's life in his village. Sadeed quickly takes over writing for his sister and even manages to write his own letters. As Abby and Sadeed learn more about each other, their letters begin to provoke resistance in their communities. Soft pencil illustrations by Mark Elliott are interspersed throughout the book.   Language Arts, Social Studies LA1, SSIII, SSIV, SSV, SSVI, SSIX Afghans

Hurricane Song
By Paul Volponi. 2008. 136 pages. Viking. (F) **Grades 8–12**

When his mother remarries, sophomore Miles moves to New Orleans to live with his dad. Miles knows he has always taken a back seat to his father's true love—jazz. After two months, Pop can't remember if it's football or basketball that Miles loves. Hurricane Katrina hits. Forced to stay in the Superdome, Miles, Pop, and Uncle Ray plan to stick together and help only each other—no one else. As conditions worsen and gangs of thugs terrorize groups of evacuees, Miles finds Pop stands up for what's right. When Pop decides to break for freedom to see if their apartment still stands, Miles makes a decision that changes both their lives. Volponi focuses on the injustices perpetrated on the primarily black residents who sought refuge in the Superdome. Quick, engaging plot, but contains explicit language and graphic descriptions of the Superdome nightmare. Music, Social Studies LA1, LA9, MU9, SSIII, SSIV, SSV, SSVI, SSVII African Americans

Joseph
By Shelia P. Moses. 2008. 174 pages. Margaret K. McElderry. (F) Grades 7–10

At 15, all Joseph wants is a normal life; he feels responsible for his alcoholic, drug-addicted mother as they move constantly from one homeless shelter to the next. Once, when they'd lived with Granddaddy, Joseph had felt safe. Now Granddaddy is dead, Daddy is fighting in Iraq, and Aunt Shirley, a lawyer, can't get her sister to give up custody of Joseph. As Joseph makes friends in his new school and joins the tennis team, he begins to see the toll his mother's addictions have taken on his life, and he makes some difficult decisions. The first-person narrative in Joseph's tenuous, almost naive voice achingly reveals the choices one boy must make if he is ever to have a life of his own. The frustration felt by the members of this strong, well-educated extended family underscores the difficulties of dealing with addiction. Health, Social Studies H2, H5, LA1, SSIV African Americans

Making It Home: Real-Life Stories from Children Forced to Flee
By the International Rescue Committee, with an introduction by Beverly Naidoo. 2005. 117 pages. Dial. (NF) Grades 4–12

Readers are introduced to children of varying ages who for one reason or another have had to flee their countries. Preceding each child's story is a brief description of his or her home country, and the political and physical upheaval caused by warring ethnic groups. From Eastern Europe to the Middle East to African countries, children have suffered death, abuse, and hunger. Some have been fortunate to escape with their families; others have been separated from their families. The common thread that runs through these stories is hope—hope for a better future, hope for returning to their home countries. Social Studies LA1, SSI, SSII, SSIII, SSIV, SSV, SSVI, SSIX Afghans, Bosnians, Burundians, Congolese, Iraqis, Kosovars, Liberians, Sudanese

Peace, Locomotion

By Jacqueline Woodson. 2009. 134 pages. Putnam. (F) **Grades 4–8**

Woodson presents characters whose situations make one want to cry, yet whose resilience inspire hope. In her continuation of *Locomotion* (2003), Lonnie corresponds with his sister, Lili, through heartfelt letters that talk about his everyday life and reflect on their family's past. Memories of Mama and Daddy are tinged with sadness at first (their deaths in a tragic house fire resulted in the siblings' current separation). He also writes about the good times the family had, and the care he feels from friends at school, his grownup foster brother, Rodney, and Miss Edna, his foster mother. Miss Edna's other son, Jenkins, is in the army, leading to Lonnie's many reflections on peace that take a new turn when Jenkins returns from Iraq in a wheelchair. Despite his determination to be upbeat for his sister, Lonnie remains fragile. This compassionate look at one child's attempts to piece together his fractured life is both heartrending and hopeful. Social Studies LA1, LA9, SSIII, SSIV, SSV, SSVI, SSIX African Americans

Ruby's Imagine

By Kim Antieau. 2008. 201 pages. Houghton Mifflin. (F) **Grades 5–9**

Ruby "talks funny" and says she talks to the birds. Believing her parents and sisters are dead, she lives in New Orleans with Mammaloosa, her unaffectionate grandmother. Ruby spends time in her garden with the birds and animals to remember her parents and sisters. Watching the birds just before Hurricane Katrina hits, Ruby knows a big storm is coming—the birds act differently and then vanish. She warns her grandmother, but her grandmother won't leave her house. Ruby and her grandmother "hunker down" in the attic as friends all around them leave. The house floods and the roof blows off, but the two are safe—albeit wet—in the attic. It is here that Mammaloosa softens and shares information with Ruby that will change her life. From chapter 1, readers understand something ominous is coming; as the story unravels they are drawn into the apprehension surrounding the lull, and they suffer with Ruby and other characters as they endure the storm. Antieau never says the characters are black or poor, but readers understand about the Ninth Ward of New Orleans. Social Studies LA1, LA9, SSIII, SSIV African Americans

Terrorist Groups (Terrorism series)
By Michael Burgan. 2010. Illus. 48 pages. Compass Point. (NF) **Grades 4–6**

In short four-page chapters with primary photographs, Burgan gives background and statistics about ten terrorist groups from around the world. There is no chronological or alphabetical order to the book, but that doesn't take away from the information. Includes a glossary, further reading, websites, a select bibliography, an index, and a note about the author. **Social Studies H1, H5, LA1, SSII, SSIII, SSIV, SSV Global**

When the Horses Ride By: Children in the Times of War
By Eloise Greenfield. 2006. Illus. No page numbers. Lee & Low. (NF) **Grades 4–8**

In this collection of twelve poems, Greenfield introduces children who have lived through war. From war in ancient China to the Iraq War, childhood hopes and dreams for a peace are paramount. Jan Spivey Gilchrist's illustrations enhance each poem by providing a backdrop and images of children. The children range from the very young to early teens, making the book appropriate for a wide audience. It personalizes the topic of war, making this an excellent choice for upper elementary and middle school classroom discussions. **Language Arts LA1, LA9, SSIII, SSIV, SSV, SSIX Global**

WORLD RELIGIONS

A Faith Like Mine: A Celebration of the
World's Religions through the Eyes of Children
By Laura Buller. 2005. Illus. 80 pages. DK. (NF) **Grades 3–7**

First-person narratives from children ages 8 through 14 help readers examine many of the traditional rituals and beliefs of religions around the world. Large, double-page spreads feature maps and photographs that depict the activities described by each narrator. Other children's photographs and thoughts underscore the world-wide nature of most religions. For example, we learn about Ramadan and Eid al-Fitr from 9-year-old Leena from Jordan; brief notes and photographs of Omar from Afghanistan and Yasmin from the U.K. add their thoughts. Prefaced by a discussion of faith and traditional beliefs, this covers Hinduism, Buddhism, Sikhism, Judaism, Christianity, and Islam. Short, one-page entries briefly look at Zoroastrianism, Shinto, Taoism, Jainism, and Baha'i. This is an engaging introduction to world religions. Social Studies LA1, SSI, SSIII, SSV AOD, Global

World Faiths series
By Trevor Barnes. 2005. Illus. Approx. 40 pages. Kingfisher. (NF) **Grades 5–12**

Barnes, a BBC religious affairs reporter, gives an unbiased view of the history and modern practices of world religions using simple two-page spreads with rich art and color photographs per topic. For each religion, he breaks infor-mation into manageable chunks. In just forty pages, he explains art, customs, education, political life, and the divisions in each group. The books are dense with text but don't appear daunting, thanks to the illustrations. Each title includes a glossary and index. Religions covered include Christianity, Eastern religions (including Hinduism, Buddhism, Jainism, and Skihism), Islam, and Judaism. This paperback series, aimed at middle school readers, serves as a solid guide to the major world faiths. Social Studies LA1, SSI, SSII, SSIII, SSV, SSIX AOD, Global

The Kingfisher Atlas of the Medieval World
By Simon Adams. 2007. Illus. 44 pages. Kingfisher. (NF) **Grades 5–8**

Double-page spreads feature maps peppered with Kevin Maddison's draw-ings of people, buildings, boats, and caravans one might find in a particular region or era. Illustrations include captions and explanations, making this an ideal browser. Maps include a locator map highlighting the world featured; on the opposite page is an extensive timeline giving the major political events for that region and era. Timelines can be compared to get a quick snapshot of the medieval world. The global coverage is refreshing; it includes African kingdoms, North and Central America, the Chimús and Incas, the Pacific, China, Japan, and Korea, Medieval India, and more. Emphasis is put on the spread of Islam and Christianity during the medieval period. Social Studies LA1, LA7, SSI, SSII AOD, Global

Life in the Medieval Muslim World series
By Kathryn Hinds. 2009. Illus. Approx. 96 pages.
Marshall Cavendish Benchmark. (NF) **Grades 6–10**

This series covers the political and social history of the Dar al-Islam, or "abode of Islam," from 622 CE to 1258 CE. This territory stretched from the Iberian Peninsula across North Africa and parts of sub-Saharan Africa; to the Arabian peninsula; through Turkey, the Middle East, parts of Central Asia; and into India. Arabic, the language of the Qur'an, was used throughout Dar al-Islam for government, law, literature, and learning. Because of this, knowledge spread quickly, causing many historians to label the period the Golden Age of Islam. We have read and recommend the four titles in the series: *The City*, *The Countryside*, *Faith*, and *The Palace*. All the books are beautifully formatted, with borders in Islamic designs, illustrations, maps, paintings, and photographs creating a visual treat. The text is well spaced, the subheadings are clear, and all graphics include explanatory captions. Most important, Hinds includes numerous primary sources and thorough chapter documentation. Each book includes a glossary, further readings, websites, a selected bibliography, source notes for quotations, an index, author and consultant information, and image credits. Social Studies LA1, SCVI, SCVII, SSI, SSII, SSIII, SSV, SSVI, SSVII, SSVIII, SSIX, VA4 Ancient Middle Eastern Peoples

Religions around the World series
By Katy Gerner. 2008. Illus. Approx. 32 pages.
Marshall Cavendish Benchmark. (NF) **Grades 4–6**

The Religions around the World series gives a broad yet brief look at the six major religions of the world. Each book presents double-page spreads that cover religious beliefs, beliefs about behavior, scriptures, religious leaders, worship practices, festivals and celebrations, important people, clothes and food, birth, growing up, marriage, death, and the afterlife. A final page in each book has a world map showing where that religion is most heavily practiced. Religions covered include Buddhism, Catholicism, Hinduism, Islam, Judaism, and Protestantism. A glossary and index are provided. As a basic, strictly nonpolitical introduction to world religions, this series will meet the needs of most middle school collections. Social Studies LA1, SSI, SSIII, SSV AOD, Global

Religions of Africa (Africa: Progress & Problems series)
By Lora Friedenthal and Dorothy Kavanaugh.
2007. Illus. 112 pages. Mason Crest. (NF) **Grades 7–12**

Over 98 percent of Africans identify themselves as followers of one of three religions: African traditional religion (ATR), Christianity, or Islam. The authors give an in-depth look at the development of all three, beginning with an informative chapter on ATR. Each of about three thousand ethnic groups has its own religious system; however, these systems have many similarities, such as belief in the existence of a supreme creator and/or spirits. Each group, too, "incorporates many ritual prayers and actions in . . . everyday life." Both Christianity and Islam took hold early in African countries and continue to grow today. However, followers often practice a tribal or indigenous religion as well. Maps, photographs, and text boxes help explain the history, and a final chapter, "Religious Conflicts in Africa," gives background information on current events. Replete with case studies, information on specific countries' wars and leaders, color photographs (some gruesome), and maps, the book is clearly organized and well written, with easy-to-follow subdivisions in each chapter. A glossary, a bibliography, websites, picture credits, and an index are provided; unfortunately, no source notes are included.   Social Studies LA1, SSI, SSIII, SSV, SSVI, SSIX Africans

7 VISUAL ARTS

Art both expresses and transcends culture. This chapter includes books about specific artists and art forms. Because many art teachers collaborate with other content area teachers, titles that we feel showcase specific artistic media and styles are found throughout this book.

Arctic Adventures: Tales from the Lives of Inuit Artists
By Raquel Rivera and Jirina Martin. 2007. Illus.
47 pages. Groundwood Books/House of Anansi. (NF) **Grades 4–7**

In an interesting format, Rivera introduces four Inuit stories and four Inuit artists. Each story is based on actual events in the life of an artist and is elegantly illustrated by Jirina Martin, who, like Rivera, has spent considerable time in the Arctic. Accompanying each tale is a biographical sketch of the particular Inuit artist, a portrait, and a sample of the artist's work. The book includes detailed notes about the stories, a map of where they took place, a glossary, further readings, acknowledgments, and photo credits. **Visual Arts, LA1, SSII, SSIII, SSIV, VA4, VA5, VA6 Inuits**

Art from Her Heart: Folk Artist Clementine Hunter
By Kathy Whitehead. 2008. Illus. No page numbers. Putnam. (NF) **Grades 4–8**

The daughter of slaves, Clementine Hunter was born in 1886 or 1887 and worked as a common laborer on the Melrose Plantation in Louisiana. About midway in her life, when Melrose had been turned into a writer's and painter's haven, she began to paint—with paint left behind after artists departed. Once several artists saw her work, they began providing her with paint and supplies. At first she sold her paintings for twenty-five cents; now they are worth thousands. Hunter wasn't allowed to attend the first two showings of her work until after the galleries closed! She died in 1988, and now her colorful folk art hangs in galleries across the country. Shane Evans' mixed-media illustrations help showcase Hunter's life and works. Visual Arts LA1, SSII, SSIII, SSIV, SSV, VA1, VA4, VA6 African Americans

Ashley Bryan: Words to My Life's Song
By Ashley Bryan and Bill McGuinness. 2009. Illus. 58 pages.
Atheneum. (NF) **Grades 4–7**

In a most compelling book, Bryan presents his life, his family, his path toward painting, and his complete satisfaction with where that path has taken him. Combining photographs from his childhood and his island home in Maine with paintings he has created through the years (or is currently painting), readers feel a connection to Bryan in a way not possible with just a book of narrative prose. The format of the book is like a scrapbook Bryan lovingly opens to share with a friend. It's as if we are walking along with him on the beach, looking for special rocks or bits of glass, as we learn hidden secrets that make Bryan the wise, caring man he is today. The book could be used on so many levels, but is particularly valuable for Bryan's artistic expressions. Language Arts, Visual Arts, LA1, SSIII, SSIV, SSV, VA4, VA5, VA6, African Americans

Beyond the Great Mountains: A Visual Poem about China
By Ed Young. 2005. Illus. No page numbers. Chronicle. (NF) **Grades 7–12**

Young integrates sparse verse, paper collage illustrations, and Chinese characters to create a unique visual experience for children and adults. The illustrations represent the Chinese characters (from Middle China of 500 BCE). It takes more than one reading to experience the full impact of the poem and art. This is a book not to be missed. Language Arts, Visual Arts LA1, LA9, SSIII, VA4, VA6 Chinese

Change Has Come: An Artist Celebrates
Our American Spirit: The Drawings of Kadir Nelson
By Kadir Nelson and Barack Obama. 2009.
Illus. No page numbers. Simon & Schuster. (NF) **Grades 5–9**

As he watched television the night Barack Obama was elected president, Nelson felt the need to create these spontaneous pen-and-ink drawings to savor his personal reaction to the events leading to the night. Using words from Obama as the impetus for each drawing, Nelson's drawings take on more meaning. Although one man's feelings are the impetus for the drawings, in their simplicity they emit powerful emotions and confirm just how far this country has come in the area of civil rights for all. Language Arts, Social Studies, Visual Arts LA1, SSII, SSIII, SSIV, VA4, VA6 African Americans

Come Look with Me: Latin American Art
(Come Look with Me: World of Art series)
By Kimberly Lane. 2007. Illus. 32 pages. Charlesbridge. (NF) Grades 5–8

Contains photographs of works by twelve well-known artists of Latin America from the eighteenth and nineteenth centuries. A short biographical sketch and brief summary of historical, political, or cultural events accompanies each work. The author also includes questions adults might use to help students appreciate the paintings and styles of each artist. The book could be used on a variety of levels: as an introduction to Latin American art and artists, an introduction to the ways artists portrayed events taking place during their lives, an overview of the use of color to express mood, a guide for students who wish to follow the style of Latin American folk art, or simply a way to appreciate a variety of artistic endeavors. Visual Arts, LA1, SSII, SSIII, SSIV, SSVI, SSIX, VA3, VA4, VA6 Latin Americans, Latinos

How I Learned Geography
By Uri Shulevitz. 2008. Illus. No page numbers.
Farrar, Straus and Giroux. (NF) Grades 3–6

In 1939, Shulevitz and his parents fled Warsaw, Poland, and lived as refugees for the next six years in the Soviet Union in Turkestan. The family shared a one-room dirt-floor dwelling with others and often went hungry. One day when Uri is 4 or 5, his father is unable to buy bread but comes home with a wall-sized map of the world. That map is what saves Uri for the remainder of their years in Turkestan. He travels far—seeing mountains and snow, a city with tall buildings, a desert, a grand palace, and other sights that help him forget his hunger and misery. When writing and painting this book in 2008, Shulevitz re-created the map and events in his early life from memory. This simple, autobiographically based picture book would be a good companion or introduction to a study of World War II.   Social Studies, Visual Arts LA1, SSII, SSIII, SSIV, SSV, SSVI, SSIX, VA4, VA6 Jewish Poles

Isamu Noguchi (Asian Americans of Achievement series)
By Caroline Tiger. 2007. Illus. 112 pages. Chelsea House. (NF) **Grades 7–12**

Born in the U.S. in 1904, Isamu Noguchi moved to Japan when he was just two due to his mother's well-founded fear that he would be the target of hostility as he grew up. Unfortunately, his father, celebrated poet Yonejiro Noguchi, had a new wife and family in Japan. Thus Isamu grew up in a small village with his mother and, later, a new sister. At 14 he traveled to Rolling Prairie, Indiana, where he attended for one summer an innovative school called Interlaken. From this point, Noguchi found a number of important mentors who helped him find his way as an artist. At 19 he held his first art show and was elected to the National Sculpture Society. Noguchi's struggles and successes with his art led him around the world. Boxed insets give readers the background to understand both artistic movements and some of the cultural touchpoints that affected Noguchi's life, such as statistics on Japanese immigration to the U.S. The main text flows well and uses a variety of primary sources that bring Noguchi's world to life. Numerous photographs add interest to this well-presented biography. Includes a chronology and timeline, a glossary, a bibliography, a list of further reading and websites, an index, picture credits, and author information.   Visual Arts LA1, SSIII, SSIV, SSV, SSVI, SSVII, VA4, VA5 Japanese, Japanese Americans, Mixed-Race Americans

M Is for Masterpiece: An Art Alphabet
By David Domeniconi. 2006. Illus. No page numbers. Sleeping Bear. (NF) **Grades 5–8**

From *A* to *Z*, Domeniconi and illustrator Will Bullas introduce art and artists to middle schoolers. Each two-page spread follows the same format: a brief poetic verse beginning with the specific alphabet letter, then text and illustrations expanding the verse. Although the book could be read as a whole, it would probably best be used piece by piece at the beginning of a unit on art techniques, art movements, or artists in an art classroom. Fascinating addition to an art collection.   Visual Arts LA1, VA1, VA4, VA5, VA6 AOD

Maya Lin (Asian Americans of Achievement series)
By Tom Lashnits. 2007. Illus. 128 pages. Chelsea House. (NF) **Grades 7–12**

Architect Maya Lin is perhaps best known for her creation of the Vietnam Veterans Memorial in Washington, DC. This book has the same conversational tone found in other titles. For details on this series' format and style, see *Isamu Noguchi*, page 222. Social Studies, Visual Arts LA1, SSIII, SSIV, SSV, SSVII, SSIX, VA4 **Chinese Americans**

My Papá Diego and Me: Memories of My Father and His Art
By Guadalupe Rivera Marín. 2009. Illus. 29 pages.
Childrens Book Press. (NF) **Grades 2–9**

Large, oversize pictures of children by Mexican artist Diego Rivera are accompanied by stories written by his daughter, Guadalupe Rivera Marín. In this intimate look at one of the world's great artists, paintings are set on a lightly designed background for each double-page spread. Across from each painting, under titles in fairly large type, Marín's story is presented in English and, below that, in Spanish. She provides interesting insider details about those who posed, objects she remembers that are in the paintings, and Mexican life and customs. The book includes a short introduction, information on where each painting is housed, photographs, author information, and a brief biographical note about Diego Rivera. Visual Arts LA1, SSII, SSIII, SSIV, SSV, SSVII, VA4, VA5, VA6 **Mexicans**

Side by Side: New Poems Inspired by Art from Around the World
By Jan Greenberg. 2008. Illus. No page numbers. Abrams. (NF) **Grades 5–12**

Greenberg says, "My quest began with an idea—to share with readers in the United States the rich tradition of ekphrasis, poetry inspired by art, written by poets from all over the world." She has collected contemporary poems from thirty-three countries and places the poems in one of four sections of the book: Stories, Voices, Expressions, and Impressions. The root of each poem is a piece of art—from figurines to a coffin to a sculpture to paintings in many media; some pieces are well known, others are not. She places the piece of art opposite two versions of each poem—one in English and one in the poet's language. She includes biographical sketches of the poets and artists and a map of the world showing the countries from which the poems come. What a springboard for student creativity! Language Arts, Visual Arts LA1, LA9, VA1, VA3, VA4, VA6 AOD

Swords: An Artist's Devotion
By Ben Boos. 2008. Illus. 82 pages. Candlewick. (NF) **Grades 4–12**

Boos gives almost everything anyone would have wanted to know (and more) about swords. Always intrigued with swords, Boos draws and paints the most intricately designed swords. He begins the book with swords from warriors and ends with swords from the Far East, Africa, and the Near East. For the most part, there is very little text other than descriptions of the various swords, but his illustrations are exquisite. Even those who aren't interested in swords will find the book captivating, almost spellbinding. He concludes the book with a note about his sources and inspirations and a long bibliography of select books he consulted. Visual Arts LA1, SSII, SSIII, SSVI, SSVIII, VA4, VA6 AOD

Romina's Rangoli
By Malathi Michelle Iyengar. 2007. Illus.
No page numbers. Shen's Books. (F) **Grades 3–6**

Assigned a class project to make something that will reflect her heritage, Romina is unsure of what to do. With the help of her family and her neighbor, Mr. Gonzales, she discovers that her Indian and Mexican backgrounds have more in common than she has realized. She brings an Indian *rangoli* design cut using the traditional Mexican *papel picado,* or cut paper. Both Indian and Spanish words are woven into the text, highlighting Romina's dual heritage. Jennifer Wanardi's bright watercolor illustrations feature *rangoli* designs and help explain other cultural details of this warm story. The author's notes give further details on *rangoli* and *papel picado,* making this a particularly useful resource for art classes. Visual Arts LA1, SSII, SSIII, SSIV, SSV, VA1, VA4 East Indian Americans, Latinos, Mixed-Race Americans

Taj Mahal (Wonders of the World series)
By Elizabeth Mann. 2008. Illus. 47 pages. Mikaya. (NF) **Grades 4–6**

The introduction tells of the love between Shah Jahan and his wife, Mumtaz Mahal. Upon her death, he constructs a temple monument to her memory. As the book unfolds, the author provides a brief look at history of the Mughal kingdom. The majority of the book is devoted to the construction of the Taj Mahal. The text and the full-page, vibrantly colored, detailed illustrations—including a map of the Mughal empire and several paintings—bring the building of the temple to life. The reader may not realize the brutality of Jahan or his sons and may be unprepared for the illustration depicting one son presenting his father the head of his favored son. The book includes a centerfold, detailed architectural diagram of the layout of the Mahal and its environs, a timeline, facts about the Taj Mahal, a glossary, a bibliography, picture credits, and an index.   Social Studies, Visual Arts LA1, SSI, SSII, SSIII, SSIV, SSV, SSVI, SSVIII, SSIX, VA2, VA4, VA6 East Indians

Vera Wang: Enduring Style (Lifeline Biographies series)
By Katherine E. Krohn. 2009. Illus.
112 pages. Twenty-First Century Books. (NF) **Grades 6–9**

Born in 1949 and raised on Park Avenue, Vera Wang learned about fashion at an early age through trips with her mother to the great houses of couture in Paris. She began working for *Vogue* magazine after graduating from college, where she met many of the top designers and quickly rose to senior fashion editor. In 1987, she was hired by Ralph Lauren, where she put her talent for design to work. She began her own company when, at 39, she designed her own gown for her wedding, opened a bridal shop, and quickly became known as a top designer of gowns for all occasions. The *USA Today* format is filled with newspaper excerpts, photographs, and "In Focus" insets that give further information on the world of fashion. The casual writing style moves quickly, giving information on Wang's family-centered private life, her travels and interests, and her thoughts on her design process. A timeline, a glossary, source notes, selected bibliography, a list of further reading and websites, an index, and photo credits are included.   Visual Arts , LA1, SSIII, SSIV, VA4, VA6 Chinese Americans

The Wall: Growing Up behind the Iron Curtain
By Peter Sís. 2007. Illus. No page numbers.
Farrar, Straus and Giroux. (NF) **Grades 5–8**

Sís has always loved to draw—even in his stroller, he had paper and crayon in his hands. As a young child at home, he drew what he wanted; once he started school, he drew what he was told; and, as an adult, now in the U.S., he again draws what he wants. In this autobiographical picture book, Sís combines a variety of all types of drawings with sparse text in the margins; double-page spread drawings; and timeline-type journal entries with drawings, photographs, or pictures as borders. On most pages he uses color sparingly, except for the red signifying Communist control. Sís shows his life in Czechoslovakia from his birth in 1948 to the fall of the Berlin Wall in 1989. His message about propaganda and censorship is powerful. His detailed drawings offer the reader many hours of intense examination. One message in his drawings that stands out is his two-page spread showing the division made by the Iron Curtain: one side showing the words we take for granted as part of freedom, the other side showing mistrust and suspicion. The front and back endpapers are black-and-white world maps with Communist areas in red. In his afterword, Sís talks about the difficulty he has explaining to his children how life in Prague was during his childhood.   Social Studies, Visual Arts LA1, SSI, SSII, SSIII, SSIV, SSV, SSVI, SSIX, VA1, VA3, VA4, VA5, VA6 Czechoslovakians, Eastern Europeans

APPENDIX A

NATIONAL CURRICULUM STANDARDS

Each title in this book has a number of curricular standards attached to it. These standards are set by national associations for their particular content field. Public school teachers are required to align their curriculum with local and state standards, most of which are aligned with national standards. Since standards can vary from district to district and state to state, we have chosen to use the broadest standards available: the national standards. We have focused on the content standards for specific curricular areas. Following are those standards; the website for the organization or association that developed and uses the standards is listed for those who would like more in-depth information.

This is a time of flux for educational standards as states adopt the Partnership for 21st Century Skills (P21) and the Common Core initiatives (see notes 2 and 3 on page 7). These groups are working with educators in all content areas to prepare students for success. While not all states have adopted these initiatives, many are incorporating them into their curriculum. Associations with content area standards are working to mesh their skills and themes with those of P21 and the Common Core. We are confident that the materials chosen for this book will meet many of the standards and will help students achieve learning objectives set forth by their school districts.

Dance (D + #) National Dance Standards. National Dance Association.
www.aahperd.org/nda/profDevelopment/standards5–8.cfm

Content Standard #1: Identifying and demonstrating movement elements and skills in performing dance.

Content Standard #2: Understanding choreographic principles, processes, and structures.

Content Standard #3: Understanding dance as a way to create and communicate meaning.

Content Standard #4: Applying and demonstrating critical and creative thinking skills in dance.

Content Standard #5: Demonstrating and understanding dance in various cultures and historical periods.

Content Standard #6: Making connections between dance and healthful living.

Content Standard #7: Making connections between dance and other disciplines.

Health (H + #) National Health Education Standards: Achieving Excellence.
Joint Committee on National Health Education Standards.
Atlanta: American Cancer Society, 2007.
See also: www.cdc.gov/HealthyYouth/SHER/standards

1. Students will comprehend concepts related to health promotion and disease prevention to enhance health.
2. Students will analyze the influence of family, peers, culture, media, technology and other factors on health behaviors.
3. Students will demonstrate the ability to access valid information and products and services to enhance health.
4. Students will demonstrate the ability to use interpersonal communication skills to enhance health and avoid or reduce health risks.
5. Students will demonstrate the ability to use decision-making skills to enhance health.
6. Students will demonstrate the ability to use goal-setting skills to enhance health.
7. Students will demonstrate the ability to practice health-enhancing behaviors and avoid or reduce health risks.
8. Students will demonstrate the ability to advocate for personal, family and community health.

Language Arts (LA + #) **NCTE/IRA Standards for the English Language Arts.**
International Reading Association and the National Council of Teachers of English
www.readwritethink.org/about/standards.html

1. Students read a wide range of print and non-print texts to build an understanding of texts, of themselves, and of the cultures of the United States and the world; to acquire new information; to respond to the needs and demands of society and the workplace; and for personal fulfillment. Among these texts are fiction and nonfiction, classic and contemporary works.
2. Students read a wide range of literature from many periods in many genres to build an understanding of the many dimensions (e.g., philosophical, ethical, aesthetic) of human experience.
3. Students apply a wide range of strategies to comprehend, interpret, evaluate, and appreciate texts. They draw on their prior experience, their interactions with other readers and writers, their knowledge of word meaning and of other texts, their word identification strategies, and their understanding of textual features (e.g., sound-letter correspondence, sentence structure, context, graphics).
4. Students adjust their use of spoken, written, and visual language (e.g., conventions, style, vocabulary) to communicate effectively with a variety of audiences and for different purposes.

5. Students employ a wide range of strategies as they write and use different writing process elements appropriately to communicate with different audiences for a variety of purposes.

6. Students apply knowledge of language structure, language conventions (e.g., spelling and punctuation), media techniques, figurative language, and genre to create, critique, and discuss print and nonprint texts.

7. Students conduct research on issues and interests by generating ideas and questions, and by posing problems. They gather, evaluate, and synthesize data from a variety of sources (e.g., print and nonprint texts, artifacts, people) to communicate their discoveries in ways that suit their purpose and audience.

8. Students use a variety of technological and informational resources (e.g., libraries, databases, computer networks, video) to gather and synthesize information and to create and communicate knowledge.

9. Students develop an understanding of and respect for diversity in language use, patterns, and dialects across cultures, ethnic groups, geographic regions, and social roles.

10. Students whose first language is not English make use of their first language to develop competency in the English language arts and to develop understanding of content across the curriculum.

11. Students participate as knowledgeable, reflective, creative, and critical members of a variety of literacy communities.

12. Students use spoken, written, and visual language to accomplish their own purposes (e.g., for learning, enjoyment, persuasion, and the exchange of information).

Mathematics (M + #) **Principles and Standards for School Mathematics.**
National Council of Teachers of Mathematics.
http://standards.nctm.org

Content Standards
1. Number and Operations
2. Algebra
3. Geometry
4. Measurement
5. Data Analysis and Probability

Process Standards
1. Problem Solving
2. Reasoning and Proof
3. Communication
4. Connections
5. Representations

Music (MUS + #) National Standards for Music Education.
National Association for Music Education.
menc.org/resources/view/national-standards-for-music-education

1. Singing, alone and with others, a varied repertoire of music.
2. Performing on instruments, alone and with others, a varied repertoire of music.
3. Improvising melodies, variations, and accompaniments.
4. Composing and arranging music within specified guidelines.
5. Reading and notating music.
6. Listening to, analyzing, and describing music.
7. Evaluating music and music performances.
8. Understanding relationships between music, the other arts, and disciplines outside the arts.
9. Understanding music in relation to history and culture.

Physical Education (PE + #) Moving into the Future: National Standards for Physical Education. National Association for Sport and Physical Education. 2004.
www.aahperd.org/naspe/standards/nationalStandards/PEstandards.cfm

A physically educated person:

Standard 1: Demonstrates competency in motor skills and movement patterns needed to perform a variety of physical activities.

Standard 2: Demonstrates understanding of movement concepts, principles, strategies, and tactics as they apply to the learning and performance of physical activities.

Standard 3: Participates regularly in physical activity.

Standard 4: Achieves and maintains a health-enhancing level of physical fitness.

Standard 5: Exhibits responsible personal and social behavior that respects self and others in physical activity settings.

Standard 6: Values physical activity for health, enjoyment, challenge, self-expression, and/or social interaction.

Science (SC + #) National Science Education Standards. 1996. The National Academies: National Academy of Sciences, National Academy of Engineering, Institute of Medicine, National Research Council.
www.nap.edu/openbook.php?record_id=4962&page=2

On July 19, 2011, the National Academies issued a press release announcing the formation of a new framework for K-12 Science standards; see www8.nationalacademies.org/onpinews/newsitem.aspx?RecordID=13165

This framework will be used to develop new science standards that will work with the Common Core standards. It is not anticipated that these standards will be in effect before the publication of this book; therefore, we have relied on the standards currently in use.
www.nap.edu/openbook.php?record_id=4962&page=104

I   Unifying Concepts and Processes
II   Science as Inquiry
III   Physical Science Perspectives
IV   Life Science
V   Earth and Space Science
VI   Science and Technology
VII   Science in Personal and Social Perspectives
VIII   History and Nature of Science

Social Studies (SS + #) **National Curriculum Standards for Social Studies.**
National Council for Social Studies, 2010.
www.socialstudies.org/standards/strands

I   Culture
II   Time, Continuity, and Change
III   People, Places, and Environments
IV   Individual Development and Identity
V   Individuals, Groups, and Institutions
VI   Power, Authority, and Governance
VII   Production, Distribution, and Consumption
VIII   Science, Technology, and Society
IX   Global Connections
X   Civic Ideals and Practices

Theatre (TH + #) **National Standards for Theatre Education. Developed by the American Alliance for Theatre and Education in cooperation with the Educational Theatre Association and as part of the National Standards for Arts Education, a product of the Consortium of National Arts Education Associations.**
www.aate.com/?nationalstandards58

Content Standard #1: Script writing by the creation of improvisations and scripted scenes based on personal experience and heritage, imagination, literature, and history.
Content Standard #2: Acting by developing basic acting skills to portray characters who interact in improvised and scripted scenes.
Content Standard #3: Designing by developing environments for improvised and scripted scenes.

Content Standard #4: Directing by organizing rehearsals for improvised and scripted scenes.

Content Standard #5: Researching by using cultural and historical information to support improvised and scripted scenes.

Content Standard #6: Comparing and incorporating art forms by analyzing methods of presentation and audience response for theatre, dramatic media (such as film, television, and electronic media), and other art forms.

Content Standard #7: Analyzing, evaluating, film, television, and electronic media productions.

Content Standard #8: Understanding context by analyzing the role of theatre, film, television, and electronic media in the community and in other cultures.

Visual Arts (VA + #) **The National Visual Arts Standards.**
National Art Education Association.
www.arteducators.org/store/NAEA_Natl_Visual_Standards1.pdf

Content Standard #1: Understanding and applying media, techniques, and processes.

Content Standard #2: Using knowledge of structures and functions.

Content Standard #3: Choosing and evaluating a range of subject matter, symbols, and ideas.

Content Standard #4: Understanding the visual arts in relation to history and cultures.

Content Standard #5: Reflecting upon and assessing the characteristics and merits of their work and the work of others.

Content Standard #6: Making connections between visual arts and other disciplines.

APPENDIX B

~~~~~~~~~~~~~~~~~~~~~~~~~~~~

CULTURES

Abenakis
Aboriginal Peoples—Australia
Acolhuas
Afghans
African Americans
African Australians
African Canadians
African Colombians
Africans
Albanians
Albanian Americans
American Indians
Anatolians
Ancient Chinese
Ancient Middle Easterners
AOD
Appalachians
Arab Americans
Arabs
Asian Americans
Aztecs
Balinese
Bangladeshi Americans
Bangladeshis
Bengalis
Beninians
Bhutanese
Brazilian Americans
Brazilians
British
Buddhists
Burmese

Cambodian Americans
Cambodians
Canadian East Indians
Canadian First Peoples
Canadians
Central Americans
Central Asians
Cherokees
Chickasaw
Chinese Americans
Chinese Canadians
Choctaw
Coahuitecas
Colombians
Congolese
Creeks
Crows
Cuban Americans
Cubans
Czechoslovakian Americans
Czechoslovakians
Deaf
Dene
Denes
Dutch
East Indian Americans
East Indian British
East Indian Trinidadians
East Indian Ugandans
East Indians
Eastern Europeans
Egyptians

English
Ethiopians
Europeans
French Canadians
French
Germans
Global
Greenlanders
Guatemalans
Haitian Americans
Hawai'ian Americans
Hindus
Icelanders
Inca
Indians
Indians of North America
Indonesians
Inuits
Inupiats
Inuvialuit
Iranians
Iraqis
Irish
Israelis
Italian Americans
Japanese
Japanese Americans
Jews
Jewish African Americans
Jewish Americans
Jewish Austrians
Jewish Cubans
Jewish Czechoslovakians
Jewish Dutch
Jewish Dutch East Indians
Jewish Eastern Europeans
Jewish Europeans
Jewish French
Jewish Germans
Jewish Hungarians
Jewish Italian Americans
Jewish Poles
Jewish Russians
Jewish South Africans

Jewish Ukrainians
Kaiyuh
Kalispels
Karennis
Kenyans
Korean Americans
Koreans
Kurds
Laotians
Latin Americans
Latinos
Levantines
Malawians
Malaysians
Maldivians
Maya
Mesopotamians
Mexicans
Middle Easterners
Mixed Race
Mixed-Race Americans
Mixed-Race Chinese
Mixed-Race English
Mixed-Race Indians
Mohaves
Mohawks
Muslim British
Muslims
Navahos
Nepalese
New Guineans
Nez Perce
Northern Paiutes
Norwegians
Ojibwa
Olmecs
Oneida
Pakistani Americans
Pakistanis
Palestinians
Persians
Peruvians
Poles
Powhatans

Romanies
Romans
Russians
Rwandans
Salish
Scots
Seminoles
South Africans
South Americans
South Asians
Southeast Asians
Spanish
Spokanes
Sri Lankans
Sudanese
Swiss

Syrians
Tabeguache Ute
Taiwanese
Taiwanese Americans
Thais
Tibetans
Ugandans
Ute
Vietnamese
Vietnamese Americans
West Indians
Western Asians
Ybo
Zimbabweans

APPENDIX C

~~~~~~~~~~~~~~~~~~~~

SOURCES FOR FURTHER
INFORMATION ON
MULTIETHNIC LITERATURE

Why Multiethnic Literature?

Agosto, Denise E., Sandra Hughes-Hassell, and Catherine Gilmore-Clough. "The All-White World of Middle-School Genre Fiction: Surveying the Field for Multicultural Protagonists." *Children's Literature in Education,* vol. 34, no. 4 (December 2003): 257–275.

Larrick, Nancy. "The All-White World of Children's Books." *Saturday Review* (September 11, 1965): 63–65; 84–85.

Rochman, Hazel. *Against Borders: Promoting Books for a Multicultural World.* Chicago: ALA, 1993.

Takaki, Ronald. *A Different Mirror: A History of Multicultural America.* Boston: Little, Brown, 1993.

———. *A Different Mirror for Young People.* Adapted by Rebecca Stefoff. New York: Seven Stories, 2012.

Yokota, Junko. "Issues in Selecting Multicultural Children's Literature." *Language Arts,* vol. 70 (March 1993): 156–167.

———. "Asian Americans in Literature for Children and Young Adults." *Teacher Librarian,* vol. 36, no. 3 (February 2009): 15–19.

Sources for Multiethnic Literature

A-Hazza, Tami and Katherine Toth Bucher. *Books about the Middle East: Selecting and Using Them with Children and Adolescents.* Columbus, OH: Linworth, 2008.

Dale, Doris Cruger. *Bilingual Children's Books in English and Spanish: An Annotated Bibliography, 1942 through 2001.* Jefferson: McFarland, 2003.

Dawson, Alma and Connie Van Fleet. *African American Literature: A Guide to Reading Interests.* Westport: Libraries Unlimited, 2004.

Derman-Sparks, Louise, Patricia G. Ramsey, and Julie Olsen Edwards. *What If All the Kids Are White? Anti-Bias Multiethnic Education with Young Children and Families.* New York: Teachers College Press, 2006.

East, Kathy and Rebecca L. Thomas. *Across Cultures: A Guide to Multiethnic Literature for Children.* Westport: Libraries Unlimited, 2007.

Ellermeyer, Deborah A. and Kay A. Chick. *Multiethnic American History through Children's Literature.* Portsmouth, New Hampshire: Teacher Ideas Press, 2003.

Gebel, Doris. *Crossing Boundaries with Children's Books.* Lanham: Scarecrow Press, 2006.

Givens, Archie, ed. *Spirited Minds: African American Books for Our Sons and Our Brothers.* New York: W. W. Norton, 1997.

———. *Strong Souls Singing: African American Books for Our Daughters and Sisters.* New York: W. W. Norton, 1998.

Harris, Violet J., ed. *Using Multiethnic Literature in the K-8 Classroom.* Norwood: Christopher Gordon, 1997.

Helbig, Alethea. *Many Peoples, One Land: A Guide to New Multiethnic Literature for Children and Young Adults.* Westport: Greenwood Press, 2001.

Kuharets, Olga R. *Venture into Cultures: A Resource Book of Multicultural Materials and Programs.* Chicago: ALA, 2001.

Slapin, Beverly and Doris Seale, eds. *A Broken Flute: The Native Experience in Books for Children.* Walnut Creek, CA: AltaMira Press, c2005.

Smith, Henrietta M., ed. *The Coretta Scott King Awards, 1970–2004.* Chicago: American Library Association, 2004.

Smith, Martha, and Liz Knowles. *Understanding Diversity through Novels and Picture Books.* Westport, MA: Libraries Unlimited, 2007.

Yokota, Junko. *Kaleidoscope: A Multicultural Booklist for Grades K-8.* Newark, DE: National Council of Teachers of English, 2001.

York, Sherry. *Children's and Young Adult Literature by Latino Writers: A Guide for Librarians, Teachers, Parents, and Students.* Worthington: Linworth, 2002.

———. *Booktalking Authentic Multicultural Literature: Fiction, History, and Memoirs for Teens.* Santa Barbara, CA: ABC-CLIO/Linworth, 2008.

INDEX

MacDonald], 94

natural disasters. *See* contemporary issues: homelessness, natural disasters, terrorism, and war

Navajos

Bird Springs (Marsden), 210–211

Code Talker: A Novel about the Navajo Marines of World War Two (Bruchac), 185

Dibé yázhí táá'go baa hane' (The three little sheep) [Yazzie], 37

Missing in Action (Hughes), 188

Neandertals: A Prehistoric Puzzle (Discovery! series) [La Pierre], 86

A Negro League Scrapbook (Weatherford), 69

Nelson, Kadir, 70, 220

Nelson, Marilyn, 5, 34, 63, 199

Nelson, S. D., 103, 175

Nelson, Vaunda Micheaux, 160

Nepalese, 78

New Guineans, 87–88

Newcomb, Rain, 94

Next to Mexico (Nails), 19

Nez Perce, 82–83

The Night of the Burning: Devorah's Story (Wulf), 133–134

the 1940s and World War II (U.S. history)

Annie's War (Sullivan), 183–184

The Baptism (Moses), 184

Best Friends Forever: A World War II Scrapbook (Patt), 184

Code Talker: A Novel about the Navajo Marines of World War Two (Bruchac), 185

Counting Coup: Becoming a Crow Chief on the Reservation and Beyond (Crow and Viola), 185

The Fences Between Us: The Diary of Piper Davis (Larson), 186

Fighting for American Values, 1941--1985 (Doak), 186–187

Freedom Train (Coleman), 187

House of the Red Fish (Salisbury), 187

Missing in Action (Hughes), 188

The Return of Buddy Bush (Moses), 188

The Tragic History of the Japanese-American Internment Camps. From Many Cultures, One History (Kent), 188–189

Weedflower (Kadohata), 189

Ninth Ward (Rhodes), 33–34

No Girls Allowed: Tales of Daring Women Dressed as Men for Love, Freedom and Adventure (Hughes), 24

No Safe Place (Ellis), 207–208

Nobody Gonna Turn Me 'Round: Stories and Songs of the Civil Rights Movement (Rappaport), 194–195

Nolan, Han, 198

North American Indians

Bear Dancer: The Story of a Ute Girl (Wyss), 160–161

The Inuit Thought of It: Amazing Arctic Innovations (We Thought of It series) [Ipellie and MacDonald], 93

North Central Asia. *See* East Asia and North Central Asia

Northern Paiutes, 177–178

Norwegians

No Girls Allowed: Tales of Daring Women Dressed as Men for Love, Freedom and Adventure (Hughes), 24

Who Was First: Discovering the Americas (Freedman), 106–107

Not a Drop to Drink: Water for a Thirsty World (Burgan), 80–81

O

Obadina, Tunde, 110

Obama, Barack, 220

Obama, Michelle, 203

O'Brien, Anne Sibley, 41

O'Brien, John, 90

O'Connell, Diane, 86, 91

O'Connell, Kim A., 201

O'Donnell, Liam, 73

You may also be interested in

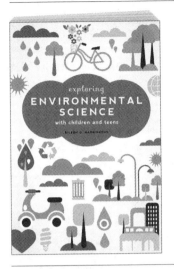

EXPLORING ENVIRONMENTAL SCIENCE WITH CHILDREN AND TEENS

EILEEN G. HARRINGTON

This book not only demonstrates the need for environmental programming but also gives those who work with children and teens the ideas and confidence they need to move forward.

ISBN: 978-0-8389-1198-3
176 pages / 6" x 9"

YOUNG ADULT LITERATURE
From Romance to Realism
MICHAEL CART
ISBN: 978-0-8389-1045-0

I FOUND IT ON THE INTERNET
Coming of Age Online, Second Edition
FRANCES JACOBSON HARRIS
ISBN: 978-0-8389-1066-5

THE READERS' ADVISORY GUIDE TO STREET LITERATURE
VANESSA IRVIN MORRIS, FOREWORD BY TERI WOODS
ISBN: 978-0-8389-1110-5

GRAPHIC NOVELS IN YOUR SCHOOL LIBRARY
JESSE KARP,
ILLUSTRATED BY RUSH KRESS
ISBN: 978-0-8389-1089-4

PICTURING THE WORLD
Informational Picture Books for Children
KATHLEEN T. ISAACS
ISBN: 978-0-8389-1126-6

GLOBAL VOICES
Picture Books from Around the World
SUSAN STAN
ISBN: 978-0-8389-1183-9

Order today at alastore.ala.org or 866-746-7252!